Mediating Globalization

SUNY series in Global Politics
James N. Rosenau, editor

*A complete listing of books in this series can be found
at the end of this volume.*

Mediating Globalization

*Domestic Institutions and Industrial Policies
in the United States and Britain*

Andrew P. Cortell

State University of New York Press

Published by
State University of New York Press, Albany

For information, address State University of New York Press,
194 Washington Avenue, Suite 305, Albany, NY 12210-2384

Production by Diane Ganeles
Marketing by Susan Petrie

Library of Congress Cataloging-in-Publication Data

Cortell, Andrew P., 1964–
    Mediating globalization: domestic institutions and industrial policies
in the United States and Britain / Andrew P. Cortell.
        p. cm. — (SUNY series in global politics)
    Includes bibliographical references and index.
    ISBN 0-7914-6441-5 (hardcover: alk. paper) — ISBN 0-7914-6442-3 (pbk.: alk.
paper)
    1. International economic relations.   2. Globalization.   3. United States—Economic
policy.   4. Great Britain—Economic policy.   5. Industrial policy—United States.
6. Industrial policy—Great Britain.   I. Title.   II. Series.

HF1359.C7 2005
337.73—dc22

                                                                        2004016216

10 9 8 7 6 5 4 3 2 1

Contents

Tables

Preface

There is no question in many observers' minds that the international system is characterized by globalization and that globalization somehow matters. For some, globalization spells the end of the nation-state and an irreversible shift in the balance of power to markets and market agents. For others, the shift is not so clear. It is to this debate that I have been drawn, for it concerns the central agent and organizational form in international relations, the state. This book does not question the notion that globalization processes characterize the international economy or that globalization has created new challenges for states. In fact, the book takes as its starting point that globalization poses challenges for states. The book's goal instead is to show that the state or, in particular, its institutional structures, continues to have meaning for understanding the nature of international relations regardless of whether some states seem overrun by the market. I seek to understand how domestic institutions mediate globalization and, by doing so, lead states to engage globalization in differing ways and with differing degrees of success.

This book combines several of my academic interests. Globalization, high technology competition, and the advanced industrial countries have been at the forefront of my research and teaching interests since entering the profession. At the same time, I have been drawn to exploring the nature and impact of domestic institutions since reading Peter Katzenstein's conclusion to *Between Power and Plenty* in one of my first graduate school courses. As a consequence, conceptualizing, researching, and writing this book have occupied much of my time over several years. In the process I have incurred a number of significant debts. My dissertation advisors at Columbia University, Helen Milner and David Baldwin, spent much time helping me to think through the international political economy literature and my understanding of institutions. Several friends and colleagues commented on portions of earlier versions of the manuscript: David Baldwin, Jeff Checkel, James Davis, Helen Milner, Sue Peterson, and Steve Solnick. I thank the anonymous reviewers for SUNY Press for their extremely insightful and constructive comments. The production staff at SUNY Press, led by Diane Ganeles and Kelli Williams, helped to turn the manuscript into a book. In addition, I have been afforded a rare opportunity over the last four years at Lewis & Clark College: the capacity to have excellent research assistance from gifted and motivated undergraduate students, including Joe-Ryan Bergoch, Aaron Forbort, Tristan Nuñez, Tanya Sloan, and Odessa Weber. Joe-Ryan, in particular, provided valuable research assistance for chapters 5 and 7. I am grateful to Lewis & Clark College, particularly the dean of the college and dean of the social sciences, for providing these students with financial support.

An earlier version of portions of chapter 2 and 7 appeared in *Polity* 30, no. 1 (1997). I gratefully acknowledge M. J. Peterson, who, as the editor of that journal, provided numerous constructive editorial suggestions. An earlier version of sections of chapter 2, 3, and 4 appeared in *Governance* 10, no. 3 (1997) and sections of chapter 4 in *International Studies Quarterly* 40, no. 4 (1996). Portions of chapter 7 appear in *Comparative Political Studies* 34, no. 7 © 2001 Sage Publications.

Throughout the writing process, I have been fortunate to have had much support and encouragement. Gordon Silverstein provided invaluable guidance on numerous issues and was always a call or e-mail away when I needed to talk. Robert Eisinger was consistently enthusiastic and insightful. Sue Peterson not only read and commented on the penultimate version of the manuscript, but also willingly re-read my attempts to address her comments. I thank her for her willingness to read my work, especially as its completion has slowed work on our other projects. Our collaborations on institutional change continue to inform my thinking of that subject in this book. My parents triggered and cultivated my academic interests, and have monitored my progress on this project with much interest. My wife, Lois, a constant support, has been an especially wonderful and insightful companion throughout the book project.

Part One

The Argument

Chapter One

Globalization and Convergence?
The Domestic Impact of Globalization

Globalization challenges a country's capacity to promote national wealth and power. For some, the appearance of a global economy, in which goods, services, and ideas move easily in and out of countries, shifts the balance of power from states to markets. Globalization then produces a "race to the bottom," in which states embrace the same strategy to attract internationally mobile capital and firms: reducing their financial and regulatory support for national economic activities and adopting liberal economic strategies more generally.

This view of the contemporary international system is widespread today. In the bestseller, *The Lexus and the Olive Tree* (1999), highly acclaimed journalist Thomas Friedman's discussions of the "Golden Straitjacket" and the "Electronic Herd" illustrate to a mass audience that states face limited options in a global economy. Mass protests by "antiglobalization" demonstrators outside meetings of the World Trade Organization (WTO), the Group of Eight (G-8) major industrial countries, and the International Monetary Fund (IMF) underscore the salience of the view that global forces, not states or domestic publics, determine national economic strategies. Scholars too have become attracted to the changes wrought by globalization. Indeed, concern with the effects of a global economy informs research across several disciplines in the social sciences and has given rise to an emerging "globalist" perspective.[1] Reflecting its recent origins and multidisciplinary character, the globalist perspective embodies a diverse set of viewpoints and arguments rather than a coherent set of hypotheses or an overarching theory.[2] Nevertheless, several prominent globalists develop similar themes regarding how globalization is thought to transform international relations (Strange 1996; Scholte 1997; 2000; Held and McGrew 1998; Held et al. 1999). One theme is most pertinent to the focus of this book: In an open, global economy, states choose their economic policies based on the predicted effects of those policies for mobile international firms and capital, and on the constraints imposed by international organizations' liberal prescriptions. Globalization, then, should make states less willing and capable to use interventionist strategies to promote their national wealth and power.

Before national governments become convinced that they are powerless to respond to the international economy, however, the globalist perspective's expectations need to be explored empirically and analytically. Such analyses are pivotal, since some globalists indicate that states may differ significantly in their responses to global economic forces. Philip Cerny (1997, 268) acknowledges, for example, that "[d]espite elements of convergence, significant divergences remain, for different states have different sets of advantages and disadvantages in the search for international competitiveness." This is an important qualification, since the onset of a borderless world is thought to have similar effects across all countries.[3] Not surprisingly, the globalist perspective generally has neglected to explore national-level factors and how they affect globalization's impact. This book explores these domestic factors, specifically the ways national institutions influence the range of policy choices available to states.[4] The book's central contention is that while globalization creates new incentives for state policy, its impact on a state's policy is mediated by domestic institutions, the rules, norms, and procedures that organize policymaking authority and establish relations between state and societal actors. These institutions create their own incentives for policymaking and, by doing so, lead states to engage globalization in differing ways and with differing degrees of success.

I examine the relationship between the state and economic globalization through a longitudinal analysis of two countries' relationships, the United States and Britain, with one of the most globalized sectors, the semiconductor industry, from the early 1970s through the mid-1990s. Throughout this period, both countries' commercial manufacturers encountered severe challenges from foreign competitors, triggering multiple debates regarding the merits of existing strategies, the need for new ones, and the nature of the global challenge facing the sector. This sectoral focus helps to shed light on a core implication of the globalist perspective: globalization limits a state's ability to adopt interventionist policies, or industrial policies, that seek to promote and retain high value-added activities within its territory. These policies seek to strengthen the position of specific firms or sectors through the use of such initiatives as research and development (R&D) subsidies, tax credits, or the regulation of markets; in doing so, the government assumes a direct role in guiding industrial activity within its borders (Hart and Prakash 1999, 245). I maintain that states still may possess the capacity to advance such strategies. Whether they have this capacity hinges on the structure of national institutions. Institutions influence the type of policies a government is likely to pursue by setting the parameters for both intragovernmental and state-societal relations. In particular, the roles and strategies of government officials and firms are mediated—shaped and hindered or empowered—by the institutions through which these actors must operate. In this regard, the book seeks to identify the domestic institutional conditions that create opportunities or set constraints for the development of more or less interventionist strategies in response to globalization. It indicates that domestic institutions frequently create conditions that can lead a country to adopt strategies that are inconsistent with globalist expectations.

The empirical chapters examine thirteen policy episodes occurring between the early 1970s and mid-1990s, and find that globalization did not lead the United States or Britain to adopt only liberal strategies or to assume a marginal role in industrial development. Until the mid-1980s, for example, the British government played an activist role in the development of the country's semiconductor industry, funneling considerable amounts of aid to national firms and foreign firms under specific conditions. Beginning in the mid-1980s, the U.S. government assumed a similarly interventionist role: it provided large-scale funding for an applied research and development consortium open only to national firms and subsequently managed the sector's trade with its primary rival, Japan. As the United States continued this interventionist strategy throughout the late 1980s and 1990s, British policies turned liberal, remaining so until the mid-1990s. Ironically, if there were evidence of convergence, it was in the period between 1992 and 1996, when both countries' governments actively sought to promote national capabilities in the sector. The empirical evidence, moreover, indicates that the two countries' strategies converged on similarly interventionist strategies as a consequence of similar domestic institutional incentives. The institutional context also shaped their use of liberal strategies, making it difficult to correlate these choices with the constraints identified to emerge from globalization.

This introductory chapter provides an overview of the book. It begins by delineating globalist expectations about how globalization constrains states' industrial strategies and discusses some of the significant logical problems in these arguments. Second, it previews the argument and the institutional perspective developed more fully in the second chapter.

Third, it identifies the reasons for selecting the semiconductor industry. The chapter concludes with an outline of the rest of the book.

The Globalist Perspective

Globalization has become a central focus of scholarship in international relations theory. While there is no consensus definition for the term, there is some agreement that globalization represents an increase in globalism, or interconnections across different regions. Robert Keohane and Joseph Nye (2000, 105) define globalism as "a state of the world involving networks of interdependence at multicontinental distances. The linkages occur through flows and influences of capital and goods, information and ideas, people and forces, as well as environmentally and biologically relevant substances. . . ." Economic globalization would represent an increase in one dimension of globalism. The following discussion largely focuses on this dimension.

The globalist perspective conceptualizes globalization, regardless of definition, as a significant determinant and constraint on state action. The mobility of capital, firms, and technology is seen to force states to adopt liberal or more market-oriented strategies, if they hope to benefit from these global entities. In effect, the advent of globalization has made it less likely that the state will play an activist role in national industrial development or its economy more generally.[5] This is thought to be the case for at least three reasons.

First, globalists expect liberal strategies due to "the multinationalization of production and the attendant credibility of firms' threats to move production from one country to another in search of higher rates of return" (Scholte 1997, 443). In effect, states' autonomy and independence are reduced thanks to the globalization of production. One factor likely to increase firms' mobility or reluctance to locate in a state is their unwillingness to pay the tax burdens necessary to fund an activist state. "Governments must thus embrace the free market if they are to compete for the investment and jobs provided by multinational firms" (Garrett 1998, 792; Friedman 1999; Clark 1999, 96-100). This perspective rests on the more basic globalist belief that mobile firms are now no longer national, but global in orientation, outlook, and organization (see Held et al. 1999, chap. 5). For example, Roger Tooze (1997, 221) explains that the global economy comprises

> a structure that is more than and additional to the 'international economy,' and is made up of firms and other entities that operate transnationally over the whole globe. The activities of

> these firms are based upon and geared towards global produc-
> tion and services for a global market, with much of their eco-
> nomic activity taking place outside of the market within their
> own global structures. . . . The strategies and purposes of these
> 'global' entities are not necessarily congruent with or support-
> ive of the strategies and purposes of the separate national gov-
> ernments of the states within which they are located.[6]

As a consequence, the emergence of a global market is expected to produce "demands for the harmonization of national polices, or common
rules that prohibit national state intervention" (Zürn 2002, 240).

Second, states are thought to have become less important and capable sites of economic policymaking. At one extreme are those globalists
who see globalization as portending the end of the nation-state as a
meaningful or significant entity in the international system (Strange 1996,
75).[7] Others, such as Tooze (1997, 221) and James Rosenau (2000, 186;
2003) for example, see global dynamics as "lessening the capacities for
governance located at the level of sovereign states and national societies."
Cerny (1997, 269-70) offers a similar assessment: "[T]he nation-state is
not dead, but its role has changed. . . . The functions of the state, although central in structural terms, are increasingly residual in terms of
the range of policy instruments and outcomes which they entail." This
transformation emerges as a result of the state's effort to make itself attractive to global firms through deregulation and liberalization (e.g.,
Baker 2000). Although there may be some disagreement on the extent of
change emerging, globalists generally maintain that globalization is "re-
constituting or 're-engineering' the power, functions and authority of
national governments" (Held et al. 1999, 8).

Others contend that international institutions, such as the WTO and
IMF, have led to the development of extensive sets of international rules designed to institutionalize liberalism at the international and national levels.[8]
In addition, nonstate actors, such as international financial markets, create
a further set of tacit rules limiting government intervention. These supranational forms of governance have further constrained the policymaking
autonomy of national governments (Cerny 1995, 625; Strange 1996; Held
and McGrew 1998, 229–30; Rosenau 2003). For example, as Jan Aart
Scholte (1997, 444) maintains, "[t]he recently created World Trade Organization marks another striking growth of suprastate governance. . . .
[M]any decisions concerning the regulatory environment for capitalism
now come to rather than from the state." As a consequence, according to
Scholte (2000, 139), states "no longer always clearly promote 'domestic'
interests against those of 'foreigners.'" Ian Clark (1999, 90) identifies the
analytical foundation of this perspective when he writes, "[t]he rules of

competition are imposed from the outside, and the economic state must conform to them if it is to succeed."

A third argument focuses on the efficacy of interventionist strategies in a global economy. Interventionist strategies are expected to be futile, when firms can form alliances with those located in other countries and, thus, share the benefits with them. Such alliances make it difficult for the intervening state to capture the benefits of doing so for its territory. Jonathan Perraton and his collaborators (2000, 297) maintain that "[m]ultinationals' ability to transfer technology abroad and the ability of foreign MNCs to tap into domestic innovation structures limit the effectiveness of national industry and technology strategies." Given the global economy, Cerny (1995, 611) writes, "the outer limits of effective action by the state . . . are usually seen to comprise its capacity to promote a relatively favorable investment climate for transnational capital—i.e., by providing an increasingly circumscribed range of goods that retain a national-scale (or subnational-scale) public character or of a particular type of still-specific assets described as immobile factors of capital." As a consequence, "multinationalization appears to have led to a shift in industrial policy away from national industrial development strategies and towards an emphasis on offering inducements for inward F[oreign] D[irect] I[nvestment]" (Perraton et al. 2000, 298).

The globalist perspective has come under fire for at least three reasons. First, a number of scholars have called into question the notion that economic factors have generally become transnational and, by implication, that national territories have become insignificant to firms (Wade 1996; Hirst and Thompson 1996; Doremus et al. 1998). These scholars often grant that firms exhibit tendencies consistent with globalization in terms of the interregionalization of production processes and interfirm networks, but point to a number of different statistics, including employment, ownership, and R&D, to note the continuing importance of firms' home locations. Chapters 3 through 7 indicate that U.S. and British semiconductor firms, albeit largely multinational in orientation, tended to identify with their national territories in the sense that they sought support from their national governments in an effort to cope with the challenges they associated with the globalization of production. In this sense, these firms' home bases remain salient to their identities and actions. That being said, I leave the debate regarding the extent of globalization to others and, instead, focus on the factors that affect whether and how these firms' governments respond to the emergence of global economic challenges. In doing so, I explore how domestic institutions influence a state's capacity to respond to increased global connections, whether hindering or facilitating its use of different types of strategies.

A related critique focuses on the nature of the challenges states are thought to confront from the globalization of production. Globalists are primarily interested in how globalization has empowered mobile capital and firms and decreased the significance of nationally defined borders, actors, and interests. As a consequence, globalists tend to explore the effects of globalization only on an aggregate level, in the process downplaying the implications of a global marketplace for states' longstanding concerns with their relative positions (see Tooze 1997; Held and McGrew 2000a; Scholte 2000, chap. 5). Those who do emphasize competitiveness issues tend to narrow their focus to a competition for mobile investors and the downward pressure this competition places on national regulations (Strange 1996; Cerny 1997; Scholte 1997; Baker 2000). Yet, the global economy enables the dispersion and diffusion of productive potential to new locations, thus producing gains for some states and losses for others, whether measured in terms of technological development, economic growth, jobs, or tax revenues. States then face incentives to reinforce the economic benefits or halt the losses associated with the globalization of production and competition (see Prakash and Hart 2000a; 2000b). Given the potentially differential impact of globalization, multiple strategies are possible, including more rather than less state intervention. Chapter 2 maintains that whether and how states respond to such incentives depends on the structure of national political institutions, which will amplify, suppress, or modify various state and societal actors' preferences for responding to global competitive challenges.

Second, some scholars have focused on the globalists' expectation of a liberal convergence. These scholars have noted that the meanings of liberalism and convergence are many and murky (Berger 1996; Hay 2000; Drezner 2001). Others note that those states experiencing the most globalization of their economies, the advanced industrial countries, do not demonstrate a liberal convergence (Garrett 1998). This book reinforces these findings; the globalist expectation of liberal policy convergence is not borne out by British and U.S. strategies toward their semiconductor industries from the early 1970s through the mid-1990s. Throughout this period, the two countries opted for strategies that varied most significantly along two indicators: first, whether the strategy required the government to disengage from or intervene in the sector; and second, whether the strategy targeted the economic environment in which all industries operated or the sector. And even when the two countries pursued liberal strategies, considerable divergence remained in the initiatives used, especially with regard to the extent to which the state sought to extricate itself from the economy or sector. Perhaps more problematic for the globalist perspective is that by the 1980s, a period of heightened globalization, the two countries' strategies diverged sharply. Whereas beginning in the mid-1980s Britain adopted a liberal strategy, the United States developed interventionist approaches to regenerate the industry in light of the acceleration in the sector's globalization.

Third, others have taken issue with the determinism of the globalist position. They have done so in several respects, calling into question the globalist expectation that states will respond similarly to a common external pressure, globalization. Helen Milner and Robert Keohane (1996, 20) write that "observations of past political change should make us wary about expecting . . . one-sided effects. Political leaders have a degree of latitude in how they respond to internationalization. In large part, this range of choice is a function of the domestic institutional framework in which they must operate." Some have noted that globalists tend to equate globalization only with the decreasing capacity of the state and, thereby, exclude the possibility that globalization may be empowering for some states. Linda Weiss, for example, maintains that globalization has the potential also to be "enabling," since "intensified competitive pressures . . . urge governments to devise new policy responses, new regulatory regimes, and similar restructuring reforms" (Weiss 2003a, 17; 1998, 208). Summarizing the findings of a collective research project, Weiss (2003b, 298) explains that "[e]nablement implies that in the face of relatively similar globalization pressures, there are countervailing pressures on governments and, often, political incentives, to intervene."

In addition, similar critiques can be lodged against the notion that globalization leads to state restructuring that only decreases state powers. The transformation of the state apparatus may be unlikely to head in a single direction, since it is fundamentally affected by the relationship between agents and institutions operating in specific national contexts, the starting point for any transformation process (Gourevitch 1996; Cortell and Peterson 2002). Domestic groups' desire for national institutional change and the types of change demanded then are likely to be significantly shaped by distinctive domestic-level dynamics, making it possible for the restructuring of the state to head in multiple directions.

Others have taken aim at the limited role for agency in the globalist perspective (Guillén 2001a). It generally expects that the states themselves, whether their structures or officials, will play little role in mediating the effects of globalizing pressures. Even if states find themselves forced to respond to events emanating from outside their borders, domestic actors still must decide that doing so is necessary. In this regard, the globalist perspective suffers from a problem common to systemic-level theories in the international relations literature more generally; it leaves underdeveloped the process by which purported systemic-level effects are translated into national-level policies. Moreover, it is possible then that convergence may have nothing to do with the systemic pressures identified and more to do with domestic-level characteristics. As Clark (1998, 497) writes, "only by a consideration of the state caught between the competing pressures emanating from both [the international and domestic] fields can the impact of globalization, and its likely future development, be understood."

Some might contend that globalists implicitly see firms as the central agents driving national policies (e.g., Strange 1996). If so, this argument rests on at least three assumptions, none of which is unproblematic on either empirical or theoretical grounds. First, it presumes that all globalized firms want liberal strategies and that their national institutional and cultural contexts play no role in influencing their preferences. Second, it presumes that firms enjoy access and influence to policymaking processes across all states and that government officials and government structures play no role in mediating their impact. Third, it presumes that the domestic context exerts no significant effect on how a state responds to the international economy.

A similar criticism can be raised regarding the globalists' expectation that interventionist strategies are unlikely to be effective. The perspective asserts that all states will find such strategies to be ineffective and that this outcome will hinder them from adopting such strategies. This expectation overlooks the role of domestic politics and the differing preferences of national actors in driving policy choice. Much literature shows that domestic-level factors can block or refract systemically derived pressures (e.g., Katzenstein ed. 1978; Katzenstein 1985; Gourevitch 1986). As a consequence, it is possible that the determinations of effectiveness derived from the international environment may be pushed aside due to domestic factors that block, overcome, or compensate for these constraints. Moreover, these same domestic factors may help to explain why several of the industrial policies advanced by the United States and Britain explored in subsequent chapters achieved their objectives.

This last critique suggests that the globalist perspective "offer[s] what might be termed an 'input' model of convergence since the institutional and cultural factors which might translate common inputs into divergent outcomes generally remain underspecified or wholly unspecified" (Hay 2000, 512). As Weiss (1999, 81) explains,

> whatever pressures are 'out there' (whether coming from above or below and whether we agree to label them internationalization or globalization), states are responding from very different institutional and ideational bases and are therefore most unlikely to be moving in a single (regulatory) direction. This is because, in an internationalized economy, path-dependency (historical linkages between institutions which create interlocked systems) still carries weight: the weight of both historically formed regime

orientations (e.g., fundamental norms about the state's role in economic and social relations) and institutional configurations (e.g., the availability of cooperative mechanisms for public-private governance).

Or as John L. Campbell (2003, 249) writes, institutions are "the mechanisms that determine how national actors respond to the pressures of globalization when they arise or are otherwise invoked."

An Alternative Approach: Domestic Institutions Matter

This final critique serves as the starting point for the historical institutionalist explanation advanced in chapter 2 to account for the types of strategies a country is likely to adopt in response to globalization. Peter Hall and Rosemary Taylor (1996, 938) note that historical institutionalists conceive the institutional context to encompass "the formal or informal procedures, routines, norms, and conventions embedded in the organizational structure of the polity or political economy. They can range from the rules of a constitutional order or the standard operating procedures of a bureaucracy to the conventions governing trade union behavior or bank-firm relations. In general, historical institutionalists associate institutions with organizations and the rules or conventions promulgated by formal organization."[9] These institutions influence policy by affecting the ability of state and societal actors to achieve their interests, by shaping the formation of actors' interests, and by the path-dependent quality of their evolution. The approach is historical in two respects. First, institutional creation and change reflects "the contingent nature of political and economic development, and especially the role of political agency, conflict, and choice in that development" (Thelen and Steinmo 1992, 12). Second, the approach conceptualizes institutions as being path dependent; that is, the composition of new institutions tends to interact with and carry forward key elements of existing institutions, including their incongruities and asymmetries. Moreover, some of the more significant institutional effects involve unintended consequences, which can be understood only over time (Pierson 1996). Taken together, these points indicate that a historical institutionalist approach expects cross-national institutional variations and that these are likely to be maintained over time (Katzenstein 1978).

Political scientists, among others, have long recognized that a country's institutions play a significant role in influencing its policies. While there are numerous ways to conceptualize institutions (see Hall and Taylor 1996), one of the more widely applied arguments in the international relations literature focuses on a state's domestic structure. Domestic structural approaches explore the institutions affecting the relationship between state and society in national policymaking processes. There is growing evidence to suggest that the basic premises associated with the conventional wisdom regarding these institutions are open to challenge in four respects.[10] First, many studies call into question the assumption that an undifferentiated institutional structure affects a country across all issue areas. Much research has shown, instead, that the state's organization and its relationship with societal and other non-state actors vary across different issue areas (Krasner 1978; Ikenberry, Lake, and Mastanduno eds. 1988; Smith 1993; Weaver and Rockman eds. 1993a). Second, a number of scholars recently have found that centralized decision-making structures may be more favorable to societal influence than decentralized structures (Suleiman 1987; Evangelista 1995; Risse-Kappen 1995a). Whereas previous arguments maintained that decentralized structures were more conducive to societal influence due to the greater number of access points they offered, research indicates that this access comes at a cost not found in centralization: multiple incompatible institutionally derived positions. Policy impact then is likely to be more difficult, since societal actors must build "winning coalitions with like-minded" officials "who constantly face countervailing forces" (Risse-Kappen 1995b, 290). Third, recent work suggests that societal access to the policy process emerges not simply from the structure of decision-making authority as traditionally argued, but more significantly from the presence of formal and conventional linkages that connect private and public sector representatives (Hall 1986; Weiss 1998, 34–36). A similar conclusion applies to the role of societal structure in determining groups' role in policymaking, since institutional linkages can substitute for weak organizational forms (see Goldstein 1988; Evangelista 1995). Fourth, existing work has generally portrayed institutions as a static constraint, subject to change only during periods of crisis, such as depressions or wars. Recent research suggests that institutional change instead may be frequent and incremental, as institutions are adapted in response to domestic or international events that call into question existing patterns of behavior or strategies (North 1990; Cortell and Peterson 1999).

The institutional approach developed in chapter 2 builds on these recent conceptual developments. My central claim is that institutions influence a state's response to globalization by affecting its capacity to advance different types of strategies, whether these are liberal or interventionist. In particular, institutions, by delimiting the roles of state and societal groups in policymaking, can foreclose some options while making others more likely. In this way, institutions mediate whether and how demands for new responses to the effects of global markets are transmitted into policy outcomes. In developing this argument, I focus on two aspects of the institutional context: the degree to which decision-making authority over a particular issue area is centralized in one or more state units; and whether decision-making bodies and administrative, legal, or customary procedures, referred to here as institutional networks, provide industry representatives with a channel through which to access government officials during policymaking. On the basis of the interaction between the two institutions, I identify six different institutional contexts within which policymaking can transpire. Each context differently affects the distribution of authority within the governmental apparatus and the flow of information between government officials and private commercial interests. I explain how each institutional context affects the ability of government officials and firms to access and influence policymaking and, by doing so, also helps to make some strategies more or less difficult to develop. In this way, institutions create their own set of opportunities and constraints, thereby influencing the ways globalization affects state policy. Chapter 2 develops this argument in detail, linking specific types of institutional contexts to different types of responses to globalization. For example, it posits that the institutional context is most conducive to interventionist strategies when this context enables an ongoing interaction pattern between firms and government officials who can operate relatively autonomously of other state units. Such policies become more difficult as the number of state units involved in policymaking increases or when institutions do not foster an interactive pattern of policymaking between firms and officials. In this regard, some states will find their policy options constrained when responding to international economic forces and this lack of policy discretion will reflect dynamics associated with their institutional contexts rather than globalization. Moreover, so long as the two institutions vary across states, we should expect states to pursue divergent paths in response to globalization.

Since institutions are unlikely to be static over time, the roles state and nonstate actors play in the policy process also are not fixed. This point is significant in at least two respects. First, since the institutional parameters affecting policymaking are mutable, a state's response to the international environment is unlikely to be fixed over time. A wide-ranging literature suggests that a host of domestic and international pressures over time can produce changes in domestic institutions, in the process producing new national capacities and policies.[11] Second, globalization may serve as one source of institutional change, transforming a state's capacity to respond to the very consequences globalization portends for states. In this regard, if there is one point of consensus in the literature, it is that globalization creates pressures that are likely to reconfigure the state. What is less clear, however, is the uniformity, direction, pace, and implications of the potential transformation across national contexts. Using the empirical chapters as my foundation, I return to issues related to the sources and consequences of institutional change in the concluding chapter, suggesting several reasons why it is difficult to pinpoint the direction or type of institutional reform arising from globalization and why we should expect cross-national divergence in the link between globalization and state transformation.

Globalization and the Semiconductor Industry

The semiconductor industry, which topped $200 billion in sales in 2001, is often identified as the quintessential globalized industry given the organization and diffusion of its production networks (Cerny 1995, 621; Held and McGrew 2000b, 249). Firms sell their products, source their inputs, partner with foreign firms, and do research and development in many different countries and regions across the globe. One implication of these dynamics has been the rise of new sites of national competency and, thus, the entrance of new firms in the industry. Thanks to a global economy, technological know-how has diffused to new competitors, thereby intensifying competition among firms for market share and technological advantage.

The semiconductor industry exhibited characteristics associated with globalization beginning in the 1960s. Globalization can be equated with transcontinental or interregional networks of interaction. David Held and Anthony McGrew (1998, 228) maintain that economic globalization exists when "[n]ational markets are increasingly enmeshed with one another as intra-industry trade has expanded and global competition transcends national borders, impacting directly on local economies. In these respects, individual firms are confronted by a potential global marketplace whilst they simultaneously face direct competition from foreign firms in their own domestic markets." Globalists often point to the dispersion of production, foreign direct investment, strategic alliances, subcontracting, joint ventures, and other forms of interfirm relationships to demonstrate the existence of interregional production networks.[12]

Beginning in the 1960s, the geographic structure of the semiconductor market became globalized.[13] In 1960, for example, the United States accounted for 75%, Europe 12%, Japan 10%, and other Asian countries—including Korea, Taiwan, Singapore, and Hong Kong—3% of the world semiconductor market (OECD 1992, 138). Over the next thirty years, the world market gradually became less concentrated, with the U.S. share dropping to just 30% and Japan's rising to 40%, Europe's to 17%, and other Asian countries' to 13%. This change reflects consumption and production patterns for semiconductor devices: relatively stronger consumption growth in the newly industrializing Asian economies, particularly Korea, Taiwan, Singapore, Hong Kong, the Philippines and Thailand, and the emergence of Japan as the largest consumer and producer of semiconductor devices

(Ibid., 138–39). Trade in semiconductor devices has long been a component of the industry given the significance of offshore manufacturing facilities and intrafirm trade. By the 1980s "[m]any firms from each of the core countries [were] investing in R&D and design centers in other advanced countries, in order to tap local software skills and provide facilities for customers to design ASICs [application-specific integrated circuits]" (Morgan and Sayer 1998, 61). More specifically, the Organisation for Economic Co-operation and Development (OECD 1992, 40) reports that "[i]n the case of both the United States and Japan, about half of total imports and exports are generated by offshore manufacturing: parts of semiconductors are exported to non-OECD or other OECD countries where they are assembled and reexported often back to the source country. The European trade data also includes a substantial share of intrafirm trade, including imports and reexports of semiconductor parts by foreign manufacturers."

Both the U.S. and British industries globalized early. With regard to production networks, U.S. firms first began using offshore assembly operations in 1961, when Fairchild began manufacturing in Hong Kong (Flamm 1985, 69). U.S. firms soon set up facilities across Europe and Asia, and the percentage of U.S. shipments involving processing abroad reached 82% by 1978 (Ibid., 83). As early as 1970, exports constituted a 26% share of U.S. domestic production and imports 9% of supplies. By 1975 these figures had grown to 34% and 19%.[14] Simultaneously, the level of foreign investment in the U.S. semiconductor market rose sharply, as European companies acquired smaller U.S. semiconductor firms (Milner 1988, 122). Thanks to an acceleration of Japanese FDI in the 1980s, by 1990 14.9% of workers in the semiconductor industry in the United States were employed by foreign-owned affiliates (U.S. OTA 1993, 55, fig. 3.2).[15] By the mid-1980s, the number of U.S.-Japan strategic alliances increased markedly, reaching nearly 100 (NRC 1992).

Since the early 1960s, the British semiconductor market has been dominated by foreign multinationals. These were initially U.S. and European firms and since the 1980s have included Japanese firms. As early as the late 1970s, some foreign subsidiaries exported from Britain to other regions of the world (McCalman 1988, 63, table 3.9). By 1983 nearly 41% of those employed in the electronics industry in Scotland's Silicon Glen were working for U.S.-based multinationals (Ibid., 61). Although British manufacturers largely produce specialized circuits for the British market, these firms have not been immune or opposed to global connections (Sciberras 1980, 284, 289; Hobday 1989, 171, 177; Hart 1992, 169–78). Foremost, these firms are largely reliant on technological developments taking place in the United States, Europe, and Japan, with some producing devices under license from foreign firms. Second, many of their personnel were trained and employed by U.S. MNCs, and U.S. personnel have been recruited to lead British firms. Third, the larger indigenous firms are themselves multinationals, manufacturing other products, and marketing and selling semiconductors abroad. Finally, they have engaged in multiple types of interfirm arrangements with U.S., Japanese, European, and Canadian firms. These agreements have included purchasing, production, and ownership arrangements. More recently, British firms have become the subject of acquisition by foreign firms.

The semiconductor industry provides a useful vantage point to examine the relationship between states and globalization. Semiconductor technology is integral to many of the industries that underpin crucial defense systems and helps to determine the pace and level of innovation in a wide range of industries in the contemporary national economy. A country's productive potential, which derives in large part from its capabilities to produce and to master leading-edge technologies such as the semiconductor, has long been thought to be an important determinant of a country's standing in international relations (Kennedy 1987; Thurow 1992; Samuels 1994). As such, some would consider the semiconductor industry to be a strategic industry (NRC 1992, 85).[16] Thanks to the dispersion of production and the emergence of new sites of competence in the sector, globalization brings unequal benefits and costs for various states and substate actors.[17] The possibility for winners and losers is likely to lead state and nonstate actors to try to shape the terms on which globalization affects them. A cross-national, longitudinal study of the sector then provides an opportunity to explore the conditions affecting the outcomes of these struggles, thereby shedding light on the relationship between globalization and state policy. That being said, I do not claim to offer a complete investigation of this relationship. That may not be possible given the multifaceted nature of globalization and its purported effects (Held et al. 1999). This book explores the relationship between the state and economic globalization through the lens of global competition in the semiconductor industry and U.S. and British strategies for coping with that competition.

Overview of the Book

Chapter 2 develops the book's institutional explanation. It begins by explaining how a country's strategy to promote national competitiveness can vary and identifies two potential responses to pressures associated with globalization. The second part of the chapter develops the book's institutional argument. It does so in two parts. It starts by delineating the two institutions at the core of the argument, the organization of decision-making authority and those institutions structuring government-industry relations during policymaking. It then explains how these two institutions affect government officials' and firms' access, influence, and strategies in the policy process. After doing so, the chapter explains how different combinations of these two institutions create opportunities and constraints for a state's response to globalization, linking the various institutional combinations to the two potential strategies identified in the first part of the chapter. The chapter concludes with an overview of the case selection strategy, particularly the focus on the United States and Britain.

Chapters 3 through 7 provide an empirical investigation of U.S. and British strategies to confront the globalization of the semiconductor industry from the early 1970s through the mid-1990s. The chapters recreate thirteen policy episodes to examine the role the institutional context plays in mediating the domestic impact of the pressures associated with globalization. Chapters 3, 4, and 5 examine six U.S. policy episodes, beginning with the Carter administration's innovation initiatives and ending with the Bush administration's renewal of the Sematech initiative in 1992. The chapters explore the impact of different institutional contexts, showing how variations in these contexts contributed to the administrations' decisions to adopt more or less interventionist strategies in response to pressures associated with globalization. These chapters also analyze several instances of the link between globalization and institutional transformation. These examples often involved a deliberate attempt to increase rather than decrease the state's capacity to advance interventionist strategies. Whether such innovations brought about these strategies hinged on the type of institutional context that subsequently emerged.

Chapters 6 and 7 explore seven policy episodes involving British governments' efforts to deal with the effects of the globalization of the semiconductor industry. The case studies begin with initiatives advanced by Edward Heath's government in the early 1970s and conclude with those developed in the mid-1990s by John Major's government. The cases show that institutional variations influenced whether the governments advanced liberal or interventionist strategies in response to pressures associated with the globalization of the semiconductor industry. These chapters also investigate several institutional reforms that both increased and decreased the capacity of the state apparatus to assume a role in the economy. These institutional variations highlight the role of several factors that can produce institutional reforms and indicate that globalization's impact on state transformation is unlikely to be unidirectional.

Chapter 8 identifies the book's central empirical and theoretical findings. The chapter begins by highlighting how the findings raise several key problems for globalists' expectations. It then considers the plausibility and explanatory strengths of several factors identified by other theoretical approaches. A third section explores the relationship between globalization and institutional transformation, identifying several sources of the institutional changes found to emerge in the United States and Britain. The chapter concludes with an analysis of the effectiveness of several of the more recent U.S. and British industrial strategies examined in previous chapters. It finds that interventionist strategies advanced by both countries were successful along several indicators. This final section suggests that given certain conditions, states may retain the capacity to use industrial policies to promote national competitiveness.

Chapter Two

Globalization, Domestic Institutions, and Industrial Strategies

Globalization creates new pressures confronting states. Most significantly, in a borderless world, firms can invest and produce almost anywhere they choose, and technology and productive potential may diffuse with these producers. The globalist perspective contends that states will respond similarly to these new economic developments: they will deregulate, liberalize, and generally reduce their roles in the economy. For a state to do otherwise, the globalists argue, risks alienating mobile international firms, which will invest their money and technology in jobs, factories, and goods elsewhere. In effect, the globalists expect states' strategies to converge on the use of liberal strategies to increase their wealth and power.

The globalist perspective is based on an analytical view similar to that of other systemic-level theories: incentives derived from the international system drive state behavior. Since the mid-1970s, scholars in the field of international political economy (IPE) have sought to explore the merits of such systemic arguments. Whether these scholars focus on the impact of interdependence, international institutions, economic pressures, or transnational entities, they generally conclude that national institutions play a significant mediating role. This chapter draws on the work of such scholars as Peter Hall (1986), G. John Ikenberry (1988; 1994), Peter Katzenstein (1978; 1985), and Thomas Risse-Kappen (1991; 1995a) to explain how the structure of national political institutions affects a country's response to globalization. It contends that the organization of decision-making authority and the structure of state-societal relations affect the policymaking resources of state and societal actors and, ultimately, a state's capacity to adopt different policies.[1] Institutions affect the ability of different actors to influence policymaking and help to make some strategies more or less difficult to develop and implement effectively. In this way, the chapter maintains that institutions create their own set of opportunities and constraints, thereby influencing the ways globalization shapes state policy. To borrow Risse-Kappen's (1994) language, globalization then "does not float freely into policy choice." Instead, globalization's effects for a particular country's policy choices are mediated by its institutions.

Before developing this argument, the chapter delineates the dependent variable, the strategies available to a country to promote national competitiveness in the face of globalization. The second section develops the book's institutional approach.

The Dependent Variable:
Strategies to Promote National Competitiveness

Globalization is thought to portend costs and opportunities for firms and states given the emergence of new sites of industrial competence and the potential mobility of firms across territories. One central difference of opinion in the globalization literature concerns the strategies available to states to confront the effects of a global economy on national competitiveness. The options identified tend to parallel the traditional dichotomy in the IPE literature, mercantilism versus liberalism (Cable 1995; Cerny 1997). Globalists, for example, expect states to respond to globalization with liberal strategies to make themselves more attractive to mobile investors. In the globalist vision, as Paul Hirst (1997, 409) explains, the task of national governments "is to provide those public services business wants, to promote the competitiveness of local firms and to attract inward investment. . . . Government can act best by getting out of the way of business by deregulating and containing public spending." These initiatives, along with opening markets and decreasing taxation, are the hallmark of a liberal strategy, since they seek to let market forces and market agents operate more freely in the economy. Those more skeptical of the globalist position argue, by contrast, that globalization does not limit states to liberal options. Instead, "various survival strategies are apparent," among them interventionist national wealth creation strategies (Cable 1995, 47; Weiss 1998; 1999). Jeffrey Hart and Aseem Prakash (1999, 243) contend, for example, that the integration of national markets creates incentives for national governments "to favor firms that located more of their value-added activities in their territorial jurisdictions."

To do so, a government might seek to sign agreements that open foreign markets to the benefit of domestic firms or design policies that seek to improve the technological capabilities of domestic firms, for example, by "enabling firms located in the country to have adequate and timely access to inputs needed to maintain their international competitiveness" (Ibid., 249). These strategies are more in line with mercantilism, or economic nationalism, since they seek to promote national competitiveness through government support for national industry.

This section identifies the central features of the various strategies available to states and the points of difference among them. In what follows, I identify the primary strategies states can use to respond to the globalization of competition: liberal strategies and industrial policies. These strategies differ in two fundamental ways: the extent to which they increase or decrease the government's role in promoting national economic development; and the extent to which they are designed to benefit specific sectors or the economic environment more generally.

At one end of the spectrum is a strategy consistent with general understandings of liberalism. In this strategy, the government fine tunes the general economic climate in which all industries operate and relies upon such initiatives as deregulation, reduced taxation, and more open markets. Such initiatives seek to reduce the transaction costs associated with doing business in the economy and "are addressed to the realization of economic objectives that affect all sectors," and, thus, are "aggregate in intent" (Tyson and Zysman 1983, 21). The emphasis here is on curtailing government involvement in the economy to let market forces benefit the most competitive entities, regardless of their nationality or sector. Such strategies of disengagement are most consistent with globalist expectations: globalization reduces both the state's role in the economy and its willingness to promote the competitiveness of specific national industries.

Liberal strategies also may involve some role for the government. Often, these comprise initiatives that establish property rights, create an educated workforce, or support basic research and development. These initiatives also include those focusing on the international environment, such as the creation of multilateral institutions and rules to promote and ensure liberal international economic strategies. These initiatives increase the role the government plays in the economy, but that role remains relatively minimal, and the benefits it provides are diffuse in the sense that they are deliberately broad or non-discriminatory.

At the other end of the spectrum are government initiatives designed to enhance national wealth creation through the promotion of specific industries operating in its territory. These interventionist or industrial policies, Daniel Okimoto (1989, 8–9) explains, "involve the government's use of its authority and resources to administer policies that address the needs of specific sectors and industries (and, if necessary those of individual companies) with the aim of raising the productivity of factor inputs. . . . The defining characteristic of industrial policy, then, is the custom design of policy instruments to fit the differing priorities, needs and circumstances of individual industries, particularly with respect to factor inputs." Robert Wade (1990, 13) offers a similar understanding; an "industrial policy aims to direct resources into selected industries so as to give producers in those industries a competitive advantage. It therefore aims to produce a different profile of industries compared to what would result from the decisions of unguided, unstimulated market agents on their own." While the latter outcome is an underlying objective of an industrial policy, the central distinguishing trait of such policies used here is that they increase the government's role in the economy and provide benefits to particular sectors.

Industrial policies generally promote industry by actions affecting the organization of markets, the prices of products, or the creation of new products and technologies. To achieve such aims, a government may use such targeted initiatives as subsidies, regulations, import protection, sponsorship of applied R&D, or procurement guarantees.[2] Some initiatives may involve the establishment of new bilateral, regional, or international rules or agreements to organize trade or investment patterns for a specific sector. These actions contrast with a liberal focus on international institutions in that an interventionist strategy attempts to establish rules that redound positively for national interests operating in a specific sector. Additional strategies may comprise initiatives that appear less interventionist but still involve a central and direct government role to assist a particular industry. These include exemptions from antimonopoly regulations, initiatives to open foreign markets, education and training initiatives, and research consortiums.

Some initiatives may be more difficult to classify as liberal or industrial policies. In such cases, the intended beneficiary is used as the primary means to classify an initiative. This coding strategy helps to get at the core issue raised in the globalization literature, whether the government seeks to promote a national capacity in a sector. Focusing on the intended beneficiary also is useful because it helps to distinguish deliberate sectoral strategies from the unintended sectoral benefits that others (Tyson and Zysman 1983, 21; Okimoto 1989) note may accompany strategies designed to improve the workings of labor, capital, regional or other markets. Looking at the intended beneficiary helps to make sense out of a related complexity: the possibility that a strategy simultaneously has multiple, distinct beneficiaries. For example, a government may respond to an industry's competitive situation by targeting the industry and specific markets, such as labor or regional development. Aid to a particular firm or industry in such cases may be contingent on locating a manufacturing site in a specific region of the country or developing environmentally safe production processes. The key criterion in coding initiatives with multiple objectives is whether a policy is crafted in response to globalization pressures affecting an industry, or whether the industry simply capitalizes on a preexisting regional or labor market initiative. The latter is an example of a liberal strategy given the diffuse and indirect nature of the benefits. The former is referred to as an industrial policy with multiple objectives given the presence of multiple, distinct intended beneficiaries.

In sum, countries' responses to the globalization of competition are distinguished using two indicators: the extent to which the government increases or decreases its role in the economy and the extent to which specific sectors or the economic environment more generally are the intended beneficiary. A liberal policy generally seeks to decrease the role of the government in the economy to the benefit of all firms regardless of their sector or nationality. An industrial policy seeks to redress a national industry's specific competitive circumstances through increased government support.

Institutions, Access, and Policymaking Authority

Political scientists have long been concerned with identifying the roles state and societal actors play in policymaking, and how these differing roles affect a country's policy choices. In exploring these factors, political scientists tend to attribute greater or lesser weight to state or societal actors. That is, explanations of the policy process tend to be dichotomous, attributing causality either to societal actors or state officials. As many (e.g., Smith 1993) have pointed out, neither approach offers a complete picture of why a certain policy was selected, since each assumes that policy decisions reflect the interests of its preferred agent. One type of approach, that focusing on the structure of domestic political institutions, seeks to avoid this strategy. It makes claims regarding the policymaking roles of state and societal actors only after examining the institutional context in which they operate. This context sets the rules of the game for policymaking, thus privileging some actors and actions rather than others in the national arena. An institutional approach then offers greater precision regarding the relative weights that should be attached to different actors in any given policy debate. In doing so, an institutional approach sheds light on not only which agents will assume the most significant role in policymaking but also, as will be argued, a country's capacity to adopt different strategies in response to globalization.

This section contends that a country's response to globalization depends on two institutions that determine the role of, and interaction between, government officials and private commercial interests (which may be national or transnational) in the policymaking process. The two institutions are: 1) the structure of state-societal relations in the issue area, particularly those institutions affecting the linkages between government officials and industry representatives; and 2) the organization of decision-making authority over a particular policy area. The two institutions are conceptualized at the issue area level, as the needs of and pressures facing different task environments are likely to contribute to distinctive institutional development in any given area (Skocpol 1985, 17; Ikenberry 1988, 236; Weaver and Rockman 1993c, 447). Thus, states may exhibit institutional similarities in an issue area, even though their institutions in other areas may differ (Thatcher 1999).

Institutional Networks

Scholars studying domestic institutions and state-societal relations increasingly focus on the network of institutional arrangements that link representatives from the state and society together during policymaking. When present, these institutions, or institutional networks,[3] fundamentally shape the coalition-building process between the two spheres. Institutional networks connect state and societal actors and "provide institutionalized channels for the continual negotiation and renegotiation of goals and policies" (Evans 1995, 59). Some scholars (Okimoto 1989; Risse-Kappen 1995a) might see institutional networks as being similar to policy networks. So long as the term "policy network" stands for the institutions connecting state and societal actors in policymaking, then the two terms have the same meaning. Yet policy network is increasingly used in a second way. Policy networks often refer to the types of relationships that arise between societal groups and governments (Marsh and Rhodes 1992; Smith 1993). To avoid the possibility that a policy network (institutional connections) may be said to determine a policy network (a type of state-societal relationship), the term "institutional network" is used here to refer to those institutional connections that link state and societal actors together during policymaking. As the discussion proceeds, it emphasizes those institutions linking government officials and industry representatives given the book's empirical focus.

Institutional networks include those arrangements, both formal and conventional, that grant nonstate representatives a direct and privileged role in the formulation of a particular area of national policy. Formal networks include advisory bodies, regulations, and other decision rules that mandate some form of state-societal consultations during policy formation. Conventional networks comprise less formalized, yet institutionalized consultative mechanisms that derive from a given polity's customary practices. Such networks include most significantly top-level government and industry recruitment patterns that involve the movement of such elites between public and private sector positions. France's system of *pantouflage* and Japan's *amakaduri* are perhaps the best examples of such linkages (Hayward 1983;

Okimoto 1989). Additionally, long-term personalized networks—such as "old boy networks"—that link the state and its society also would be classified as conventional networks (see Katzenstein 1978). Other standard operating procedures and cultural or social norms are included in this category of institutions if "they have been established by either an explicit or a tacit agreement . . . whether or not they have been written down and decided upon in a formal procedure" (Rothstein 1996, 146).

How Institutional Networks Matter

The presence of any one of these institutional networks increases the ability of societal actors to channel their preferences to decision-makers during policymaking. Simply put, an institutional network provides a societal interest group with a legitimate and, in some cases, a relatively stable communication channel through which it can provide government officials with advice and information. For this reason, the presence of this institution provides an interest group with the expectation of access to centers of decision making and influence therein. In doing so, the network creates incentives for the group to work with authoritative officials to redress its demands. In other words, the existence of a network may depoliticize the interest group's actions, as there is some presumption of a long-term relationship and the benefits that may accrue from it (e.g., Katzenstein 1985, 91–94). As Stephan Haggard, Sylvia Maxfield, and Ben Ross Schneider (1997, 41) note, research on corporatism, social pacts, and concertation draws a similar conclusion. This research finds that these structures of business-government relations "[provide] a forum for negotiation between representatives of business, government, and labor that can resolve the strategic dilemma of government-business cooperation. By creating opportunities for repeated interactions, such institutions lengthen time horizons and create trust."

Policymakers are likely to perceive institutional networks as serving two purposes, both furthering either their agency's mission or their electoral prospects. First, networks offer a means to gain technical or other expert information from societal representatives to develop more effective policies. Weiss (1998, 58), for example, writes that such networks are important because "[i]n so far as public and private decision-makers get together to exchange information and to coordinate actions, information gaps are minimized and each generally ends up making better decisions than if trapped in isolation. . . . [T]he economic bureaucracy therefore has a vital mechanism for acquiring production-related information and for coordinating agreement with the private sector in order to design and implement policies better." Second, networks enable officials to anticipate societal reaction to proposed strategies, thereby helping the government to mobilize support for its policies.[4] Peter Evans (1995, 41, 69, 248) identifies these factors in making a case for why state officials might value close government-industry relations. He (1997, 70) observes that "[b]ureaucratic capacity will always be inadequate to produce transformation on its own. No conceivable formal organization could successfully deal with all the innumerable intricacies involved in promoting economic transformation. The state needs business first of all as a source of decentralized intelligence about what is possible. Even more important, any transformative project that the state might contrive must in the end be implemented largely by private capitalists."

Whether viewed from the state or societal perspective, an institutional network can—as the literature on policy networks contends—produce a degree of interdependence between the two sectors; information and support are exchanged for a privileged position in policymaking.[5] This pattern of interaction not only fosters bargaining and negotiation over the direction of policy, but also the accommodation of conflicting objectives among the participating policymakers and societal groups, leading them to develop shared interests and goals (Okimoto 1989, chap. 3). At other times, as several observers (Cawson, Holmes, and Stevens 1987, 14) point out, "[t]he close relationship which develops [in this institutional context] between certain groups and state agencies means that the agency may act as the client group's advocate, and the group may undertake certain quasi-official functions."

Without recourse to an institutional network societal actors are likely to find it more difficult to assume a regular role in policy development. Accordingly, societal actors may be forced to utilize extrainstitutional channels to influence policymaking. These avenues may include strikes, demonstrations, media campaigns, election contributions, or the manipulation of public opinion more generally. In the absence of institutional networks, the role societal actors ultimately assume is a function of their ability to mobilize public opinion to convince state officials that their electoral prospects will be adversely affected, if they do not respond in a manner broadly consistent with the group's interests (Risse-Kappen 1991, 504, 510–11).

Institutional networks are important not simply for providing a linkage between the state and its society, but also for what they indicate about the country's normative beliefs. Institutions, as sociological institutionalists note, tend to emerge from and reflect national normative understandings and values regarding the appropriateness of certain relationships and actions (Ikenberry 1988; Risse-Kappen 1994; Hall and Taylor 1996). In this respect, institutional networks provide insight into fundamental norms about the state's relationship with society-based economic actors. In particular, the absence of networks indicates that the country is ideologically oriented toward an arms-length relationship between government and industry in policymaking whereas the presence of institutional networks is suggestive of national norms supportive of public-private coordination of economic activities. Given that institutions "reflect a set of dominant ideas translated through legal mechanisms into formal government organizations" (Goldstein 1988, 181), institutions are likely to infuse the preferences and expectations of state and societal actors in terms of the responsibilities of each sector with respect to globalization and to the policies that should follow. For example, the absence of institutional networks is likely to be associated with an understanding that the appropriate scope of state economic activity is not inclusive of the development of strategies that advance a particular sector's individual competitive interests; the converse is likely to be true if such networks exist. These institutions then give rise to what Mauro Guillén calls "strategies of action" or "resources for action." Guillén (2001a, 14) writes that these institutions become "sense-making frames that provide understandings of what is legitimate, reasonable, and effective in a given context." In effect, institutions provide insight into those national ideas and practices that are salient in the issue area.

The presence of an institutional network provides societal actors with access to policymaking, but it does not guarantee that their preferences will translate readily or completely into the policy process or outcomes. Access should not be equated with influence by definition. Influence also depends on the organization of decision-making authority that prevails during the policy debate.[6] This is the second component of the argument advanced here.

The Organization of Decision-making Authority

The organization of decision-making authority over a particular area of policy varies in terms of its relative centralization. The organization of decision-making authority refers to the number of individual state units involved in determining policy for a specific issue area. This institution captures the degree of independence and, thus power, government officials in different aspects of the state enjoy in relation to each other with respect to policy outcomes.

The degree of centralization is determined by two dynamics. First, the greater the number of agencies, departments, or institutions that have jurisdiction over a particular area of policy, the more authority is decentralized. The centralization of decision-making authority increases, by contrast, "as other agencies are effectively precluded—by formal procedure or by political arrangements—from influencing policy choice" (Solingen 1993, 280). Centralized structures can take two primary forms depending on the specific distribution of authority. One form is best captured by Etel Solingen's term "lateral autonomy," which measures an agency's autonomy in relation to other parts of the state; "it is thus a relational property of the state unit with respect to others and should not be confused with state autonomy as a whole" (Ibid.). In this respect, "[a]n agency with higher levels of *lateral autonomy* has greater capacity to define and carry out policy independent of the interference of other units" (Ibid.). A second form of centralization may result when decision-making authority is concentrated in the head of the government as opposed to a bureaucratic agency or other state unit. In this case, decision-making authority is "executive-centered."

Second, a state unit possesses greater independence when it controls the policy instruments needed to advance its own interests. Important among these instruments, for example, are an agency's budgetary, legal, or technical capabilities. In the issue areas examined here, the key policy instruments involve the control of financial resources and technical expertise. Policy instruments, it should be noted, need not be applied for an agency to attain its objectives; they also can be withdrawn or left untouched. The key point then in determining a state unit's autonomy with regard to policy instruments is the extent to which it controls the use or nonuse of different instruments.

How the Organization of Decision-making Authority Matters

The organization of decision-making authority affects government officials' capacity to advance their preferences and the government's capacity to speak with a single voice. As Hall (1986, 19) explains, "organizational position also influences an actor's definition of his own interests, by establishing his institutional responsibilities and relationship to other actors. In this way, organizational factors affect both the degree of pressure an actor can bring to bear on policy and the likely direction of that pressure."

As much research has shown, bureaucratic agencies tend to disagree about "what policy in a given circumstance serves the long-term national interest" (Cohen 1987, 42). The incongruity among different departments results because the stance of a particular government official tends to reflect his or her position in the bureaucracy or the policymaking apparatus more generally (Allison 1971; Art 1973). That is, policymakers tend to favor policies that are consistent with, or maximize, their department's preexisting institutional interests and culture, not all of which will be perceived to be enhanced, for example, by addressing an industry's demands to respond to globalization pressures. Accordingly, the participation of several functionally differentiated departments in the policy debate tends to produce bureaucratic disagreement regarding the correct strategy to pursue (Cohen 1987, 45; Atkinson and Coleman 1989, 51; Solingen 1993, 283). Scholars studying the United States suggest that the potential for conflict of interests to emerge among government officials is not limited simply to those arising from their positions within different bureaucratic agencies; rather, it also prevails at a higher level of generality, affecting relations between the legislature and the executive (Pastor 1980, 53). David Lake (1988, 36–38) locates the conflict of interest in the differing constituencies of these entities; whereas the legislative branch is "representative" of society, the executive branch "is the sole authoritative foreign policymaker and the only national actor mandated to preserve and enhance the position of the nation-state within the anarchic and competitive international system."

An official's position in the governmental apparatus then creates distinct pressures for the type of policy preferred. This observation suggests that as the organization of decision-making authority becomes more decentralized, the diversity of interests among government officials increases, and the capacity of any individual official to advance his or her preferences decreases. As discussed in the next section, this dynamic also affects the influence societal actors can wield in the policy process. Put otherwise, the structure of decision-making authority determines the extent to which an institutional network empowers societal actors' preferences.

Decision Making in Different Institutional Contexts

The interaction of the two institutions creates six distinct types of institutional contexts with particular characteristics. Table 2.1 depicts each context and its implications for the policymaking influence of state and nonstate actors. The discussion that follows begins with the three contexts in which an institutional network is present and then proceeds to those in which they are absent.

Table 2.1
Six Institutional Contexts

| Institutional Networks | *Organization of Decision-making Authority* | | |
	Executive-Centered	*Decentralized*	*Lateral Autonomy*
Present	TYPE I Top executive-interest group cooperation	TYPE III Societal actors enjoy access to the policy process, but their leverage over policy is limited due to intra-governmental divisions	TYPE V Agency-interest group cooperation
Absent	TYPE II Executive autonomy	TYPE IV Bureaucratic bargaining	TYPE VI Agency autonomy

A societal group's influence can increase when an institutional network links the group's representatives to a decision-making structure that concentrates authority, either in the executive (Type I) or laterally in an individual state unit (Type V). In these two contexts, intragovernmental conflict is reduced, since the authoritative policymakers have "greater capacity to define and carry out policy independent of the interference of other [state] units" (Solingen 1993, 280). Nonetheless, these officials are not expected to operate autonomously from the societal group's representatives that the institutional network integrates into the policy process. Instead, a convergence of interests can arise out of the interaction between these state and societal actors. In this regard, the institutional network affords the private sector representatives a privileged and influential position in policymaking, not only fostering the ongoing exchange of information and ideas between them and government officials, but also making it dif-ficult to determine who is influencing whom. For example, the societal group, as R. Kent Weaver and Bert Rockman (1993b, 28–29) note, "may be better placed to ensure that [some] decisions are never made to begin with."

Meanwhile, the network provides the authoritative decision-making unit with the ability to integrate societal representatives into the development of policies. This allows government officials the opportunity to formulate strategies that will be more effectively implemented and/or reduce the possibility that societal groups will use extrainstitutional channels to discredit the executive and his or her government. Since state units with countervailing interests assume an insignificant role in policymaking, the power of the state can be put behind decisions derived from this state-societal interaction.

In a Type III context, the decentralized decision-making structure reduces the ability of societal representatives to utilize an institutional network to translate their preferences into policy. As several observers explain, "[t]he reason for this pattern is that [this structure] provides multiple points of influence or access for interest groups . . . as well as veto points" (Feigenbaum, Samuels, and Weaver 1993, 99). As far as private sector interests are concerned, the downside of this structural context is two-fold. First, the societal group faces the difficult task of convincing many functionally differentiated state units of the merits of its demands. Due to these units' role in the policy process, if any one remains opposed to the group's demands, it can act as a barrier to the achievement of the group's interests. In short, in this type of setting, as Mark Peterson (1993, 793) observes, "stymieing action" is more prevalent than an interest group's success in "guiding" its demands through the multiple veto points. Second, the proliferation of state units tends to produce bureaucratic conflict or immobilism. As Michael Barzelay (1986, 110) explains, "[f]or the simple reason that no two agencies are likely to have identical missions, some incompatibility between the[ir] institutional interests is likely to emerge." Even if each of the participating state units favors responding to the group's demands, conflict regarding the appropriate response may still emerge as a result of each unit's organizational and role influences. Resolving the differences among these state units entails a bargaining process that may at the least modify or undermine the societal group's objectives. This outcome results, Michael Atkinson and William Coleman (1989, 51) note, because "bureaucratic pluralism encourages . . . decision making that is based on least common denominator criteria. . . ."

State officials' autonomy from societal interventions increases when an institutional network does not connect societal representatives to them. The possibility for state autonomy emerges in each of three institutional contexts. When decision-making authority is concentrated in the top executive and institutional networks are lacking (Type II), the head of the government can advance strategies that he or she believes reflect the government's mandate or are most appropriate for the country in the particular situation. In a decision-making structure characterized by lateral autonomy (Type VI), the authoritative agency independently can pursue policies in keeping with its understanding of its institutional mission, culture, and objectives. In both contexts, the empowered officials enjoy the decision-making power to consult with private sector interests, if they so desire. However, the absence of institutional networks suggests that such consultations are unlikely, since they do not resonate with national expectations of legitimacy. Additionally, state autonomy is possible when decision-making authority is dispersed and institutional networks are absent (Type IV). In this context the state may not appear to act as a capable entity, since the increased "division of policy authority . . . may increase bargaining costs and reduce effective bargaining space. Requiring the agreement of additional players implies, all else equal, a greater diversity of interests and hence greater disagreement over changes to the status quo" (Heller, Keefer, and McCubbins 1998, 157).

In sum, a focus on these two institutional components suggests that a policy debate can take place in any one of six contexts, depending on the two institutions' combination and configuration. Each context produces different effects for the influence state officials and societal actors can wield over policy. It should be recognized that in reality each context is likely to vary somewhat from the idealized dimensions depicted in Table 2.1. In some cases multiple institutional networks may be present, whereas in others only one will connect private and public representatives together during the formulation of policy. Additionally, rarely will decision-making authority be concentrated in a single agency given the inherent complexity of most issues. For this reason, decision-making structures are expected to differ in terms of their degrees of centralization.

The institutional contexts identified in Table 2.1 are not assumed to affect an issue area indefinitely. Instead, the two institutional components are mutable. That is, there is likely to be variation over time with regard to the type of institutional structure that affects an issue area within a particular country. Accordingly, the institutional constraints and opportunities that prevailed during one policy episode may be different during a subsequent policy episode. The possibility for institutional transformation does not imply that institutions are likely to be epiphenomenal. This is true for at least three reasons. First, institutions are unlikely to be changed at will. Much research indicates that institutional reform tends to be difficult, incremental rather than radical, and several causal conditions need to be present to enable agents to alter the institutional parameters they face (Gourevitch 1996; Risse, Cowles, and Caporaso 2001; Cortell and Peterson 2002). Second, existing institutions tend to structure the possibility and scope for change (Skocpol and Weir 1985, 118). As Mark Thatcher (1999, 18) writes, "when institutional change does take place, existing institutions affect its form. They influence the ideas, interests, resources, and strategies of actors engaged in reform. Institutional modification does not begin '*de novo*,' but involves adaptation of, or reaction against, existing institutional arrangements." Third, the possibility that institutions can be altered does not mean that agents will achieve their preferences in doing so. Success is likely to be elusive, because an altered institution creates new incentives and constraints, which may create new obstacles that militate against the achievement of the reformers' interests (Moe 1990; Lindsay 1994; Pierson 1996).

Toward an Understanding of National Responses to Globalization

Like other historical institutionalists, I do not claim that institutions are the only determinant of a country's response. In particular, an institutional approach allows us to determine how a particular policy debate will play out, but does not provide complete information a priori regarding the content of the debate (Hall 1986; Thelen and Steinmo 1992; Immergut 1992). That is, institutions may affect agents' preferences and actions, but they do not determine them. To offer some preliminary expectations regarding how different contexts affect a country's response to the globalization of the semiconductor industry, I adopt two premises regarding the content of this debate. First, I assume, like others examining state interactions with globalization, that firms and governments "seek to cope with economic globalization because they perceive it as changing their economic and political landscapes, thereby creating new opportunities and threats" (Prakash and Hart 2000a, 1). Second, firms are assumed to be motivated to seek policies that benefit them in light of increasing competition in foreign and domestic markets.[7] Both assumptions suggest that pressures associated with globalization produce gains and/or losses and that actors within the national arena hope to capitalize on opportunities or compensate for vulnerabilities. In doing so, these dynamics can lead actors within the national arena to favor either interventionist or liberal strategies. The central goal of the following discussion is to explain how states' capacity to capitalize on or compensate for globalization pressures depends on the institutional context shaping the policy debate. Phrased otherwise, I seek to show that these institutions are themselves constraining or enabling, thereby mediating the opportunities and threats globalization may produce.[8]

In what follows I explain the policies that are likely to flow from each of the institutional contexts discussed in the previous section. Like that one, the following discussion begins with the three contexts in which an institutional network is present and then proceeds to those in which they are absent. The discussion of the first two contexts starts from the assumption that firms in the sector or government officials whose focus is industry-related identify vulnerabilities or threats from globalization and these pressures create incentives to favor interventionist strategies. It then takes up the alternative assumption and weaves the two sets of demands into the discussion of the subsequent four contexts.

Generally, centralized decision-making structures tend to be more conducive to industrial policies than decentralized structures. This dynamic reflects the differing degrees of autonomy accorded to state officials in the two structures; centralized structures provide a limited number of state units with authority over the issue area and, thus, the capacity to act independently to assist an industry to respond to globalization. Similarly, the presence of institutional networks is likely to produce more interventionist policies than a context lacking networks. This expectation reflects several dynamics. Networks empower industry representatives during policymaking and, thus, afford policymakers information regarding which strategies are most likely to succeed. The presence of institutional networks also indicates that close government-industry relations are seen as appropriate within the national arena, and this appropriateness can serve as reasons for embracing interventionist initiatives. Taken together, these propositions suggest that industrial policies are most likely to be developed in an institutional context characterized by the presence of institutional networks and the centralization of decision-making authority (Types I and V).

These two contexts provide industry representatives with direct access to those state officials—whether the executive or agency officials—who can operate independently of other officials in formulating policy. Consequently, industry representatives will find themselves institutionalized into the policy process, leading policy formation to be characterized by a close working relationship between the authoritative policymakers and industry representatives. While this interactive process fosters the convergence of interests across the two spheres, state officials may try to accommodate industry, since it is likely that their goals and understanding of viable strategies may emerge from their interaction with this group. These contexts are then conducive to the development of strategies that are tailored to the specific demands or needs of industries seeking to cope with globalization. It is possible, however, that a decision-making structure characterized by lateral autonomy (Type V) will produce more interventionist strategies than an executive-centered structure (Type I). Since the authoritative agency tends to define its interests and success in terms of the well-being of the groups it is designed to serve (Lake 1988, 36), it will be less constrained by strategic and other considerations that can lead the executive to temper his/her support for specific sectors.

If firms or officials do not perceive vulnerabilities from globalization, but instead see opportunities, they may favor the strengthening of global interconnections. Under such conditions, the role of the government in the economy is likely to decrease most markedly when an institutional network is present and the decision-making structure is characterized by lateral autonomy (Type V). This context enables a close working relationship between industry representatives and the authoritative officials. These officials will have detailed information regarding the strengths of the industry and the possible effects of liberalization initiatives for this and other sectors. Given its lateral autonomy, these officials can pursue desired strategies, whether national or multilateral, to advance the sector's immersion in the global economy without the intervention of other officials. As a consequence, initiatives adopted in a Type V context may go far in minimizing the government's role in the sector. Strategies advanced in a Type I context, in contrast, are likely to be more restrained, since the executive's view of the implications of such actions is mediated by other concerns, such as other interests in the polity or the country's relationships with other countries or international entities.

An institutional context characterized by a decentralized decision-making structure and the presence of an institutional network (Type III) empowers numerous government and industry representatives in the policy process. The access afforded industry representatives enables them to pressure policymakers to help them capitalize on, or compensate for, globalization's effects on their competitive position; alternatively, industry representatives' role in the policy process can serve as a resource for those policymakers who see the necessity of a policy response. In this regard, these officials have access to technical information to support their positions and are able to design strategies that reflect sectoral developments and appear relevant to the success of the sector. Moreover, norms legitimating cooperative policymaking also offer justifications for the use of policies that call for the state to support a particular industry's individual interests. However, the bureaucratic pluralism creates constraints and opportunities for the influence of individual government officials and industry representatives. In particular, officials' focus on their own institutionally derived objectives will crowd out the industry-specific concerns triggering the policy debate. If this pluralism is extensive, the government may be unable to offer any response, as arriving at a consensus among the many empowered agencies becomes difficult. Otherwise, the decentralization of decision-making authority produces a lowest common denominator approach regardless of globalization's perceived impact.

In a Type III context, support then is easiest for initiatives designed to make the economic environment more attractive, especially those reinforcing the educational, training, and R&D infrastructure, given their negligible impact on each state unit's extant interests. For example, the patchwork of competing institutional interests is likely to work against a significant reduction in the government's role in the economy, since some state units are likely to favor the maintenance of regulations or the creation of new ones to safeguard their varied constituents. Similarly, if vulnerabilities are identified, industrial policies can emerge, but these will be designed to achieve multiple objectives, including some unrelated to the sector involved (e.g., labor and regional markets or environmental protection).

An executive-centered structure devoid of networks (Type II) enables the executive to develop policies autonomously of societal interventions and other state units. As a result, the type of strategy pursued largely depends on the executive's willingness to intervene in or disengage from the economy, which is a function of a number of factors, including his or her ideological proclivities or electoral calculations. We might expect the executive in the United States and Britain to be less willing to intervene due to both countries' liberal proclivities (Krauss and Reich 1992; Wilks 1983). More generally, the absence of an institutional network in this context may further reduce the willingness of an executive to intervene given his/her distance from, and lack of knowledge of how globalization impacts particular sectors. The disincentive to intervene is reinforced by what the lack of networks suggests about the standing of close government-industry relations in the national arena: such actions do not resonate with prevailing norms. Even with these constraints, however, the institutional context still empowers the executive to act autonomously to advance the strategy s/he deems most appropriate. Thus, either of the policy options are possible in this context and these choices may vary over time.

When an agency enjoys lateral autonomy and no networks are present (Type VI), the agency can act autonomously of other state units and societal pressure. Given the absence of connections between the agency and the affected industry, however, the agency lacks the information necessary to craft what it hopes will be effective industrial policies. Such policies are further hindered, since the arms-length nature of government-industry relations is likely to infuse officials' understandings of appropriate strategies. The dearth of information also restrains the agency when it perceives that globalization affords opportunities. Without networks, the agency lacks an intimate understanding of the strengths of national industry generally speaking, creating obstacles for the use of initiatives that minimize the government's role in the economy, especially those that portend cross-sector effects. Regardless of the agency's view of globalization's impact, the agency's imperfect information makes likely the use of tax initiatives or liberal strategies that seek to support education and training or research and development. These initiatives can lower the costs of doing business in the economy or facilitate an increase in investment and innovation with minimal deleterious consequences for national industry. Additionally, the agency's lateral autonomy enables it to respond unilaterally to its initial policy choices, suggesting that there could be an action-reaction dynamic in which additional measures go beyond those initially selected. Over time, this may lead to increased strategies to immerse the country in the global economy. However, the absence of networks remains a significant constraint on the agency's assumption of a direct role in the sector, since such strategies are unlikely to be viewed as legitimate in light of national norms demarcating government from industry.

An institutional context characterized by decentralization and the absence of institutional networks (Type IV) limits a state's capacity to advance new strategies. First, those departments whose institutional missions are most closely associated with industry or commercial concerns lack the sectoral information necessary to develop successful policies and the capacity to act autonomously from other state units. Second, direct state support for national industry does not resonate with national norms given the absence of institutional networks. Third, the various other state units and/ or agencies accorded authority over the issue are unlikely to propose, or to take the lead in formulating, initiatives that seek to promote industrial competitiveness. Instead, the attention of these officials will be consumed by issues that are more consonant with their preexisting institutional interests and priorities. Taken together, these three dynamics suggest that this institutional context minimizes the state's capacity to develop new initiatives, leading it to leave in place existing strategies.

In sum, the combination of the two institutions illuminates a state's capacity to advance different types of strategies in response to globalization pressures. This capacity is a function of how the institutional context affects the role and influence state officials and industry representatives play in the policy process. Due to the constraints and opportunities afforded by different institutions, a cross-national convergence on the need for liberal strategies nevertheless may lead states to pursue divergent paths with regard to whether and, if so, how they seek to immerse the country in the global economy. A similar dynamic is likely to emerge when intervention is preferred, since not all contexts enable industrial policies. This discussion indicates that if states find their policy choices constrained in responding to international economic forces, their lack of discretion may have more to do with their institutions than dynamics associated with globalization.

As noted above, state capacity may change over time, as the two institutions are not immutable. Over time, different institutional contexts may prevail in the same issue area, thereby creating opportunities for different policies. Institutional dynamism is especially likely as the state engages globalization. As many note (e.g., Clark 1999; Guillén 2001b), globalization is likely to produce a restructuring of the state's policymaking authority and capacity, since it creates new pressures and developments that raise the costs associated with an extant institutional context and the benefits that could accrue from change. Chapters 3 through 7 find that both the United States and Britain frequently advanced institutional reforms in response to globalization dynamics. The concluding chapter explores the sources of and variation in the institutional changes the two countries advanced in response to globalization pressures.

Case Studies and Methodology

Chapters 3 through 7 apply this chapter's argument to empirical examinations of thirteen policy episodes involving U.S. and British responses to pressures emerging from the globalization of competition and production in the semiconductor industry. The analysis focuses on policy debates involving whether and, if so, how to support the capacities of firms located within the United States and Britain. The policy episodes revolve around competitive pressures impacting the firms' development of commercially oriented manufacturing technologies; these firms include domestic- and foreign-based multinationals, those likely to develop global interests and, thus, possess the potential for the mobility globalists expect. In addition, the cases focus on the commercial domain, since "commercial technologies and the industries that produce them are considerably more globalized than the defense industrial sector" (Held and McGrew 1998, 226). Each case study is organized around a separate policy debate concerning the appropriateness of existing policies, regardless of whether the policies are changed or new ones developed, and whether government officials or firms trigger the debate. I examine six U.S. cases covering the period between 1977 and 1997. For Britain, I examine seven policy debates that took place between 1970 and 1996.

The empirical chapters do not feature all six of the institutional structures identified in this chapter. No cases examine the Types I, IV, or VI institutional structures. The book's cross-national longitudinal study then enables a test of only three of the six institutional contexts. This limitation emerges for two primary reasons. First, the absence of policy episodes taking place in these structures reflects the fact that the institutional contexts identified in Table 2.1 are analytical possibilities and are not intended to be representative of those that affected U.S. and British policies in the three decades under review here. Second, existing institutions tend to structure the direction of change, making some types of reforms more or less likely (Thelen and Steinmo 1992). Such path dependence suggests that a wide variation in each country's institutional contexts is unlikely in the twenty-five year period examined here. Nevertheless, the cases explored in chapters 3 through 7 include examples of institutional structures that vary across all three structures of decision-making authority and both structures of state-societal relations. As a consequence, the cases provide variation across the independent variables. Additional case studies still are required to provide a complete test of the institutional argument.

There is also variation across the dependent variable, a country's policy response to the globalization of competition. Although such variation is crucial to explore the validity of the globalist perspective's expectations regarding liberal convergence, the cases were not selected on this basis (King, Keohane, and Verba 1994, chap. 4). I examine the semiconductor industry because globalists generally identify it as having been one of the most globalized sectors since the late 1960s. Starting from this presumption, then, reduces the possibility for debate about the international dynamic. Since globalization generally is thought to be intensifying over time, a longitudinal study of the sector sheds light on whether states learn certain lessons in response to their initial responses to globalization and subsequently shift future strategies in the way globalists expect. I examine the United States and Britain because they provide a hard test for the argument advanced here. On the one hand, the purported similarities in these countries would lead us to expect them to be an easy confirmation of the globalist view. First, scholars have commonly identified both states as lacking the policy instruments and institutional capacity to harness market forces to the state's advantage. As such, the United States and Britain would be expected to find the external environment constraining. Second, both are thought to have a long-standing preference for liberal economic policies. Both states are expected to welcome rather than resist the globalization of industry. The conventional wisdom regarding the two countries' liberal predilections suggests that if a liberal convergence emerges, it is most likely to include these two countries. Third, as noted in chapter 1, both countries' semiconductor industries and markets experienced significant internationalization during the period of accelerating globalization, the period since the 1960s. On the other hand, these purported similarities provide a difficult test of the historical institutionalist argument offered here. That is, international and national factors would seem to be pushing the United States and Britain to converge on liberal strategies. National institutions should not produce divergent strategies, let alone enable either to adopt interventionist strategies.

Although the cases are treated individually, some interdependence is likely to exist among them. In particular, government officials' responses to previous sectoral developments can set the stage for further government interventions. In a sense, then, one policy episode may be premised on a previous one. A second form of interdependence among the cases also may exist. Developments in an earlier policy episode may infuse the preferences of government officials or societal actors regarding whether to seek a change in the institutional context during a subsequent policy episode. This snowball effect is useful in understanding the evolution of institutions, as well as the factors that can lead agents to want to alter their institutional contexts.

Conclusion

This chapter starts from the perspective that for globalization, like other systemic dynamics, to affect national policy, it must be acted upon by agents who must work through national political institutions to achieve their preferences. I develop a historical institutionalist approach to explain how these institutions affect a state's response to globalization. Focusing on the presence or absence of institutional networks and the organization of decision-making authority, the chapter identifies six potential institutional contexts within which policymaking can occur. Each context uniquely structures government-industry and intragovernmental relations and, as a consequence, makes different policy responses more or less feasible. The next five chapters test this argument by examining U.S. and British reactions to the globalization of competition in the semiconductor industry. If the two countries do converge on a similar strategy, this convergence is expected to reflect the impact of similar institutional conditions rather than just the pressures associated with the globalization of competition.

Part Two

The United States

Chapter Three

Liberal Convergence: The Carter and First Reagan Administrations

The 1970s were marked by the emerging globalization of competition in the semiconductor industry. Most notably, U.S. manufacturers began to confront intense competition in the U.S. market from technologically adept Japanese firms. In response to these new realities, the Carter and Reagan administrations advanced liberal strategies. This convergence is surprising given the ideological differences of the two administrations and, thus, some globalists may see this period as significant confirmation of their arguments. Attributing this liberal convergence to the pressures and constraints of globalization, however, misses the important role domestic institutions play in producing the outcome.

In the two cases examined in this chapter (see Table 3.1), neither government officials nor industry representatives uniformly sought liberal strategies or a decrease in the government's role in the economy or sector more specifically. In fact, both policy episodes were initiated by government officials who believed more interventionist strategies were required given the pressures globalization created for U.S. industries. The choice of liberalism ultimately reflected the constraints imposed by the institutional context shaping each policy episode. In particular, the evidence indicates that proponents of interventionist initiatives were thwarted not by the effects of globalization, but instead by the decentralized structure of decision-making authority shaping the two policy episodes.

Table 3.1
Policy Episodes, Institutional Contexts, and Policy Choices

Cases	Institutional Context			Nature of the Policy-making Process	Outcome
	Institutional Networks	Decison-making Structure	Type		
Innovation Initiatives (1979)	Present	Decentralized	III	Industry access and intra-governmental divisions	Liberal strategy
High Tech Working Group (1982)	Present	Decentralized	III	Industry access and intra-governmental divisions	Liberal strategy

The chapter begins with a short overview of the competitive position of the U.S. semiconductor industry prior to 1978 and identifies the catalyst for the competitive concerns that came to be associated with the sector. It then examines, chronologically, the policy debates surrounding each administration's choice of strategy.

An Emerging Competitive Challenge

Technological innovations in the semiconductor industry from the late 1950s to the 1970s were largely driven by American firms. American dominance began with the creation of the integrated circuit in 1958 and continued throughout the 1960s and the early 1970s, thanks in part to the dynamism of the country's computer industry, a major source of demand for semiconductor devices.[1]

As a result of American technological dominance, U.S. firms were able to control an overwhelming proportion of the world market for semiconductors throughout much of the 1960s and 1970s. For example, in 1975 U.S. firms accounted for 98% of the U.S. market for integrated circuits and 78% of the West European market; by contrast, the U.S. share of the Japanese market was 20% (Borrus, Millstein, and Zysman 1983, 175). The small size of the U.S. share of the Japanese semiconductor market did not become a galvanizing issue for the American industry until the competitive strength of Japanese semiconductor and electronics firms rose during the 1970s. In this period, Japanese manufacturers increased their share of the world market, largely at American firms' expense and much of it in the U.S. market. To compound matters for U.S. firms, the technological capability of Japanese manufacturers was generally recognized to be approaching that of American firms (Japanese Challenge 1977, 73). The abilities of Japanese firms would improve, thanks to the Japanese government's decision to target the industry. In 1976 Japan's Ministry of International Trade and Industry (MITI) established the Very Large Scale Integration (VLSI) project. Its goal was to help Japanese manufacturers develop the next generation of integrated circuits, which would be used in computers. To this end, MITI contributed about $300 million to the project between 1976 and 1980 (see Callon 1995).

The emerging strength of Japanese firms and the Japanese government's interest in semiconductor technology led American firms to see the Japanese industry as a potential threat to its dominance. As Kenneth Flamm (1996, 138) writes, "[a] surge in exports of Japanese chips to the U.S. market, similar to those already seen in consumer electronics and automobiles, seemed likely." Wilfred Corrigan, president of Fairchild Corporation, captured the sentiments of the U.S. industry when he noted, "[i]t's better to address the problem now than wait until it gets too big" (Japanese Challenge 1977, 72). American firms attributed much of the competitive success of Japanese firms to "unfair" trade practices.

The U.S. industry's unfair trade complaints fell into two broad charges. First, Japanese firms were thought to sell their products for prices that appeared to be way below their cost of production. In other words, some charged that Japanese firms "dumped" their products in foreign markets in an effort to gain market share. Second, U.S. firms found it difficult to export their products to the Japanese market. U.S. firms attributed their minimal share of the Japanese market to such nontariff barriers as "buy Japanese" practices, technical standards, and government promotion initiatives that excluded foreign firms. To put more weight behind these charges, five leading U.S. semiconductor firms formed the Semiconductor Industry Association (SIA) in 1977.[2]

The Carter Administration's Industrial Innovation Initiatives

The heightening of the competitive pressures facing the U.S. industry coincided with the Carter administration's decision to review the government's support for industrial innovation. This policy review was triggered by administration officials who believed that the government could do more to support research and development. Nevertheless, the Type III institutional structure shaping the policy episode limited the administration's policy alternatives, leading it to adopt a liberal strategy to reverse the declining rate of U.S. high technology industries' investment and innovation. The evidence shows that the decentralized decision-making structure reduced the ability of industry representatives to influence the policy process and suppressed the concerns of those policymakers who had been instrumental in initiating the policy debate.

Institutional Context

Soon after President Carter took office in 1977, members of the administration voiced concerns about problems U.S. industries were encountering in meeting their capital requirements (*Wall Street Journal* 1977; Senate 1978a; House 1980a). Frank Press, director of the president's Office of Science and Technology Policy (OSTP), Secretary of Commerce Juanita Kreps, and National Science Foundation (NSF) Director Richard Atkinson concluded that the government was not doing enough to support industrial research and development. Moreover, these officials maintained that the government's existing tax and regulatory policies may even have hampered the competitiveness of the country's high technology industries (Silk 1978). In response to such deficiencies, these officials recommended that the administration increase its support for R&D, whether through direct subsidies, tax credits, or regulatory changes. They argued that to do otherwise would lead to the continued decline of U.S. manufacturing exports in world markets, a development these officials believed would have negative consequences for the performance of the entire economy.[3] Moreover, OSTP Director Press maintained that "some foreign governments were doing much more than the United States to support civilian research and development" (Silk 1978). Specifically, Press cited Japan's decision to allocate $300 million to microelectronic research through the VLSI program, and the West German practice of "providing from 50% to 95% of the research and development funds for those civilian industries requesting aid and judged to be important to the economy as a whole." Some in the Commerce Department argued that these developments necessitated that "R&D and federal investment policy in the future should be targeted to backing the so-called high-technology winners that would provide the muscle for U.S. competitiveness in the world market" (Barfield 1982, 35).

In early 1978 NSF Director Atkinson forwarded President Carter a report showing that U.S. high technology industries' spending on R&D had declined between 1976 and 1977.[4] President Carter was troubled by this decline and instructed Press to investigate it. In fact, Press passed the president's request on to Commerce Secretary Kreps, who subsequently forwarded the query to Dr. Jordan Baruch, assistant secretary of commerce for science and technology. Baruch returned the query to President

Carter with a simple margin note that the decline was due to unusually high interest rates. According to one source, President Carter and Stuart Eizenstat, Carter's chief domestic policy advisor, were not satisfied with this response and requested that a full-scale investigation be undertaken. An interagency committee, placed under the direction of the Commerce Department, was empowered to conduct a comprehensive review of issues and problems related to industrial innovation, and to recommend an appropriate policy response based on its findings.

Reflecting the cross-cutting nature of the problem, the diversity of existing federal programs, and the jurisdiction of departments, a committee was established comprising twenty-eight federal agencies (House 1980b, 11). As a result, an extremely decentralized decision-making structure served as the forum in which the administration would review and propose initiatives to spur industrial innovation. In addition, an institutional network was created to provide the review committee with an understanding of the private sector's specific needs. This institutional network, the industrial innovation review's "private sector advisory panels" consisted of more than five hundred representatives from business, labor and public interest groups. Of these five hundred private sector participants, only one member represented the semiconductor industry.[5] Consequently, the administration's industrial innovation review, as this inquiry was called, transpired within a structure characterized by the decentralization of decision-making authority and the presence of an institutional network.

Administration officials, it would seem, established a decision-making process exclusively for the evaluation of existing government support programs for industrial development. This structure was not created from scratch so to speak, but reflected existing institutional parameters. With regard to the distribution of authority, those departments that enjoyed some jurisdiction over or role in existing policies were accorded a role in the policy review. The private sector advisory committee system also reflected existing institutional patterns in the issue area; the Department of Commerce, the department overseeing the review, had an extensive network of advisory committees that it used to seek industry advice regarding its strategies.[6]

Industry Preferences

The private sector advisory committees developed numerous proposals that called not only for modifications in existing federal policies, but also for the development of new policies to spur industrial innovation. These recommendations included initiatives that would affect such issues as federal research and development programs, tax policy, trade policy, and antitrust laws. Several of the private sector advisory committee's recommendations involved calls for changes in long-standing government policy. These proposals included modifications in existing antitrust policies to allow for cooperation in such precompetitive areas as basic research, creation of an R&D tax credit and an increased investment tax credit, and increased federal support for commercially relevant R&D.[7]

Given the unusually large and diverse collection of interests represented by the private sector advisory panels, it is surprising that these panels' recommendations were similar to the preferences of U.S. semiconductor manufacturers. At this time, the industry saw greater government support for its capital and R&D needs as being essential, if U.S. semiconductor manufacturers were to maintain their technological lead over their European and especially Japanese rivals. While the industry was concerned about its European competitors, it saw Japan as "the country of our greatest and most immediate concern, because of its target industry strategy" (SIA 1978, 56). In this regard, the Japanese government's VLSI project was seen as paying significant dividends, since by early 1979 Japanese firms captured nearly 50% of the American market for the best-selling and most advanced standard circuit at that time, the 16K dynamic random access memory circuit (DRAM) (Can Semiconductors 1979, 66).[8] The U.S. semiconductor industry hoped that the Carter administration would adopt the following initiatives to help it fend off the Japanese challenge: establish tax credits for year-to-year increases in research expenditures by high technology firms; create new incentives for R&D taking place in the United States; liberalize depreciation rules; increase funding for industry-university research in specific high technology areas; and increase funding for commercially relevant semiconductor technologies.[9] Even though the private sector advisory panels' recommendations did not completely reflect the SIA's policy proposals, they captured their basic thrust: to get the U.S. government to increase both its direct and indirect support for high technology innovation. However, due to the fact that these advisory panels were linked to an extremely decentralized decision-making structure, it was unlikely that their recommendations would be acceptable to all the participating federal agencies. Moreover, it was unlikely that the many different state units would be able to reach a consensus regarding what steps would be acceptable to increase industrial innovation.

Policy Response

The private sector advisory panels, on completing their deliberation process, sent their recommendations to the Commerce Department. The Commerce Department could not, however, independently act on the private sector advisory panels' recommendations. Instead, the Commerce Department synthesized the private sector's proposals and then forwarded them to the interagency review committee. Here the proposals "ping-ponged back and forth" among the twenty-eight different executive agencies and departments that were involved in the industrial innovation review (House 1980b, v). The president's domestic policy staff finalized the document ultimately presented to the president (Stanfield 1979, 1442; see Eizenstat, McIntyre, and Press 1979). This decision-making structure created obstacles for those officials who wanted the administration to do more to foster industrial innovation since the administration "was never of one mind on the subject." Instead, it comprised "various shades of opinion about the actual gravity of the [innovation] problem and about the steps that must be taken—particularly by the federal government—to correct it" (Barfield 1982, 34).

As expected, various agencies adopted different perspectives that reflected their preexisting institutional interests (Eizenstat, McIntyre, and Press 1979). During this process, the private sector's original policy proposals underwent continual revision (House 1980b, v). After eighteen months of development and subsequent interdepartmental bargaining, a set of draft policy recommendations was presented to the president for his approval in October 1979. The large number of departments involved in the policy review made it impossible for the interagency committee to reach a consensus on a number of issues. On several of them, the interagency committee asked President Carter to choose unilaterally among several different options. For example, with regard to improving the U.S. patent system, the interagency committee offered four separate proposals. These options each reflected, as the *Memorandum for the President* noted, the range and inconsistency of the agency preferences involved in the policy review (Eizenstat, McIntyre, and Press 1979, 15).

The president's "Industrial Innovation Initiatives" were announced at the end of October 1979. These initiatives included (Senate 1980, 51–67):

- Asking Congress to create a uniform patent policy for innovations derived from federal support and calling for a policy granting "exclusive licenses in specific fields of use" when the licensee "agrees to commercialize the innovation."

- Instructing the Justice Department "to clarify its position" on industry cooperation "to dispel" the notion that antitrust law "inhibits innovation." The plan did not include any changes in existing antitrust laws.

- Adding $10 million to an NSF program enabling small businesses to develop feasibility studies.

- Adding $20 million to an NSF program supporting "R&D projects that are proposed and jointly funded by industry-university research teams." These funds were to be allocated in the 1981 fiscal year budget.

- Promising that federal procurement programs would seek to buy more innovative products by establishing specifications based on performance rather than design.

- Promising to increase the "flow of knowledge from federal laboratories and R&D centers to industries" not normally associated with them.

The Carter administration opted for a strategy then that sought to spur industrial innovation by nominally improving the institutional foundations of the U.S. market. This program represents a liberal strategy, since it sought to increase the transparency of existing regulations and provided limited, additional, nonselective support for precompetitive economic activities.

This program was not enthusiastically received by its intended beneficiaries. To many U.S. high technology industries, the program did not go far enough in addressing any of the existing disincentives to innovation and investment they faced (Levine 1979, 3). Within three months of the program's announcement, the U.S. semiconductor industry called on the government to take further action on the question of industrial innovation. In particular, the industry called on the government to pursue policies that would have a more direct impact on the industry's capital investment, its R&D, and university research that was explicitly linked to commercial applications.[10]

The Carter administration advanced a liberal response to the emerging globalization of competition. The restrained nature of this response is consistent with globalist expectations, but the limited nature of the government's role reflects the influence of national, not international, constraints. The Type III institutional structure militated against a more interventionist strategy for two reasons. First, decision-making authority was decentralized across twenty-eight total executive agencies and departments. As a result, the decentralization of decision-making authority enabled executive agencies that did not give priority to the reallocation of federal resources to U.S. industries to wield influence in the policy debate. This structure led the administration to adopt innovation initiatives that did little to address the concerns voiced by its own officials about declining federal support for industrial development that had prompted the debate.

A second obstacle to the development of industrial policies was the limited role private commercial interests were able to play in the policy process. Even though private commercial interests were represented on the advisory panels, this institutional network did not facilitate the translation of their demands into the eventual policy decision. These panels were involved only in the preliminary stages of the policy process. Much of the substantive debate concerning the potential innovation initiatives took place among the members of the interagency review committee, a process that largely excluded industry or other private sector representatives.

The decentralized nature of decision-making authority further reduced the influence of the private sector advisory panels' recommendations by amplifying the diverse interests of the participating government officials. In fact, due to the play of bureaucratic politics that occurred among the functionally differentiated executive departments and agencies, the content of the industrial innovation initiatives was largely a function of the interests of government officials, and not necessarily of those who instigated the policy review.[11] This fact was not lost on members of the Carter administration. In forwarding the interagency committee's recommendations to President Carter, members of the domestic policy staff advised the president that the industrial innovation initiatives did not reflect the preferences of the private sector: "In light of the fact that the study could not respond completely to the interests of the private sector, we believe it is important to characterize the Domestic Policy Review as revealing only the first steps in meeting our commitment to this issue. Perhaps the most significant action you can take is to provide a signal to the private sector that innovation is important and that it is our federal policy to seek to preserve it and promote it in the years ahead" (Eizenstat, McIntyre, and Press 1979, 4). As the semiconductor industry's reaction noted above suggests, the administration's policy was indeed viewed as just a first step. Unfortunately for the semiconductor industry, a revision in the government's industrial innovation initiatives did not emerge until 1987. This delay proved to be problematic for the industry's competitive position, as global competition intensified in the interim.

The High Technology Working Group Agreements

It was not until the early part of the Reagan administration that a policy debate involving the competitive pressures facing the semiconductor industry emerged again. This debate concerned the appropriate market-opening objectives the administration should seek in its consultations with Japan during the "High Technology Working Group" (HTWG).

These negotiations consumed much of the period between early 1982 and the end of 1983. They focused on U.S. industries' claims that Japanese firms practiced unfair trade and that there were nontariff barriers blocking U.S. firms' entrance to the Japanese market. Given that a Type III institutional structure also shaped this policy episode, the administration ultimately advanced a liberal strategy.

Global Competition and Industry Distress

By the end of 1981, Japanese firms seemed to be on the verge of technological preeminence in the industry. They carried their success in the 16K DRAMs into the next DRAM generation. They not only beat their U.S. counterparts to the market with the 64K DRAM, but eventually captured 70% of the U.S. market for this chip. These were dramatic turns of events for U.S. manufacturers: as recently as 1978 they had captured nearly 80% of the global DRAM market (Tyson 1993, 106, fig. 4.2; SIA 1983, 7). Although DRAMs represented only a small percentage of the total semiconductor market, these devices were considered, at this time, to be the foundation for most future advances in integrated circuit technology (Tyson and Yoffie 1991, 6-7; International Trade Administration 1983). Because DRAMs have a fairly simple design and are produced in high volumes, they serve as a testing ground for designers who seek to pack more circuits on smaller pieces of silicon, and for manufacturers trying to perfect delicate manufacturing processes.[12] Without experience manufacturing DRAMs, both American and Japanese manufacturers insisted they would not be able competitively to manufacture more complex semiconductor products.[13]

Alarmed by the rapid success of Japanese semiconductor firms, U.S. semiconductor manufacturers intensified their efforts in 1981 to lobby Washington for policies that would help them to compete more successfully against their Japanese competitors. In seeking government assistance to confront Japanese competition, semiconductor manufacturers called on the Reagan administration and Congress to press Japan to remove its nontariff barriers to the import of U.S. semiconductor devices and to make it more difficult for Japanese semiconductor manufacturers to dump their products in the U.S. market.[14] The industry did not request that the administration impose tariffs to ameliorate their competitive difficulties. The lack of such calls reflects, as noted in chapter 1, the international orientation of the American industry, both in terms of its sales and production in foreign markets. Milner (1988, 124) reports, moreover, that many U.S. firms used their offshore plants to export to the United States. Thus, any U.S. tariff would disadvantage American as well as foreign firms.

On the dumping issue, industry representatives maintained that Japanese companies priced their semiconductor devices below the cost of production in foreign markets in an effort to gain market share. If confirmed, such practices would constitute dumping and contravene not only U.S. trade laws, but also Japanese obligations under the General Agreement on Tariffs and Trade (GATT). According to some in the industry, if these Japanese practices continued, the U.S. industry would be obliterated, because it would not have sufficient revenues to make the investments necessary to develop new generations of semiconductor chips.[15]

Led by Motorola Chairman Robert Galvin, some American firms pressed for the monitoring of Japanese trade practices (Robertson 1982, 1, 4). According to one SIA report (1983, 104), a monitoring system would "give 'early warning' of export drives, and [would] be available to alert the U.S. government to possible predatory export trends by Japanese firms as well as the continuing existence of barriers to market access to Japan." To add credibility to the monitoring system, the report continued, "[t]he U.S. government should provide assurances that it will take appropriate action under the U.S. trade laws if monitoring reveals the existence of unfair trade practices."

On the market access issue, the SIA pointed out that, even though Japan had instituted liberalization measures during the 1970s, these initiatives had not increased U.S. manufacturers' share of the Japanese market.[16] In 1981 the industry's share remained unchanged from its 1973 level of 10%. To U.S. manufacturers this level of market penetration was proof that import barriers existed. During the same time period, the U.S. industry accounted for well over 50% of U.S. and European semiconductor markets (SIA 1985, fig. A2). The SIA called for three policies regarding access to the Japanese market. First, the industry asked that the two countries move forward with their Tokyo Round agreement to reduce tariffs on semiconductors to 4.2% by April 1982; the SIA also asked that these tariffs be completely eliminated soon thereafter. As far as the SIA was concerned, this was the least significant of their policy recommendations. In the association's words, "the major significance of the tariff reduction would be to serve as a symbolic reaffirmation of the commitment of the United States and Japan to compete on an equal basis in an open international market. Additionally, it would signal a commitment to eliminate all remaining restrictions on high technology items" (SIA 1981, 23). True access hinged on making it harder for Japan to distort its market to its firms' advantage (SIA 1983). The industry's second demand involved equal national treatment in the Japanese market. The SIA (1981, 23) called for "treatment equivalent to domestic firms, in areas such as access to financing at competitive rates, bureaucratic processing of subsidiary filings with the

government, and ability to recruit top Japanese engineering talent."
Third, the industry wanted the Japanese government to "take affirmative steps to compensate for its past discriminatory practices. Such an
'affirmative action program' would help to alleviate a significant disadvantage which impedes American companies seeking to successfully
function in the Japanese market today" (SIA 1981, 23).

Institutional Context

In presenting its case to the Reagan administration, the SIA sought to persuade officials at the Office of the United States Trade Representative
(USTR) of the merits of its position. The USTR, thanks to a series of congressionally instigated institutional reforms, has become the locus for the
development of trade policy as well as the defender of the rights granted
to U.S. industries by international agreements. The SIA found the USTR's
office receptive to its concerns. It helped that the industry was linked to
the trade representative's office by an institutional network created by the
SIA's use of former government officials as lobbyists. One of the lobbyists
hired by the SIA was Alan Wolff, formerly deputy United States trade representative in the Carter administration.[17] Wolff's position as a former
high-ranking USTR official provided the SIA with privileged access to
current trade officials. In fact, at the beginning of 1982, Wolff informed
Richard Heimlich, then an assistant United States trade representative, of
the increased competitive pressures facing the U.S. semiconductor industry and its desire to gain greater access to the Japanese market.[18]

The SIA indicated to the USTR that it was interested in filing a Section 301 unfair trade practices petition against the Japanese government.
Douglas Irwin (1996, 32) reports that William Brock, the USTR at the
time, "advised the SIA against filing a petition because the case appeared
weak. While the Japanese had captured a large share of the DRAM
market, the U.S. share of the world semiconductor market was still
roughly twice Japan's share, and the industry appeared to be in reasonable financial health as well. Thus, the semiconductor industry was
viewed as fundamentally sound and Japanese competition healthy for the
industry. In this context, Brock reported the administration consensus
that a Section 301 action would not be viewed favorably."

As an alternative, Heimlich indicated that the USTR could best help
to resolve the semiconductor industry's trade complaints through bilateral discussions with MITI officials. He suggested to Japanese officials
that they recommend the initiation of high-level discussions covering the
two countries' trade differences. Heimlich believed that his Japanese
counterparts would seize his suggestion as an opportunity to deflect
the growing resentment in the Congress regarding the then $16-billion

imbalance in the two countries' bilateral trade relationship. He also concluded that the administration would welcome the proposal, since it too needed to restore congressional support for free trade policies. Through Heimlich's good offices, at the beginning of April the United States and Japan established the High Technology Working Group to discuss their trade differences.

David MacDonald, the deputy United States trade representative, explained in congressional testimony that the working group was set up to "make specific recommendations . . . [to maintain] the competitiveness of our industries . . . [by] eliminating barriers and distortions to trade in high technology goods . . ." (House 1982, 12, 22). Given the working group's origin, not all high technology industries were to be the focus of the consultations. Three were slated for discussion: semiconductors, telecommunications equipment, and computers. Flamm (1996, 154) reports that "the principal issue on the U.S. side was access to . . ." the Japanese semiconductor market.

The establishment of the HTWG represented an ad hoc reaction by both countries to a looming, contentious issue in their trade relationships. The U.S. government conventionally relies on interagency groups to deal with new problems in the realm of international economic policy (Cohen 1994, 89–93). Many of these interagency committees have been statutorily created under the chairmanship of the USTR and tend to be quite inclusive, involving as many as twelve additional executive agencies. For the HTWG, a similar structure was employed. In this case, representatives from ten departments and agencies, almost every executive agency with some responsibility for trade or high technology issues broadly defined, were included in the development of U.S. negotiating objectives.[19] The working group also included the participation of industry representatives, a practice common with regard to the USTR's development of U.S. trade policy, especially for market opening and fair trade initiatives.[20] A Type III institutional structure then shaped this policy episode.

Policy Response

Thanks to this institutional network, the U.S. delegation received much of its sector-specific information from an industry advisory committee, which in turn enabled the industry to assume a privileged role throughout the evolving negotiations (Madison 1982). Even so, the decentralization of decision-making authority impeded the semiconductor industry's capacity to translate its preferences into policy outcomes and thwarted the efforts of USTR officials to use the working group to address the semiconductor industry's concerns. In effect, the institutional context militated against the development of a strategy that would target the semiconductor industry's demands. Clyde Prestowitz, a former Commerce Department official and cochair of the U.S. working group delegation, (1988, 154) recalls that the decentralized decision-making structure necessitated that a compromise position had to be worked out among the many departments that comprised the U.S. delegation before negotiations with Japan could begin:

> The consensus was that while it was appropriate to request better market access, asking for a specific market share or sales volume [for U.S. semiconductor manufacturers] would violate free market doctrine, and thus would be unacceptable. Similarly, with regard to dumping, collecting data on the volume of shipments was acceptable, but not on prices, because in the view of the Justice Department that might violate antitrust laws on price fixing. . . . Thus, before talking to the Japanese, we had limited ourselves to asking simply for a more open market, whose meaning we did not define, and a system of gathering statistics on semiconductor shipments. Moreover, [this negotiating stance] was strongly influenced by State and the National Security Council, which would not allow—even as a tactic—the suggestion of any retaliation if Japan did not respond favorably for fear that the overall relationship between the two countries might be harmed.

Due to the play of bureaucratic politics within the working group delegation, the Reagan administration asked Japan simply to provide all U.S. high technology industries with greater access to Japanese markets. A specific solution to the semiconductor industry's trade complaints appears to have been rejected, because such a strategy was inconsistent with the institutional missions of several of the departments included in the U.S. working group delegation. The Reagan administration's negotiating team then sought a general opening of the Japanese market, a strategy approximating a liberal strategy's emphasis on open markets, and possessed little leverage to achieve its goal.

As the U.S. proposals were cast in terms that did not call for the Japanese to make great concessions, an agreement was reached in November 1982. The agreement, which was actually nothing more than a set of recommendations, included a system for collecting data on semiconductor shipments and a promise from the Japanese government "to develop possible concrete measures to promote imports of high technology goods" (SIA 1985, 6). The agreement also called for regular meetings between the two countries "to spot potential high technology problems and to make recommendations to avert them." This "work program" was to deal individually with the three sectors, starting with the semiconductor industry (Lehner 1982).

This first HTWG agreement did not redress the industry's specific recommendations. The one component of the agreement that targeted the U.S. semiconductor industry—the system to monitor semiconductor shipments—could not stop Japanese manufacturers from dumping their products, since it did not monitor the prices of Japanese semiconductor devices. The inadequacy of this system reflected the fact that its design was influenced more by the differing interests of the departments involved in the policy debate than by the needs of the U.S. industry.

The industry, frustrated by the inadequacy of this agreement, hoped that the work program would bring a more concrete resolution to its complaints. According to Timothy O'Shea (1988, 48–49), Commerce and USTR officials hoped to use the subsequent negotiations as a means to provide the industry with its affirmative action program. These officials proposed the idea of negotiating for a guaranteed share of the Japanese market for U.S. producers. Such a strategy, however, was blocked by other members of the interagency committee on the basis of its contravention of free trade ideals. In Prestowitz's (1988, 155) words, "the invocation of free trade doctrine by most of the U.S. government agencies [in the interagency committee] made it impossible to negotiate for concrete results." Accordingly, when the HTWG negotiations continued in April 1983, the U.S. delegation once again found its negotiating writ limited. Not surprisingly, the second HTWG agreement also fell short of achieving the industry's demands.

This agreement included the acceptance of recommendations to discourage high technology piracy and to move toward the elimination of both countries' tariffs on semiconductors. The latter element was the result of an American proposal, which was clearly in line with the free trade preferences of the interagency committee. When finally implemented by the two countries in 1985, this represented the most tangible gain the industry received from the HTWG's negotiations. A third aspect of the agreement comprised "a confidential chairman's note." In this secret side letter, the chief MITI negotiator, Yukiharu Kodama, confidentially promised to his U.S. counterparts, James Murphy, an assistant USTR, and Prestowitz, that "MITI would encourage the major Japanese chip users to buy more U.S. chips and to develop long-term relationships with U.S. suppliers" (Prestowitz 1988, 156). In effect, Kodama pledged to use his persuasive powers to make certain that Japanese firms increased their purchases of semiconductor devices from American producers by some unspecified quantity. Since Kodama's promise was nothing more than a personal declaration, it had little to no effect on American firms' market share.

The HTWG agreements indicate how the institutional context can affect domestic actors' policy influence and, subsequently, a country's policy choices. An institutional network enabled the semiconductor industry to place its demands squarely on the administration's agenda; another enabled the industry to transmit its preferences to authoritative policymakers during the bilateral negotiations. Even though these institutional networks privileged the semiconductor industry's trade complaints in the policy process, the participation of several functionally differentiated departments directed the U.S. delegation to other concerns, thus, limiting its range of policy alternatives. In the process, the industry's concerns, which had prompted the formation of the working group, were subordinated to those of the participating policymakers. The constraints imposed by this structural context limited the types of strategies the United States could advance to assist the industry.

Conclusion

This chapter finds that the Carter and Reagan administrations each advanced liberal strategies in response to the growing globalization of competition in the semiconductor industry. While the emergence of such a liberal convergence seems to support globalist expectations, the pressures globalists associate with the open global economy did not drive the policy choices examined here. Both administrations' choices instead reflected constraints emerging from the domestic institutional context. As subsequent chapters illustrate, different institutions produce different policy outcomes, indicating that these domestic-level factors mediate globalization's impact on national policy choices.

The Carter administration's innovation initiatives were prompted by government officials' concerns that the United States needed to increase its support for industrial innovation, if it were to remain competitive. Similarly, the HTWG was established to work out a bilateral agreement to open Japanese markets for the benefit of the American industry. In effect, the initial goal in both cases was to develop more interventionist strategies and an explicitly targeted one in the case of the HTWG. The evidence indicates that proponents of such initiatives were thwarted due to the decentralized structure of decision-making authority shaping the two policy episodes. This institution enabled multiple bureaucratic interests to assume an authoritative role in policymaking, bringing competing concerns to the fore. This conflict of interests made it difficult for proponents of interventionist strategies to direct the process to their preferred outcome. Nevertheless, these officials were able to persuade their colleagues that responding to challenges associated with globalization was necessary; the multiple state units involved in developing the Carter administration's innovation initiatives and the Reagan administration's HTWG strategy could agree, however, only to nominal changes in the general economic environment affecting industrial activity. In these cases, then, the institutional context helped to limit what strategies were possible. However, as the next chapter indicates, once this context changed during the second Reagan administration, so too did U.S. policies.

The two cases underscore how institutions steer policy choice in another respect. Both examine policy episodes in which the institutional structure was created to deal with specific developments triggered by the globalization of competition. Neither institutional structure, however, represented a break with existing structural parameters. Instead, both reflected prevailing parameters and practices, carrying forward these characteristics and their extant constraints and opportunities for policymaking. In doing so, these institutional contexts made it unlikely that either administration would radically modify existing strategies.

Chapter Four

Industrial Policy Without Limits?
Reagan's Second Term

By President Reagan's second term, the globalization of the semiconductor industry reached unprecedented levels, and U.S. firms found it hard to remain competitive. The administration responded to these developments with interventionist trade and investment strategies targeting the U.S. industry: the 1986 United States–Japan Semiconductor Trade Agreement and the 1987 Sematech initiative. The trade agreement launched the U.S. strategy of managed trade, where the United States seeks a guaranteed share of a foreign market for its firms. While the Sematech initiative may have been less precedent setting, it was unusual in that it involved an annual $100 million government subsidy to an industry consortium that sought to improve the technological capabilities of national private commercial manufacturers. The empirical findings then do not support globalist expectations. Instead of the government reducing its significance in the economy, in the mid-1980s the Reagan administration developed industrial policies that called for it to assist the industry confront the pressures of globalization.

Table 4.1 depicts the two policy episodes discussed in this chapter, the institutional contexts, their dynamics, and the type of policy advanced. The two case studies demonstrate that the institutional context affected the administration's response to the industry's globalization. Institutions determined the roles and influence of industry representatives and government officials in the policy process. In doing so, institutions created

Table 4.1
Policy Episodes, Institutional Contexts, and Policy Choices

| Cases | Institutional Context | | | Nature of the Policy-making Process | Outcome |
	Institutional Networks	Decison-making Structure	Type		
U.S.–Japan Semiconductor Trade Agreement (1986)	Present	Lateral autonomy	V	Agency-industry cooperation	Industrial policy
Sematech (1987)	Present	Lateral autonomy	V	Agency-industry cooperation	Industrial policy

opportunities for and constraints on the types of policies that could be advanced. Each case includes institutional variation within it, helping to reinforce how differing contexts impact policymaking. The trade case involves a change in the organization of decision-making authority over time. The Sematech case indicates that institutions may vary across different stages of the policy process; variation occurred in the policy development and budget appropriation phases of the process.

The 1986 U.S.-Japan Semiconductor Trade Agreement

Following the HTWG, the competitive success of Japanese semiconductor manufacturers reached new heights. Much of this success came at the expense of American firms. To reverse their competitive decline, U.S. semiconductor firms resorted to U.S. trade laws to file unfair trade practices and antidumping complaints against Japan in the spring of 1985. Until the fall of 1985, the Reagan administration seemed unmoved by the industry's petition. This position largely reflected the structure of decision-making authority. At this time, the administration's response to Section 301 unfair trade petitions was developed by an interagency committee that was quite decentralized. Once this authority structure was altered to approximate one of lateral autonomy, the administration changed its strategies, ultimately filing its own antidumping complaint against Japanese semiconductor trade practices.

This policy episode is discussed in two main sections. The first delineates the components of the Type III institutional context that shaped the policy debate until the middle of September 1985. The second section begins with a discussion of President Reagan's decision to modify the existing structure of decision-making authority in late September and create a Type V context. Subsequently, the section examines the consequences of the altered structure for the administration's response to the semiconductor industry's unfair trade practices petition.

Institutional Context I: Decentralization

By the end of 1984, the U.S. semiconductor industry was in the midst of its worst slump, thanks in large part to the competitive success of Japanese firms in the U.S. market and the limitations of the HTWG agreements. This competitive challenge is illustrated by several statistics. First, by 1985 U.S. semiconductor manufacturers' share of the Japanese market remained at its 1973 level of 10%.[1] Second, Japanese firms continued to dump their semiconductor devices in the American market, subsequently forcing all but two U.S. firms out of the DRAM market.[2] These two developments contributed to a third: By the end of 1984 Japanese firms had captured over 90% of the American market for the next generation, standard memory circuits, the 256K DRAM (Chips 1985). This triumph enabled Japanese manufacturers, for the first time, to overtake the U.S. industry to capture the largest share of the world semiconductor market (Tyson 1993, 105, fig. 4.1). The Japanese share of the world market at this time was 45.9%, whereas the U.S. share was 41.5%.

Japan's domination of the U.S. market for the 256K DRAM coincided with expressions of increasing concern in Congress over the growing trade imbalance with Japan (House 1984; Senate 1984). The influence of Congress on U.S. trade policy is registered most significantly in drafting U.S. trade laws and serving as a bully pulpit for distressed industries. It has been longstanding congressional practice—beginning with the 1934 Reciprocal Trade Agreements Act—to delegate much of its constitutional authority over trade policy to the executive branch, especially its authority with respect to "product-specific trade barriers" (Destler 1992, 65–66). Nevertheless, congressional trade prerogatives aided the U.S. semiconductor industry to influence the administration's trade policy.

Congress's interest in trade policy heightened in the mid-1980s due to the dramatic rise in the trade deficit from about $36 billion in 1982 to $143 billion by 1986 (see Ibid., chap. 4). As the largest proportion of this deficit was a function of the U.S.–Japan trade relationship, Congress became interested in the difficulties U.S. industries were having in selling their products in Japan. For example, in March 1985 the Senate voted 92–0 in favor of a Republican-sponsored nonbinding resolution that condemned Japan's trade practices as "unfair" and called on President Reagan to retaliate by curbing imports of Japanese autos to reduce the then $37 billion U.S. trade deficit with Japan (*Cong. Rec.* 1985a). Soon thereafter the House voted 394-19 in favor of a broadly similar resolution (*Cong. Rec.* 1985b).

To capitalize on what appeared to be rising sentiment for strong executive action against Japan, the SIA filed under Section 301 of the 1974 Trade and Tariffs Act (as amended) an unfair trade practices petition against the Japanese government on June 14, 1985. Section 301 enables private parties to petition the executive branch to initiate an investigation "of any foreign governmental act, policy or practice that burdens or restricts U.S. commerce and either violates international obligations or is determined to be unjustifiable, unreasonable or discriminatory." Section 301, then, is an institutional network. It is a formal rule that provides private parties with the legal right to petition the U.S. government to act on their behalf, particularly with regard to "unfair" and "inequitable" market access.[3] In fact, as one observer notes, Section 301 is unusual because "it provides domestic interests a statutory right to petition the government to espouse their claims in the international arena" (Hansen 1987, 1123).

To achieve a change in Japanese trade practices, the SIA's 301 petition outlined specific negotiating objectives for the Reagan administration. The SIA asked the Reagan administration, as it had at the time of the HTWG: 1) to press the Japanese government to eliminate its nontariff barriers, so that its domestic industries would buy more semiconductor devices from U.S. manufacturers; and, 2) to develop with Japan a cost-price model that would limit dumping by monitoring Japanese pricing practices (Wolff et al. 1985, 99–101). The industry would accept nothing short of resolution of both issues, as it saw them as intricately interwoven. Ellis Krauss (1993, 267) explains that lack of "access was seen by U.S. industry as a key to [Japanese firms'] competitiveness in the American market: the protected home market enabled Japanese chip-producers to . . . undercut American manufacturers . . ." by underpricing their chips in the U.S. market. For the SIA, moreover, the "antidumping cases . . . provided the U.S. leverage for negotiating market access."

The SIA hoped that a Section 301 trade complaint would lead the Reagan administration to initiate negotiations with Japan on the market access question. Yet, recognizing that Section 301 provides the president with some discretion about how to respond to a petition, one American firm decided to file its own antidumping complaint against several Japanese semiconductor firms. On June 24 Micron Technology filed an antidumping suit against seven Japanese semiconductor manufacturers. Micron, together with Texas Instruments, were the only American firms that had not stopped producing 64K DRAMs. The suit asked for countervailing duties of 94% to be imposed on the seven firms for dumping 64K DRAMs in the U.S. market. Micron hoped to make certain that the Reagan administration resolved the industry's trade concerns. If this claim were validated by the United States International Trade Commission (ITC) and the Commerce Department, antidumping duties would be imposed on Japanese semiconductor devices before the end of July 1986.

This additional complaint had two important consequences for this policy episode's denouement. First, it created a second, later deadline by which the industry's complaints would be resolved by either a negotiated settlement or the imposition of retaliatory tariffs.[4] Second, it enhanced the institutional position of the Commerce Department relative to other departments. As a result of the 1979 Trade Act, Commerce is charged with investigating the merits of antidumping petitions. In particular, it has the responsibility to determine whether products were being sold in the United States at less than their fair value.

The rules and procedures set forth by U.S. trade laws provided semiconductor manufacturers with an institutional network through which to channel their interests into the policy process. By setting forth a specific procedure for processing the industry's claims, Section 301 and the antidumping laws acted as institutional networks. These rules enabled the industry to transmit its policy preferences to relevant USTR and Commerce Department officials who were charged with processing the industry's petitions.

Section 301, for example, mandates the administration not only to take account of the views of the affected industry, but also to seek advice and information from the petitioner in preparing to settle the dispute. As Bart Fisher and Ralph Steinhardt (1982, 605) note, this statute "effectively establish[es] a cooperative relationship between the public and private sectors." More conventionally, given the USTR's ability to reject petitions, most petitioners consult with the office before filing. Not surprisingly, the USTR came to share the industry's understanding of the situation. For example, the USTR agreed that the industry's complaints were legitimate and that an alteration in Japanese trade practices was in order.[5] In fact, United States Trade Representative Clayton Yeutter "personally shot down efforts by unidentified American and Japanese interests" who had sought to settle the Section 301 petition soon after it was filed. Yeutter (Robertson 1985, 4) revealed that "Japan [had] proposed giving a little more market share to the American industry. Some American firms were inclined to say 'We'll take a little more market share, pay our legal fees and walk away.'" Yeutter rejected such a settlement, because he apparently believed it would turn out to be just another quick fix; instead, Yeutter wanted to negotiate a long-term solution to the two countries' semiconductor trade conflict. Yeutter's identification with the industry's interests is not unexpected, given that Section 301 requires the USTR not only to take account of the views of the affected industry, but also to seek advice and information from the petitioner in preparing to settle the dispute. In fact, O'Shea (1988, 63) reports that throughout the policy episode, USTR officials "relied heavily on SIA representatives for technical information and input on Japanese proposals. One USTR official said the connection was so close that 'we sometimes joked about getting the phone company to put in a direct dial telephone.'"

Commerce Department officials also favored a strong response to the industry's petition. On at least two occasions during the spring of 1985, the Commerce Department appeared to act as the industry's official government advocate. For example, Lionel Olmer, under secretary of commerce for international trade, reported in early June that his department had evidence that Hitachi was then dumping a specialized type of microchip in the U.S. market (Chira 1985). The convergence of interests between this department and the industry emerged as a result of several institutional networks. Most recently, the industry filed antidumping petitions, which Commerce officials were charged with investigating. But Commerce officials also had been linked to the industry as a result of both groups' participation in the HTWG negotiations. Additionally, the department's ongoing ISAC provided a long-standing means of communication between representatives from the two spheres. This third institutional network has been credited with enabling the industry to assume a direct role in the department's policy process; the industry was able not only to supply commerce officials with "technical information," but also to keep "the heat on the department" regarding the importance of its concerns.[6]

Had the USTR office complete discretion to decide how the administration should respond to the industry's Section 301 petition, it would appear that an attempt would have been made to redress the industry's complaints. However, the USTR does not enjoy such discretion. This decision is instead taken under the aegis of the cabinet-level Trade Policy Committee. Its Section 301 committee is chaired by the USTR and typically includes representatives from at least ten executive departments.[7] The decentralized decision-making structure, however, again militated against a strategy that explicitly addressed the industry's concerns. These departments tended to advance arguments that reflected their own institutional interests, particularly how strong action by the administration might conflict with their existing initiatives or philosophies.

Economists on the committee from the OMB, Treasury, and CEA used several arguments to block administration action in support of the industry's petition. One argument maintained that the semiconductor industry's competitive troubles reflected managerial shortcomings. A second focused on the fact that Japanese subsidies and dumping lowered the price of their semiconductor devices, which only benefited American consumers (Graham 1992, 225). Irwin details two additional arguments. Some of these economists did not find the industry's complaints legitimate: "defunct government policies, vertical integration (like IBM and AT&T), and long-term relationships hardly seemed to constitute actionable unfair trade practices." Moreover, they feared that resolution of the industry's petition might lead to "a worldwide cartel with the government fixing prices and arranging market shares by fiat" (Irwin 1996, 42, 43). Officials representing the National Security Council (NSC) and State Department opposed the petition, because it would lead the administration to label Japan an "unfair trader." Such an action, they argued, might offend the Japanese, which in turn might jeopardize Japanese support for other U.S. initiatives, especially the Strategic Defense Initiative (Prestowitz 1988, 150; Yoffie and Coleman 1991, 5; Graham 1992, 225).

In response to the SIA's Section 301 petition, the interagency committee recommended a strategy that reflected its members' conflicting interests. In July 1985 the USTR was authorized to begin negotiations with Japan on the market access issue. But the trade representative was not authorized to find Japan in contravention of U.S. or international trade laws (Prestowitz 1988, 160). This decision clearly accommodated the committee's dissenting members, who feared the implications of a successful petition. Without confirming the existence of Japanese firms' unfair trade practices, the trade representative lacked the bargaining leverage necessary to convince Japan to alter its trade practices. Nonetheless, thanks to the institutional network created by Section 301, the industry's complaints would occupy a prominent position on the USTR's agenda until June 1986, the time by which the statute required a resolution of the petition either through negotiations with Japan or the use of retaliatory sanctions.

Institutional Context II: The Trade Policy Strike Force

During the summer, the semiconductor industry's trade petitions proceeded through the bureaucratic process and, concurrently, bilateral negotiations sought to resolve the petitions amicably. In August the Commerce Department reported that the U.S. trade deficit had increased to the unprecedented level of $135 billion. This figure increased congressional attention to trade issues. Many in Congress—both Republicans and Democrats—had sought to capitalize on the soaring deficit to reorient the administration's trade policy. Congress's primary weapon involves its ability to pass trade legislation. Numerous trade bills were introduced. Many were protectionist in orientation, while others sought to reduce executive autonomy over trade policy through institutional changes. The administration's critics hoped to alter trade laws so as to force the president to take a more aggressive stance to unfair trade practices.[8]

This congressional pressure eventually led the administration to take defensive actions. It launched several trade initiatives to regain control over the direction of the country's trade policy. None of these actions, however, included action on the semiconductor industry's trade complaint.

On September 7, in an unprecedented action, the administration self-initiated three unrelated Section 301 petitions. Indicative of the globalization of U.S. trade relations, these actions concerned Japanese treatment of U.S. tobacco products, U.S. firms' difficulties in the Korean insurance market, and Brazil's laws regulating the informatics industry (Reagan 1985).[9] In a high-profile speech two weeks later, the president announced a three-pronged strategy to reduce the trade deficit (State Department 1985). First, President Reagan declared that his administration would work to lower the value of the dollar, so that U.S. products could become more competitive in foreign markets. Second, he called for a new round of GATT trade talks. Third, he formed a cabinet "strike force" "to uncover unfair trading practices . . . and develop and execute strategies and programs to promptly counter and eliminate them" (Ibid.).

The third action was most relevant as far as the semiconductor industry's petition was concerned. Foremost, the president's establishment of a trade policy strike force modified the administration's existing structure of decision-making authority over trade policy. The strike force replaced the interagency Section 301 committee with a more centralized structure of decision-making authority. Now, the secretary of commerce was put in charge of a policy process that consisted of officials from the USTR and the Departments of Commerce, Treasury, State, Transportation, and Agriculture (Stokes 1985, 2865–66). The strike force, then, centralized the policy process; it reduced the number of potential veto points over the administration's trade policy choices and, in the process, generated a new set of parameters affecting policy choice. Principally, this institutional innovation enabled Commerce and USTR officials to exercise greater control over the direction of the administration's trade strategy. In this respect, the strike force produced a decision-making structure approximating lateral autonomy.

The creation of the strike force did not, however, reflect the Reagan administration's acceptance of either the need for a more interventionist trade strategy in general, or the need to resolve the semiconductor industry's trade petition in particular (Merry 1985). In other words, there is no evidence linking the strike force to the prior decision to enhance the administration's capacity to pursue an industrial policy. This is true for three reasons.

First, as one observer notes, the president's speech was "plainly [intended] to blunt bipartisan congressional efforts to impose quotas and raise tariffs to protect American jobs" (Weinraub 1985). On the one hand, the speech itself emphasized "the unfairness issue [because it] seems to have grated most on lawmakers, leading to protectionist bills" (Pine and Shribman 1985). On the other hand, the formation of the strike force was a visible means of demonstrating to Congress that the administration was committed to doing something about the trade deficit. In effect, the creation of the strike force was intended to derail congressional efforts to pass protectionist trade legislation or reduce the executive's autonomy over the direction of the country's trade strategies. Second, the strike force's purview was intended to be quite narrow. As O'Shea (1988, 60) points out, "[i]t had been decided that the strike force would follow up on [the three] Section 301 cases self-initiated by the administration earlier in the month. But it was not clear what else the strike force would do."[10] Third, the speech indicated President Reagan's deep-seated commitment to liberal trade. To many observers the speech provided further evidence that the Reagan administration had decided to spurn an "America-first" strategy in favor of taking the lead in crafting multilateral solutions to international economic problems (Pine and Shribman 1985, 12; Pine and Merry 1985, 56). Taken together, these three factors suggest that in forming the strike force, the administration had not decided to embrace an industrial policy, managed trade, or the resolution of the semiconductor industry's petition. Nonetheless, as the next section demonstrates, by centralizing decision-making authority, the strike force led the Reagan administration to develop a strategy that would lead to the resolution of the industry's trade petitions.

Policy Response

Exercising the prerogatives associated with the department directing the strike force's activities, Commerce officials decided that its first task should be to resolve the SIA's Section 301 petition.[11] The decision to give priority to the semiconductor industry's demands appears to have resulted from two factors that increased the salience of the industry's interests in the domestic political arena. First, shortly before the strike force's creation, the ITC ruled that Japanese semiconductor firms had dumped 64K DRAMs in U.S. markets and, in doing so, had injured U.S. manufacturers.[12] Second, within two weeks of the strike force's creation, three leading U.S. semiconductor firms filed additional antidumping complaints against Japan with respect to erasable programmable read-only memory circuits (EPROMs).[13]

To address the industry's grievances, Commerce and USTR strike force members concluded that the U.S. government should file its own trade complaint against Japanese semiconductor manufacturers.[14] If the administration self-initiated a trade petition, these officials reasoned,

Japan would see that the administration was unwilling to allow unfair trade practices further to disadvantage the U.S. semiconductor industry. As a result, it was expected that Japanese officials would be more amenable to a mutually acceptable solution to the U.S. industry's complaints. If Japan did otherwise, it risked the imposition of penalty duties, which the president was unlikely to suspend, since his administration had filed the antidumping complaint in the first place.

Among the strike force members, the Departments of Treasury and State were initially unreceptive to the strategy. Krauss (1993, 267–68) explains that "[o]ne key to State's ultimate support was that . . . the State personnel involved . . . perceived that State needed to shore up its credibility in Congress and [in] the executive branch by defining American interests more broadly to include economic as well as political and security concerns." Treasury officials tended to view dumping as good for the American consumer, since this practice led to lower prices. Responding to the Treasury's objections, Commerce Secretary Malcolm Baldrige argued that if the Reagan administration did not resolve the industry's Section 301 complaint, this decision would suggest that the administration was not interested in enforcing U.S. trade law and the rules of international trade that the United States had put so much energy into constructing and reinforcing.[15] In the end, Treasury officials agreed that the Reagan administration had to enforce the rules of international trade and related U.S. trade law. In December 1985 the Commerce Department, acting on the strike force's recommendation, initiated an antidumping complaint against Japanese pricing practices with respect to DRAM chips of a density of 256K and higher (Auerbach 1985b). The choice of chips in this petition sought to gain maximum leverage for U.S. negotiators. Japanese firms had the technological lead in DRAMs, and as 256K DRAMs were currently the most advanced density, the petition uniquely included any future generations that might come on the market while the current petition was under review. Last minute interventions by other officials and the Japanese led the White House to try to stop the petition. This effort failed, after Baldrige cited his legal right to proceed as part of the responsibilities accorded to the Commerce Department by the strike force and the 1979 Trade Act.[16] In effect, the secretary of commerce was accorded lateral autonomy over the policy area.

As this was only the second time that the U.S. government had self-initiated a dumping complaint, the USTR was armed with what must have appeared to Japanese officials as the administration's unequivocal desire to redress the U.S. semiconductor industry's trade complaints.[17] Officials from MITI soon visited several SIA members to determine what initiatives were necessary to settle the dispute and thus avoid Japanese firms' payment of the antidumping penalties (Robertson 1986, 12). By July 1986

USTR negotiators were able to achieve an agreement in which Japan acquiesced to the industry's demands. The United States and Japan agreed to a five-year Semiconductor Trade Arrangement (STA). This agreement comprised two core components: 1) MITI officials promised to "encourage" Japanese manufacturers to increase their purchases of foreign-made chips to 20% of the Japanese market over a five-year period; and, 2) a price monitoring system was established to make sure that Japanese firms did not sell semiconductor products at less than their fair market value in sixteen countries, including the United States, Europe, and Asia. In return, the Reagan administration suspended the dumping findings. In the event of Japan's failure to comply with either the dumping or market access provisions, the administration retained the right to impose antidumping duties.[18] In contrast to the HTWG agreements, this one had a built-in enforcement mechanism. This feature illustrates the importance of the strike force; with fewer departments involved in policymaking, the USTR was not forced to temper its actions to accommodate the position of dissenting agencies, as it had during the HTWG negotiations. Instead, it had the capacity to craft what it perceived would be an agreement that would resolve the industry's trade complaints.

The agreement led both governments to assume a large role in the industry's subsequent evolution. First, the price monitoring system was to be overseen by Commerce Department officials, and dumping determinations would be established by Commerce and the ITC based on price statistics supplied by Japanese firms. MITI also was to help enforce the price floors by monitoring Japanese firms' export prices. Some (see Tyson 1993) contend that MITI implemented a cartel to minimize the losses to any individual Japanese firm. The second aspect of the agreement, a guaranteed share of the Japanese market for U.S. firms, was not expected to happen spontaneously. The STA called on the Japanese government to establish "an organization to provide sales assistance and other assistance to promote long-term relationships between Japanese purchasers and foreign producers" (SIA 1987, 4). In March 1987 the Japanese government established the International Semiconductor Cooperation Center, which would "stimulate inter-nation exchanges in the semiconductor field through promotion of sales of overseas semiconductors and other activities" (Ibid., 8). In effect, the agreement, which sought to open the Japanese market, required the Japanese government to organize the purchasing patterns of its national firms. Both aspects of the agreement indicate then that the industry's globalization led to an increased role for both countries' governments.

It also should be noted that the agreement showed little regard for the constraints created by the GATT system. A similar agreement was unlikely to be negotiated under GATT auspices, given this institution's emphasis on multilateralism and nondiscrimination. In fact, the Europeans were not pleased that Japan and the United States sought to establish price floors in their market and others, and lodged a GATT complaint in September 1986 against the price monitoring system. The system was found to be unacceptable, leading the two countries to modify it slightly. But even the Europeans resorted to their own processes for a preferred remedy; European firms filed antidumping complaints with the European Community (EC) against Japanese firms in December 1986. Through this mechanism the EC was able to negotiate its own price monitoring system with Japan in late 1989.

By November the monitoring system overseen by the Department of Commerce indicated that Japanese firms were not in compliance with the agreement. Some dumping appeared in third country markets. While these largely Southeast Asian markets were not the prime revenue sources for either countries' firms, they served as intermediary sites through which low-priced Japanese firms' devices could be repackaged and shipped by a non-Japanese company to the United States. By the end of March, the administration retaliated; it imposed tariffs of 100% on four Japanese-made electronics products containing Japanese-made semiconductor devices.[19] The administration applied this punishment, President Reagan (1987, 383) stated, because "the health and vitality of the U.S. semiconductor industry is essential to America's future competitiveness. We cannot allow it to be jeopardized by unfair trading practices." After this action, Japanese firms stopped dumping their products.

Ultimately, the SIA's Section 301 petition led the Reagan administration to promote the competitiveness of U.S. manufacturers in relation to their Japanese counterparts. In fact, the STA represents a radical step for an administration committed to a noninterventionist international economic policy. Not only did the administration acquiesce to a managed trade system in this sector, but it also employed retaliatory tariffs to ensure Japanese compliance with this system. The foregoing suggests that this strategy reflected the opportunities the institutional context created for some state and societal representatives to achieve their interests. Commerce and USTR officials enjoyed uniquely important roles throughout the debate, due to their departments' central roles in responding to unfair trade petitions. Thanks to the presence of institutional networks, the industry played a privileged role in the policymaking process at these departments. Initially, these departments' discretion to prosecute the industry's claims to the fullest was limited by the inclusion in the administration's trade deliberations of several other executive agencies, which did not share their view that the industry's complaints needed to be redressed. However, the president's decision to centralize the trade policy process eliminated from policymaking departments with conflicting preferences and increased the capacity of

Commerce and USTR officials to advance a strategy that explicitly sought to redress the semiconductor industry's concerns. The strike force then increased these departments' capacity to exercise lateral autonomy.

The emergence of this institutional context was made possible by the general decline in the competitiveness of U.S. industries due to globalization and the congressional outcry that followed the rising trade deficit. It is evident in the language of President Reagan's (1985) statements in September 1985 that congressional trade action was the catalyst for his decision to establish the strike force and to seek the opening of foreign markets. While the president made no mention of the semiconductor industry's Section 301 petition, his decision to create a more centralized decision-making structure made it possible for the semiconductor industry's petition to be included among the administration's efforts to reduce the trade deficit.

The Sematech Initiative

The Semiconductor Manufacturing Technology initiative or Sematech was advanced as globalization of competition in the semiconductor industry intensified. With American firms falling behind their Japanese counterparts, and the Europeans and other Asian countries targeting the semiconductor industry, the Reagan administration contributed $500 million to an industry consortium designed to help American firms hone their manufacturing skills. In an ironic twist, one of the country's more liberal-oriented administrations advanced one of the country's more mercantilist strategies to promote the competitiveness of a commercial industry. In what follows, I show how the Type V institutional context helped to make this policy outcome possible; in particular, I illustrate how this context created opportunities for close government-industry collaboration and provided the Department of Defense (DoD) with lateral autonomy. While the structure of decision-making authority became more decentralized in the appropriation phase of the policy episode, the DoD's initial involvement framed the debate in national security terms and diminished the capacity of other state units.

Intensifying Global Competition

By the beginning of 1986, the position of the U.S. semiconductor industry relative to its competitors reached an all-time low. Laura Tyson and David Yoffie (1991), for example, report that the three largest semiconductor manufacturers in the world had for the first time become Japanese;[20] the Japanese share of the world semiconductor market had risen to

45.9%, out-pacing the U.S. share by nearly 5%; the Japanese semiconductor market had grown substantially larger than the American market, and the Asian market accounted for nearly 50% of world demand; and Japanese firms were the first to produce the most advanced memory chips for the next two technology generations, the one and four megabit circuits. In addition, the gap in capital spending between Japanese and U.S. manufacturers had reached nearly a billion dollars in 1985 (U.S. NACS 1992, 23, fig. 5).

Also becoming apparent at this time was the declining competitiveness of American semiconductor equipment manufacturers.[21] These firms build the machines used to manufacture semiconductor devices. The United States had long dominated this sector of the industry, but beginning in 1980 American firms began to lose market share precipitously. Being generally small firms, they found it difficult to accumulate the revenues necessary for technological development and thus were unable to stay technically competitive. By mid-decade, American semiconductor manufacturers found themselves increasingly dependent on foreign firms, especially Japanese firms, for the equipment needed to produce semiconductor devices. While there were national security concerns to this dependence, industry observers were more concerned with what this presaged about U.S. semiconductor firms' ability to remain technologically competitive. Since Japanese equipment manufacturers tended to have close relationships with Japanese semiconductor producers, there was likely to be much synergy between them when it came to technological development. The potential loomed that American firms would be left behind as a result of this process.

To make matters worse, the globalization of semiconductor production and competition intensified, as countries in several regions established large-scale, government-funded initiatives targeting the sector. For example, in the mid-1980s the EC, whose members accounted for about 11% of the world market, launched several community-wide collaborative research programs to increase their firms' competitiveness (Sandholtz 1992). These initiatives included the European Strategic Program for Research and Development in Information Technology (ESPRIT) and the European Research Coordination Agency (EUREKA), which together included more than $2.5 billion in funding. A third initiative, the Joint European Submicron Silicon Initiative (JESSI), was planned as an eight-year, $2 billion collaboration among Siemens, Philips, and SGS-Thomson. Additionally, the governments of Taiwan and South Korea intensified their efforts in the industry (Wade 1990, 103–8, 312–18). In late 1986 the Taiwanese government provided nearly half the $135 million start-up costs for the creation of the Taiwan Semiconductor Manufacturing Corporation. The Korean government, whose firms accounted for 6% of the global market, created two programs. A first provided $350 million of cheap credit for semiconductor manufacturers in 1982. In 1986 national firms joined together to develop the four-megabit memory chip, and the government next supplied them with $175 million in low-interest loans and grants. These programs complemented the $1.2 billion invested in semiconductors between 1983 and 1986 by Korea's national champions (U.S. OTA 1991, 320). While the Europeans, Koreans, and Taiwanese were secondary players in the global industry, these programs suggested that this might not be the case in the future.

In the face of such global developments, an IBM study group concluded not only that IBM and the American semiconductor industry as a whole were dangerously close to becoming dependent on Japanese firms not simply for semiconductor devices, but more fundamentally, for the leading-edge manufacturing equipment that produces semiconductor devices.[22] As the director of the study group summarized, "[i]f we can't be sure that we can produce the most advanced chips we now make in Fishkill and Burlington and around the world today, then our capability for technological excellence and cost performance in our end products is threatened" (Warshofsky 1988, 6).

The SIA took up the IBM report in June 1986 and by November agreed to establish a collaborative semiconductor production organization. The industry association advocated a collaborative response for two core reasons. Foremost, it was seen as enabling U.S. manufacturers to obtain greater gains from their available R&D resources (Senate 1987c, 175). Through large-scale production of next generation DRAMs, the industry hoped that the collaborative venture would equip American manufacturers with advanced manufacturing technologies, hone their manufacturing skills, and lower their overall production costs in a more efficient way than any one firm could achieve through its own efforts.[23] Second, such collaborations were thought to underpin the competitiveness of Japanese firms, and as other countries recently had started similar programs, the United States remained "one of the few technologically advanced nations which have not organized a government program for the development of semiconductor technology for commercial applications" (Senate 1987a, 128). Consequently, the SIA adopted the position that existing strategies were not appropriate in the face of the globalization of the industry (e.g., House 1987c, 27).

The SIA estimated that initial financial requirements for the proposed consortium would be more than $250 million a year, a figure beyond what American semiconductor manufacturers alone could meet. Consequently, as Andrew Procassini, the SIA president explained, "government participation will be sought, but not for the entire financial burden of the project . . ."

(Bambrick 1986, 19). Jon Cornell of Harris Semiconductor and a SIA director reiterated this position, stating that "we do not have $200 million a year and it is our view that we should certainly support [the consortium] to the extent to which we can. We are going to need support from the government to do this" (Senate 1987a, 165). Although many of the details had not been finalized by the end of 1986, the SIA dubbed its proposed consortium Semiconductor Manufacturing Technology, or Sematech.

The Institutional Context Affecting Policy Development

At the same time that the industry proposed its consortium, a government-led study of the semiconductor industry was undertaken for the DoD by the Defense Science Board (DSB). In late December 1985 the secretary of defense asked the DSB, an advisory body to the secretary of defense, to set up a Task Force on Semiconductor Dependency. The task force included representatives from the industry, former government officials, and the military.[24] The task force's contingent of semiconductor industry officials facilitated discussion and interaction between its members and those officials working on the SIA's consortium initiative.

The DoD established the task force out of concern for the erosion of the technological prowess and leadership of the American semiconductor industry and charged it with investigating the U.S. industry's level of technological development, its capacity for future development, and its relative competitiveness. The DoD was most interested in how the U.S. industry's technological and competitive status would influence the department's ability to source domestically the state-of-the-art semiconductor products that were necessary for the continued technological superiority of American weapons systems. On the basis of its findings, the task force was authorized to generate a set of policy recommendations for the secretary of defense. The task force then provided U.S. semiconductor manufacturers with an institutional network by which their representatives could assume semiofficial status in policymaking.

The DoD enjoyed lateral autonomy during this phase of policy development. It set up the task force, and it appointed its members. The task force would report its findings to the secretary of defense, who independently would decide how the department should proceed. Based on this process, the DoD intended to propose a strategy to rescue the U.S. semiconductor industry, which was likely to involve some portion of the department's budgetary resources. However, other government units would become involved during the budget authorization and appropriation process. Among these were the Congress, most importantly the House and Senate authorization and appropriations committees, and the White House.

Policy Response

The task force released its recommendations in February 1987, three months after the industry announced its plan. Its proposals were premised on the conclusion that the United States was rapidly losing its technological and competitive edge in semiconductor manufacturing and equipment. The report attributed this in part to the globalization of production. As far as the task force was concerned, these developments implied that "the United States could be denied timely access to these militarily critical devices in wartime or . . . forced to rely upon technologically and operationally inferior alternatives. . . . The task force views this as an unacceptable situation" (U.S. Defense Science Board 1987, 2).

Aware of recent efforts to promote the American industry's competitiveness, such as the trade agreement with Japan, the task force (Ibid., 6) concluded that opening the Japanese market and ending dumping "by themselves will not solve the problems that beset the U.S. semiconductor industry." Instead, it concluded (13) that additional "steps to preserve [the American industry's] vitality must be taken with dispatch." Its "principal and most crucial" idea was the establishment of an industry consortium, limited only to "firms having beneficial ownership in the United States" (12). This "Semiconductor Manufacturing Technology Institute would develop, demonstrate, and advance the technology base for efficient, high yield manufacture of advanced semiconductor devices. . . . Such an institute could have an important impact not only on the DoD but in the commercial market as well when member firms transfer technology to their own applications" (11). The task force called on the government to contribute $200 million annually over a five-year period to support such a consortium and recommended that American firms contribute at least $250 million to capitalize the consortium.[25]

Several additional steps were proposed, including the establishment of a government-industry-university advisory group. This group was envisioned to be led by the Office of Science and Technology Policy and include representatives from several executive agencies. Its writ was to be broad: "to formulate a comprehensive and coherent strategy for legislative, administrative, and management action to reverse the trend toward the export of semiconductor manufacturing and technology leadership" (Defense Science Board 1987, 13). That being said, one member of the DSB task force hoped that this national advisory committee on semiconductors "would monitor the competitiveness of the U.S. semiconductor technology base and develop R&D strategies and tactics to assure U.S. leadership in the industry" (SIA Readies 1987, 6). This proposed advisory committee, which was modeled after the National Advisory Committee on Aeronautics, the predecessor of the National Aeronautics and Space

Administration, was designed to fill a void in the policy process, both at the interagency level and in terms of linking the cabinet and the industry.

The U.S. semiconductor industry reacted enthusiastically to the task force's recommendations. For example, Jon Cornell of Harris Semiconductor, declared that "Sematech is the basis by which we can indeed put the United States back into a leadership role, enhance and preserve the infrastructure of this country and establish manufacturing excellence. . . . It is clear that [without Sematech] the U.S. semiconductor industry will become the next victim of the economic assault by the Pacific Rim, or [with Sematech] the first survivor" (Senate 1987a, 144–45). While there were negative reactions from some U.S. semiconductor manufacturers to the proposal,[26] fourteen firms representing 80% of American semiconductor production capacity agreed in early March to become members of a consortium. Together, these firms pledged nearly $100 million in annual contributions to the consortium.[27] Later in 1987 another eighty-four semiconductor equipment manufacturers formed Semi/Sematech. This consortium would supply Sematech with production equipment and, in doing so, work with its members to advance the U.S. semiconductor equipment industry's technology and products.[28]

DoD reaction to the task force's recommendations was also favorable, which was pivotal in translating them into policy. In fact, even before the DSB report was officially published, Secretary of Defense Caspar Weinberger recommended in December 1986 that $50 million be earmarked for an undefined semiconductor technology initiative in fiscal years 1988 and 1989.[29] In this regard, the DoD's lateral autonomy was based not simply on the independence to respond to the task force's recommendations, but also on the budgetary resources at its command. According to Robert Costello, assistant secretary of defense for acquisition and logistics, the DoD was willing to allocate more money to the semiconductor initiative. "[W]e put the $50 million in because we did not know what the numbers were going to be. We had to say yes, there is a real requirement. First of all [this action says] to the industry get your act together. What are you going to do? What do you think the real problems are? They should know better than we do, because they are the experts. Then, once we have consensus, we need to do some multi-year funding" (Senate 1987b, 3358–59). By December 1986, however, the SIA had not conclusively outlined how the proposed consortium would operate, who would direct it, what its costs would be, or even which firms were likely to participate. Moreover, at this time the SIA's proposal differed from the task force's; the DSB recommended that the consortium be used to improve the industry's manufacturing capabilities whereas the SIA envisioned the consortium to be a large-scale producer of memory chips.

Over the next three months industry representatives and DoD officials ironed out the specifications of the Sematech consortium.[30] In this process, government officials acted as much more than a passive register of the industry's preferences (Senate 1987b, 3286). By late May the industry announced that the consortium's primary objective would be along the lines suggested by the DSB: "to do the R&D needed to develop future generations of semiconductor processes, materials and tools, and test equipment and transfer that equipment to domestic industry" (Senate 1987c, 173). Each firm would have to apply the innovations to its own commercial chip production needs. Given that a number of Sematech members produced abroad and had joint ventures with foreign firms, several steps were going to be taken to limit the likelihood that technology would be transferred to such firms. Sematech's membership would be "limited to firms based in the United States and owned and operated mainly by Americans"; it would rely on U.S.-owned firms for manufacturing equipment, require that offshore production occur only in facilities that are 51% U.S.-owned, and license its technology developments first to American firms (Mayer 1989, 18). Whether or not such actions were consistent with the GATT do not seem to have been a consideration.

The DoD's decision to propose and fund a cooperative research program for commercial technology marked a departure from the previous role U.S. governments had assumed toward the semiconductor industry or, for that matter, toward any commercial high technology industry.[31] First, the consortium would entail direct government funding of commercially oriented industrial R&D. Second, the government would be jointly funding the consortium with industry. Third, competitors would be allowed to use federal funds to develop relevant technologies cooperatively. In effect, the Sematech initiative would single out the semiconductor industry as a candidate for a U.S. experiment in Japanese-style industrial policy.

Approving Sematech's Budget

The Defense Department's decision to use its budget to support the task force's proposal introduced other state units into the policy debate. The White House had to approve the DoD's budget request, which enabled other agencies to weigh in. In addition, the House and Senate Armed Services Committees enjoy oversight powers over defense R&D programs, since they are responsible for authorizing all Defense Department R&D budgets. As a consequence, the appropriations committees and other members of Congress also were involved in the policy process.

In March 1987 Congress began hearings on the merits of the Sematech initiative and the competitive and technological status of the U.S. semiconductor industry. A month later, the House and Senate Armed Services Committees voted to fund the consortium, with the Senate committee raising the DoD's initial $50 million allocation for a semiconductor consortium to $100 million annually over five years, contingent upon a similar contribution from the industry. As noted, in March the fourteen charter members of the consortium had identified a similar figure for their possible combined, annual contribution. As a consequence, the Senate committee was responding to ongoing industry and DoD efforts to solidify plans for the consortium and endorsed their strategy because it had "been persuaded by the Defense Science Board study on U.S. Semiconductor Dependency, and subsequent testimony before this committee, that there is a critical need to improve U.S. semiconductor manufacturing technology to maintain a viable U.S. semiconductor industry." In addition, the committee (Senate 1987d, 114) was "persuaded that there is a proper role for the government in encouraging long-term, high-risk research on semiconductor manufacturing technology and . . . recognizes the need for immediate action. . . ."

Sematech received bipartisan backing in the Congress. Members of Congress on other committees with jurisdiction over the issues raised directly or indirectly by the Sematech proposal—trade, competitiveness, and antitrust—sought to exercise their oversight capacity by holding hearings on the proposed consortium.[32] The sentiment expressed at these hearings indicated that a consensus was emerging that globalization had posed problems for the industry and the U.S. economy more generally, and that existing strategies had proved ineffective and needed to be altered. This reaction might help to explain why House backers of Sematech first introduced funding legislation in March 1987 as part of the Omnibus Trade Bill. The House-passed trade bill ultimately authorized $500 million over five years for Sematech; a Senate trade bill included similar funding. However, as other issues ultimately delayed that bill's passage, Sematech funding eventually was reintroduced as part of the Defense appropriations bill in the summer of 1987.

During the spring of 1987, a number of executive departments and agencies, including officials at the OSTP, OMB, and the Commerce Department, remained unconvinced that a federally funded consortium was the answer to the industry's problems. This opposition was voiced after President Reagan submitted his budget to Congress, indicating that these agencies had failed to derail the DoD request in the administration's internal discussions. For example, while the Commerce Department thought that "[t]he concept of the semiconductor industry cooperating to meet competitive challenges is sound," it "would oppose any Federal subsidy for such an organization . . ." (House 1987b, 12). OMB officials were of the opinion that the industry had not proven that a consortium would be more than a short-term government hand-out.[33] Similarly, OSTP officials argued that "the case hasn't been made that Sematech or something like it would prevent the U.S. from becoming more dependent on foreign chip suppliers" (Blumenthal 1987, 12). In fact, OSTP Director Dr. William Graham was simply not in "favor of subsidizing the semiconductor industry" (Senate 1987b, 3284).

Although these administration officials opposed the Sematech proposal, they played a minimal role in the budgetary debate. Their weakness resulted for two primary reasons. First, once the DoD had defined the competitiveness of the American commercial semiconductor industry as an issue of national security, it was hard for other executive officials to make the counter argument, given the DoD's technical expertise in that area. Second, this difficulty was compounded, since the DoD was willing to devote some of its $5.5 billion Science and Technology budget to improve the country's commercial semiconductor industry. This conclusion also might explain the peripheral role President Reagan played in the debate, even though the plan contravened his preference for a limited public sector role in industry affairs. In late December 1987 President Reagan signed the Defense Budget in which the funding for Sematech had been appropriated, and by May 1988 funding began.[34] A second recommendation of the Task Force on Semiconductor Dependency also was adopted: The National Advisory Committee on Semiconductors (NACS) was established as a government-industry council to devise a national semiconductor R&D strategy. As the next chapter shows, this committee helped to keep semiconductor issues squarely on the Bush administration's agenda.

Sematech: Salient Forces Reconsidered

As the semiconductor industry became increasingly globalized, U.S. government and industry officials largely favored an interventionist rather than a liberal response. One might view this response as an exception to the outcome globalists expect, given that the U.S. economy was experiencing severe globalization pressures during this time. Not only did the industry face an increase in global competition, but the U.S. trade deficit reached unprecedented levels as a result of new competitors from several regions, the high dollar had ushered in an increase in FDI, and, then, the declining dollar had led to an increase in foreign acquisitions of American firms. The American industrial base seemed to be the only one suffering from globalization. As a consequence, the country's apparent declining competitiveness helped to make the Sematech decision possible by making authoritative policymakers willing to intervene. What level of decline was necessary for government officials to prefer such a policy? It is difficult to specify with any degree of certainty how much decline was necessary. But throughout the debate, three developments enjoyed much salience, both in public statements and internal documents.[35] First, the

U.S. share of the global market for DRAMs, a widely used memory chip and one seen as a technology-driver for the industry, had fallen precipitously in recent years (Senate 1987b, 3323; House 1987a, 176–77). Second, for the first time, Japanese firms, rather than their U.S. counterparts, captured the largest share of the worldwide semiconductor market. The direct implication of this development was that U.S. firms, both commercial and defense-oriented, were relying on more Japanese semiconductor devices in their end-products. Third, the Japanese market for semiconductors had grown larger than the U.S. market, indicating that Japanese users were likely to drive future innovations in the industry. Moreover, the Asian market now accounted for 50% of the world market. These developments suggested to observers that technological developments in the industry were being driven by events outside the United States. This negative turn of events heightened concerns among government officials about the threats globalization posed to the country's industrial base and to the semiconductor industry in particular.

Subsequent cases suggest that the adoption of an industrial policy in response to heightening globalization pressures is not an exception. Instead, a pattern emerges across the policy episodes discussed in this and subsequent chapters: a Type V institutional context empowers those actors most interested in developing policies that compensate for or capitalize on globalization's costs and benefits. In the Sematech debate, the DoD's lateral autonomy eliminated the need for compromise and bargaining among competing, functionally differentiated departments, and enabled the DoD to develop and propose a strategy that addressed the specific problem it had identified. In addition, the presence of an institutional network, the DSB Task Force on Semiconductor Dependency, enabled industry representatives to assume a central role in the task force's investigation and influence its conclusions. Even more important as far as facilitating the translation of the industry's preferences into policy outcomes was concerned, the task force reported directly to the secretary of defense, who was in a position independently to decide how to respond to the task force's recommendations. As a result, these recommendations provided the basis for how the DoD would respond to the semiconductor industry's declining competitiveness. This network also provided the DoD with the capacity to develop a proposal that would have the industry's support and be effective in meeting the department's goals with respect to a technologically advanced industrial base. In effect, the institutional network created a degree of interdependence between the public and private sectors, fostering the development of a policy both supported in response to the industry's apparent vulnerability due to globalization.

The causal significance of the centralized decision-making structure is well illustrated by the experience of another government-led investigation that was charged with recommending, at about the same time, an appropriate response to the declining competitiveness of the country's semiconductor manufacturers. Due to its structure, this NSF-led interagency study ultimately assumed only a marginal role in the Sematech debate. According to the chair of the policy review, this interagency committee was paralyzed by the competing concerns and biases of the twelve different executive agencies that participated in the deliberations.[36] The committee's paralysis not only delayed the release of its report until November 1987, well after the Defense-led debate had transpired, but also led its report to be devoid of any concrete recommendations. In fact, due to the twelve institutional missions involved in the policy review, the committee could not agree on what, if anything, the government should do about the apparent technological and competitive decline of the country's semiconductor industry. Moreover, the NSF's report did not even take a position on the Sematech initiative that appeared, by November, to be a fait accompli. The experience of this NSF-led report suggests that the DoD's initial lateral autonomy played a pivotal role not only in placing the Sematech proposal on the policy agenda, but also in structuring the subsequent policy debates.

Conclusion

The Reagan administration identified interventionist trade and investment strategies as the best way to help national semiconductor firms cope with the globalization of competition in the sector. The institutional context played a significant role in bringing about these strategies and, thus, mediating the effects of globalization on U.S. policy choices. In both policy episodes, the presence of institutional networks enabled the industry to put its preferences for interventionist strategies directly on the administration's agenda. These networks linked the industry to government officials who were responsible for trade and investment initiatives and who were receptive to a new strategy in light of the globalization of competition in the sector. Interaction with industry representatives soon led these officials to endorse and champion the need for strategies designed to redress the competitive challenges faced by American semiconductor firms. Given that these officials possessed or would possess the lateral autonomy to act on their preferences, the administration ultimately advanced industrial policies in both policy episodes.

The policy debates surrounding the STA underscore how variation in the structure of decision-making authority can affect policy choices. Initially, the dispersion of authority over the direction of the administration's strategy produced bureaucratic bargaining and a compromise position that sought to maintain the status quo. The establishment of a trade policy strike force in September 1985 reduced the competing state interests involved in policymaking, enabling officials who shared the industry's concerns to advance a strategy responding to them. This example of institutional change indicates that globalization can lead to state restructuring when authoritative agents see costs in existing institutions and benefits from an altered context for their ability to achieve their preferences. President Reagan's creation of the strike force was not designed to advance an industrial policy. Instead, he advanced this innovation to preempt his congressional opponents from making more extensive changes that might reduce his control over the direction of trade policy. Given the existing structure of authority over trade, the president enjoyed the capacity to transform the institutional context in a way that met his preferences; however, he could not control the consequences of the change, since it empowered officials who preferred an interventionist strategy. This case suggests that the consequences of state transformation rest on how the newly reformed institutions reshape policymaking possibilities.

The STA and Sematech pose difficulties for several globalist expectations. U.S. semiconductor firms, for example, looked to the American state for support and, in the process, identified themselves and their interests as American rather than global. Reagan administration officials similarly saw the industry as an American entity, crafting policies that sought to benefit American firms while explicitly excluding non-American firms. In this regard, the two strategies led the U.S. government to become more involved in the industry's evolution. This increased role is evidenced not simply in terms of the sector's technological development, but also in terms of its relations with foreign firms and markets. Moreover, the Reagan administration encouraged the Japanese government to become involved in its market, an objective the administration was trying to reverse in other sectors. Additionally, the U.S. government's interventionist role was neither one-time nor short-term. Both strategies required it to play an ongoing role for at least five years, whether as a member and supporter of the Sematech consortium or as a monitor of prices and market access in the STA. The next chapter examines the policy debates that emerged when this five-year time period came to a close, indicating that the government's role might extend beyond the initial period.

Chapter Five

Intervention and Institutional Change: The 1990s

This chapter examines the policy debates surrounding the renewal of the U.S.–Japan Semiconductor Trade Agreement in 1991 and Sematech in 1992. These episodes were set in motion by the coming end of the policies' initial five-year terms and the failure of the trade agreement to achieve its market share objectives. Like their predecessors, the renewed policies provided large-scale benefits to American manufacturers in an effort to promote their competitiveness, as the industry's globalization continued. The empirical findings then do not support globalist expectations. Instead of reducing the government's significance in the economy, in the late 1980s the Bush administration developed industrial policies that continued its predecessor's strategy of assisting the industry to confront the globalization of competition. The chapter shows that the institutional context affected the administration's choice of strategies. Institutions determined the roles and influence of industry representatives and government officials in the policy process. In doing so, institutions created opportunities for and constraints on the types of policies advanced in response to the globalization of competition.

Table 5.1 indicates that different institutional contexts affected each policy episode, yet the Bush administration's strategies were relatively similar across the episodes in terms of their interventionist nature. However,

Table 5.1
Policy Episodes, Institutional Contexts, and Policy Choices

| Cases | Institutional Context | | | Nature of the Policy-making Process | Outcome |
	Institutional Networks	Decison-making Structure	Type		
U.S.–Japan Semiconductor Trade Agreement (1991)	Present	Lateral autonomy	V	Agency-industry cooperation	Industrial policy
Sematech Renewal (1992)	Present	Decentralized	III	Industry access and intra-governmental divisions	Industrial policy with multiple objectives

the intended beneficiaries of the policies varied, reflecting differences in the structure of decision-making authority across the two policy episodes. The argument developed in chapter 2 expects centralized decision-making structures to be more conducive to industrial policies than decentralized structures. This dynamic reflects the differing degrees of autonomy accorded to state officials in the two structures; centralized structures provide a limited number of state units with authority over the issue area and, thus, the capacity to act independently to assist an industry to respond to globalization. The first case examining the trade agreement's renewal supports this claim. When the organization of decision-making authority is decentralized, reaching consensus among the numerous state units involved in policymaking is expected to be difficult, thereby necessitating a lowest common denominator approach. If an industrial policy emerges from such a structure, it too will embody such constraints and be designed to achieve multiple objectives, including some unrelated to the sector involved. A similar dynamic appeared in the second case examined in this chapter. Sematech's funding was renewed, but a portion was earmarked for other pursuits.

Both policy episodes are set in motion by institutional changes congressional reformers launched at the end of the Reagan administration's tenure. The National Advisory Committee on Semiconductors (NACS), a government-industry expert committee, was created to help the next administration to develop a national semiconductor strategy. The Super 301 process sought to remedy problems congressional reformers saw in existing trade procedures and to ensure that the new administration would give priority to how other countries' trade practices impacted U.S. industries' competitiveness. The chapter indicates that the NACS fell short of its intended goal, largely because it was not institutionalized into the policymaking process. The Super 301 process had a more significant impact, largely because it empowered an authoritative executive agent and provided industry officials with access to it.

The Battle for Access Continues:
Renewing the Semiconductor Trade Agreement

Within a year of its signing, the STA produced mixed results. The Reagan administration's sanctions against Japanese firms stabilized prices of imported DRAMs. This price stabilization followed an upward trend, which hurt those U.S. firms relying on Japanese chips. Perhaps more important as far as chip producers were concerned, their share of the Japanese semiconductor market did not exhibit much upward change. Due to Japan's failure to meet the terms of the 1986 agreement, the U.S. industry twice sought to persuade the Bush administration to identify Japan as an unfair trader under the newly devised Super 301 process. Ultimately, the administration developed another interventionist response to the industry's globalization, reflecting the opportunities created by the institutional context shaping this policy episode. The Type V institutional context—characterized by lateral autonomy and institutional networks—enabled industry representatives to enjoy direct access to the USTR, the agency given primary responsibility for formulating the Bush administration's international trade policy, particularly its response to unfair trade practices. Government officials were not passive registers of industry demands, however; the USTR, the agency enjoying lateral autonomy, had strong preferences regarding the appropriate semiconductor trade strategy, and the success of the industry depended on matching its demands with the USTR's other trade objectives. The following section begins with a brief overview of the origins of the institutional reforms that made the USTR and the Super 301 process salient in the policy episode. The chapter then examines how the Type V institutional context affected the administration's response to the industry's growing globalization.

Institutional Context: Creating the Super 301 Process

In the spring of 1985, the dollar reached an unprecedented high, 67% above its 1980 value, causing severe dislocations for many trade-exposed sectors of the U.S. economy.[1] The ever increasing trade deficit was seen as evidence of these problems. As the dollar and trade deficit climbed, I. M. Destler (1992, 122) writes, "the [Reagan] administration seemed to do nothing, and seemed not even to recognize that there was any problem to address." Congressional opponents of the president's strategy sought to restructure the institutional context and reorient the administration's strategies. Numerous bills were proposed to slow imports, increase U.S. exports to certain countries, or reduce executive autonomy over trade policy through institutional changes. The Reagan administration's critics hoped to alter trade laws so as to force the president to take a more aggressive stance to unfair trade practices. Japan was the implicit target of many of these proposals since the deficit with Japan comprised more than one-third of the total U.S. trade deficit. Several proposals sought to increase legislative authority over future administrations' trade policies through an enhanced, yet congressionally directed USTR.

In September the administration sought to placate its critics by working to lower the dollar and self-initiating several Section 301 petitions. For many in Congress these actions were too little and too late, and underscored their belief that the trade policy process needed to be restructured. Initially, the decentralization of decision-making authority, especially the separation of powers system, reduced the capacity of the administration's congressional opponents to advance institutional innovations. In early 1986 the House Democratic leadership sponsored trade legislation that would have "curbed presidential discretion in trade-remedy cases, mandated retaliation when other nations did not open their markets . . . and provided (in the famous 'Gephardt amendment') for quotas in cases of countries—[at the time] Japan, Taiwan, Germany—running large bilateral surpluses with the United States" (Destler 1992, 90). The House overwhelmingly passed this bill (HR 4800), but President Reagan promised to veto it. In the Senate a bipartisan coalition supported a proposal to limit presidential discretion in implementing trade laws, but lacked the votes for its passage. After the Democrats captured control of the Senate in 1986, the Congress passed a bill reforming trade and exchange-rate institutions that would limit executive discretion (see Bello and Holmer 1990).

The Omnibus Trade and Competitiveness Act of 1988 (Public Law 100-418) modified several procedures affecting the formulation of U.S. trade policy. The institutional changes built on existing institutions by imposing new constraints on executive autonomy. Destler (1992, 95) writes that the 1988 law "did not impose direct congressional control over trade. Rather it . . . statutorily enhanced [the] USTR with multiple provisions aimed at setting the USTR's agenda and stiffening its spine." For example, the Act (Sec. 1601), amending the 1974 Trade Act, stated that the USTR shall "have primary responsibility for developing, and for coordinating the implementation of, United States international trade policy. . . ." In effect, the Act sought to give the USTR lateral autonomy over the issue. In addition, the Act (Sec. 1302) revised Section 301 to create "Super 301." This statute required the USTR during 1989 and 1990 to identify publicly "priority countries," those with the most pervasive trade barriers, and "priority practices," "including major barriers and trade distorting practices, the elimination of which are likely to have the most significant potential to increase U.S. exports." Within three weeks, the USTR was to begin negotiations to eliminate the priority practices barriers with all designated priority countries. If the foreign government failed to curtail its offending practices, the president was required to retaliate. Super 301 made certain that unfair trade practices were directly and immediately on the incoming Bush administration's agenda as the first 301 designates were to be announced by May 31, 1989. In addition, the leading congressional proponents of the act "made it clear that they expected Super 301 to be used and Japan to be named a priority country" (Mastanduno 1992a, 242). For the next two years, the Super 301 process framed the policy debates surrounding the semiconductor industry and its continued struggle to cope with the globalization of competition.

Globalization and Industry Distress

The 1986 U.S.–Japan semiconductor agreement required that the foreign share of the Japanese semiconductor market reach at least 20% by July 1991, a substantial increase from the 8.6% share foreign producers held in 1986.[2] By 1989 the foreign share had moved to 11%, of which about less than one percent was attributed to non-U.S. firms. The slow pace of the rise in the foreign share of the Japanese market did not reflect a lack of effort on the part of U.S. firms, which located elements of the production process in Japan to cater to the specific needs of Japanese firms. An SIA survey of its members found that between the signing of the agreement and March 1988, its members had opened twenty new design, test, and quality centers in Japan and increased their personnel and sales expenditures there. Moreover, all U.S. companies joined the International Semiconductor Cooperation Center, a Japanese government organization created to promote sales between Japanese users and foreign suppliers of semiconductor devices (SIA 1988, i–ii, appendix B). In 1988 the Electronics Industry Association of Japan (EIAJ), whose sixty members purchased about 75% of all semiconductors in Japan, formed the EIAJ Users' Committee of Foreign Semiconductors. It held regular discussions and meetings with its counterparts in the SIA to increase its members' use of foreign devices (SIA 1990, 7–11, appendix 5). Some of these meetings led to cooperative ventures involving the transfer of technology from Japanese firms to their U.S. counterparts (see SIA 1988). For example, Hitachi was reported to have entered into technology exchange agreements with Texas Instruments on DRAM joint development and with VLSI Technology on SRAMs. NEC also inked technology transfers with AT&T and National Semiconductor. Such exchanges were expected to increase these U.S. firms' sales to Japanese manufacturers, since the U.S. firms now would have the products demanded. The SIA (1988; 1990) did not deny that progress was being made to gain access to the Japanese market, but pointed out that the bulk of the progress was being made with regard to the purchasing patterns of only the ten largest Japanese firms, which represented only half the Japanese market. In addition, its data showed that Japanese manufacturers continued to resist designing U.S. chips into their products. The industry claimed that such outcomes were evidence of the continued existence of market access barriers, especially since U.S. firms were the leading suppliers of microprocessors, logic devices, and application-specific integrated circuits.

The 1986 agreement's fair market values (or what were termed foreign market values) for DRAMs eventually abetted dumping complaints. But in doing so, the agreement helped to produce an increase in the price of semiconductor devices in the U.S. market. This price increase adversely affected the competitiveness of American DRAM users, predominately electronics and computer firms (Flamm 1996, chap. 5). In response to the higher prices, several U.S. firms attempted to reenter the market for this chip through a cooperative venture, U.S. Memories.[3] Even with the support of IBM, U.S. Memories collapsed in January 1990 due to insufficient financial support. The U.S. firms benefiting most from this aspect of the agreement were the two still in the market for this chip, Texas Instruments and Micron Technology; they reaped benefits in the form of higher profits, thanks to the now higher, minimum DRAM price. In addition, the DRAM price increase led firms from other countries to enter the market, thus increasing the competition in this sector. These included such firms as Samsung, Lucky Goldstar, and Hyundai from South Korea, Siemens from Germany, and several Taiwanese firms. One indication of the industry's globalization was that in early 1991 South Korean firms became the subject of U.S. firms' dumping complaints.

As the U.S. industry focused on gaining access to the Japanese market, Japanese firms were expanding their presence in Europe in light of the European Union's Single European Act. Although U.S. firms had twenty-two production facilities in Europe and Japanese firms only five, the Japanese share of the European market was increasing, largely at the expense of U.S. firms. The Japanese share grew from just 9.8% during the 1982 to 1986 period to 19.5% in 1988. During this same period, the U.S. share dropped from 53.3% to 44.8%.

More generally, the agreement produced some positive developments for the U.S. industry. For the first time in a decade, U.S. firms gained market share in 1990, while their Japanese counterparts lost market share. U.S. firms accounted for 39.3% of the worldwide market, up from 37.3% in 1989. Japanese firms still accounted for a dominant share of the world market: their share fell from 50.4% in 1989 to 47.1% in 1990. The decrease in Japanese market share reflected changes in the global industry. First, thanks to the STA's price mechanism, Korean firms were enticed to enter the market for DRAMs and gained market share at the expense of Japanese firms. Second, U.S. firms increased their technological prowess in microprocessors, and neither Motorola nor Intel, the two dominant firms in the market, allowed other firms to manufacture their chips, thereby reducing price competition.

Given these global patterns of competition and the status of the 1986 agreement, U.S. semiconductor firms wanted to hold Japan accountable to its promise of a 20% market share for foreign firms. They did so for two primary reasons. First, access to the largest semiconductor market in the world brought with it added revenues that could be put toward R&D and enhanced competitiveness. One Intel official explained the relationship between access and R&D: "This year alone, foreign semiconductor sales in Japan probably will be more than $1 billion higher than if the pre-Arrangement trends had continued. For U.S. companies this translates into $137 million in new R&D, $130 million in capital investment . . ." (Senate 1991a, 12). This official noted that the continuing gap between actual access and the 20% figure translated into about a billion dollars in lost annual sales. The loss of such revenue was especially concerning in light of the public sector programs in Europe, South Korea, and Taiwan (see chap. 4) that not only supported U.S. firms' foreign competitors' R&D, but also excluded U.S. firms. Second, industry officials saw 20% as the point at which they could secure a sustainable foothold in the Japanese market. U.S. firms' goal was not simply an increase in Japanese purchases of U.S. chips, but the development of close relationships with Japanese firms, so that U.S. firms' chips would be designed into Japanese products, thereby establishing long-term relationships (Senate 1991b, 22).

Policy Response

The industry, keen to get Japan to adhere to its market access promise, petitioned the USTR to use its Super 301 powers to get Japan to comply with the 1986 agreement. That is, the industry capitalized on the institutional network afforded by the Super 301 process to place its preferences on the USTR's agenda. For all intents and purposes, the industry's preferences were already well-known to the USTR, as the industry enjoyed institutionalized access to the USTR, given the latter's role in overseeing Japanese compliance with the STA. Thanks to its privileged position in the policymaking process, the industry succeeded in getting the USTR to include the Japanese semiconductor market among the National Trade Estimates Report of foreign trade barriers for 1989. This was one of thirty-four Japanese unfair trade practices included in the report. Nevertheless, the SIA failed to get the Bush administration to file a Super 301 petition to seek the remedy of the trade barriers alleged to characterize Japan's semiconductor market. Instead, the administration launched Super 301 investigations of Japanese practices in supercomputers, satellites, and wood products as well as cases against Brazil and India (see Bush 1989b). President Bush also proposed the formation of a Structural Impediments Initiative (SII), involving the establishment of an interagency committee that would begin negotiations with its Japanese counterparts to address structural impediments to the Japanese market.[4] This action gave evidence of the constraints the administration faced in light of Congress's Super 301 initiative. Although Congress succeeded in putting unfair trade practices and their elimination on the administration's trade agenda, the administration possessed some room for maneuver. And in this respect, Leonard Schoppa (1997, 71–75) concludes that the SII represented a less aggressive alternative for an administration that felt compelled to take strong action against Japan's alleged unfair trade practices, but was largely opposed to doing so ideologically and saw such a course as having the potential to alienate an important ally.

The industry's failure to get the administration to advance a Super 301 petition on its behalf was largely a function of the preferences and calculations of Carla Hills, the Bush administration's USTR. Even though the industry was privileged in the policy process, and Hills had promised at her confirmation hearing to work with the private sector to craft trade policy, U.S. semiconductor manufacturers failed to convince Hills that their preferred strategy was necessary. Hills had assumed office supporting the STA and the industry's desire for strong action in response to unfair trade practices. She stated at her confirmation hearing in January 1989 that "with respect to the semiconductor dispute with the Japanese . . . [w]e are disappointed, very disappointed, with how the Japanese have carried out their agreement in that area. It is difficult to believe that they could get to the 20% level by 1990 at their current rate, so we are very concerned about that." Moreover, she explained that she "would like to have you think of me as the USTR with a crowbar, where we're prying open markets, keeping them open, so that the private sector can take advantage of them" (Senate 1989). This perspective did not lead Hills to see the necessity of a second trade action. As she stated after the Super 301 designation in April 1989, "there was no need to layer on another semiconductor 301 case. We will continue to negotiate under the present agreement" (quoted in Robertson 1989). In this respect, the original 301 petition provided the USTR with the authority necessary to negotiate the elimination of the market access obstacles and the right to retaliate for their nonremoval. Michael Mastanduno (1992b, 738) observes that the administration saw making the semiconductor issue a Super 301 case as being "superfluous" since "[t]he United States was already investigating Japanese burdensome practices and, in effect, negotiating to eliminate them." Moreover, a Super 301 designation might lead the Japanese to void the 1986 agreement by adding unnecessary confrontation. And Hills saw such an outcome as portending troubling consequences for her central objective at the time: a successful conclusion to the Uruguay Round negotiations.

The industry filed a similar petition a year later. This action was filed amid improvements in Japan's trade practices. For example, Japan's purchases of foreign chips climbed from 11% to 13.5% in the last year. In addition, the ongoing SII was thought to be making progress, given that the U.S.–Japan trade deficit was decreasing. In April the USTR included neither the semiconductor industry nor Japan among the list of trade barriers for Super 301 status. Hills (House 1990) explained that no Super 301 cases were launched against Japan, because it "moved farther and faster on outstanding trade issues than any of our major trading partners this past year. And we continue to have at our disposal the regular 301, which is not one iota different than the Super 301, save for the fact that your negotiator has the capacity to choose the time of when to use." In response to a question regarding the U.S.–Japan semiconductor agreement and the industry's absence from the 301 list, Hills remarked that: "Japan has made progress in opening its market, but clearly this has not been good enough. A free and open (Japanese) market would result in far greater foreign penetration than the current levels. I intend to do everything I can in the remaining 15 months of the Semiconductor Agreement to increase the foreign participation in the Japanese market to acceptable levels" (quoted in Robertson 1990).

Throughout this episode, other government officials sought to assume a role, particularly with regard to whether Japan should be included among those cited for Super 301 violations. The administration discussed the annual Super 301 decisions in its Economic Policy Council (EPC) in May 1989 and April 1990. President Bush (1989a) identified the EPC as his primary cabinet-level advisory body for domestic and international economic policy. There was considerable division among the council's half-dozen cabinet officials in May 1989. The conflict largely reflected the fact that officials from State, Treasury, and CEA were unsupportive of Super 301. Hills and Commerce Secretary Robert Mosbacher "supported at least the modest use of Super 301 to maintain the administration's credibility with Congress and as a signal to trading partners of the United States that the administration was resolved to open markets by whatever means necessary" (Mastanduno 1992a, 242–43). At the same time, Hills "was also concerned about how the Super 301 decision would affect the willingness of America's trading partners to cooperate in bringing the Uruguay Round of the GATT talks to a successful close by the end of 1990—her top priority" (Schoppa 1997, 31). As a consequence, the USTR had to select carefully its Super 301 designations; in effect, she was unlikely to include a "superfluous" case that also could portend negative consequences for existing market access commitments. Moreover, given the positions of the other participating state units, they were unlikely unilaterally to advocate for it.

The April 1990 meeting was considerably less divisive, since Hills chose not to include any countries or practices for Super 301 designation. As Mastanduno (1992a, 256) explains, "[t]he 1989 designations had earned the United States widespread criticism in multilateral forums, and the final bargaining to complete the Uruguay Round was to begin in the summer of 1990. Super 301 would be a major distraction, an excuse for recalcitrant governments not to make concessions in that forum." Mosbacher disagreed with this strategy, arguing that Japan should be named so as to keep the pressure on that country to make further market opening progress (see Barnes 1990). Hills was of the opinion that such a strategy would send the wrong message to Japan in light of its recent market opening progress in the SII. The president again endorsed Hills's preferred strategy. His statement (see Bush 1990) announcing the strategy referred to Japan's positive efforts to address U.S. "concerns involving supercomputers, satellites, and wood products" and that he looked "forward to substantial progress . . . on a variety of other trade issues." Although the unfulfilled semiconductor agreement went unmentioned, the president directed Hills "to review both the status of existing section 301 investigations and related initiatives in important markets such as Japan." In effect, while Hills encountered some opposition to her preferred strategy in the EPC, she was able nonetheless to steer the strategy through this body.

Also weighing in on the use of Super 301 was Congress. It had created the statute to get the executive branch to act tougher on trade and assert U.S. trade rights in general. Judging from resolutions and committee hearings, Congress wanted the administration to act tougher specifically on the issue of access to Japan's semiconductor market. As the annual Super 301 designations were coming due, Congress sought to make its preferences known to the administration. For example, in May 1989 both houses of Congress passed identical resolutions calling on "the President and the USTR, pursuant to statute, to take all measures necessary to achieve compliance with the Agreement" (see *Cong. Rec.* 1989a; 1989b). A similar action followed in late March 1990 in response to the USTR's apparent unwillingness to identify the semiconductor trade issue as a Super 301 designation. This time several senators proposed the Trade Agreements Compliance Act, indicating that Congress would seek further constraints on the executive's trade authority (*Cong. Rec.* 1990). These congressional actions provided the USTR with a sense of congressional preferences and frustration, but did not constrain Hills's autonomy. The 1988 Trade Act empowered the USTR and instructed it to identify priority unfair trade practices and work for their resolution. The Act did not identify which practices or how many of them needed to be identified; instead, in delegating responsibility to the executive to take strong action on unfair trade, Congress accorded much latitude to the executive in determining how to proceed. And in this respect, Hills preferred not to designate semiconductors under her office's Super 301 authority.

The SIA's public response to its second Super 301 setback suggests that it understood that if it wanted the USTR to advance its interests, it would have to work within the existing STA. As SIA President Procassini stated, "in many ways, we are better off with the existing regular 301 case, which can instigate enforcement at any time. A Super 301 case could have diverted enforcement for a year while the new investigation and negotiations were underway" (Robertson 1990). Why it took the SIA a year to come to this realization, given its close relations with the USTR, is unclear. One explanation may be that the SIA followed the advice of the other department to which it was closely linked, Commerce. Commerce Secretary Mosbacher tended to be supportive of interventionist actions (i.e., for the "FSX" fighter jet program and high definition television [HDTV]), and had made statements calling for tough action on the semiconductor agreement.

In the spring of 1990, the SIA shifted course and sought to advance a strategy consistent with USTR preferences. With the foreign share of the Japanese market expected to reach 13.5% by the end of 1990, the SIA gathered support for a five-year extension of the agreement and an extension of the 20% target to the end of 1992. The industry was now of the opinion that the Japanese government and industry had over the past two years "put in place an aggressive market access program" and that a second agreement would continue these positive developments (SIA 1990, 2). To reduce the division among U.S. semiconductor users and producers in light of the price increase that followed the 1986 agreement, the SIA reached a consensus with the Computer Systems Policy Project (CSPP) regarding the scope of a potential second agreement.[5] The 20% market access figure remained an objective, but the data collection component was not to include a floor price. In October 1990 the SIA, together with the CSPP, asked the USTR to seek a renewal of the 1986 agreement.[6] In January, the USTR initiated negotiations with MITI along the lines suggested by the SIA.

As the negotiations ensued without resolution, Congress again took an interest in the issue. The Senate Finance Committee's Subcommittee on International Trade held hearings to demonstrate support for the SIA's position. Forty-five members of the House, including Majority Leader Richard Gephardt (D-MO), sponsored a bill demanding the administration seek clear market access commitments from the Japanese (*Cong. Rec.* 1991). More general congressional outcry emerged when the bilateral trade deficit worsened. With this activity in the background, in June 1991 Japan agreed to a new five-year semiconductor trade agreement to take effect in August (USTR 1991). The Government of Japan noted that it "recognizes that the U.S. semiconductor industry expects that the foreign market share will grow to more than 20 percent of the Japanese market by the end of 1992" and that "the Government of Japan welcomes the realization of this expectation." It also included a fast track procedure for monitoring any dumping complaints, which did not necessitate the government to set chip prices or collect price data. In exchange for Japan agreeing to include the 20% market access figure in the text of the agreement, the United States removed the $165 million in sanctions the Reagan administration had imposed for Japan's noncompliance with the market access component of the 1986 agreement.

This second trade agreement ultimately met U.S. objectives. Foreign firms' share of the Japanese semiconductor market surpassed the 20% mark by the July 1992 deadline, remaining above that figure ever since the fourth quarter of 1993, and eventually reaching an unprecedented 30% in 1997 (USTR 1997). The monitoring system also helped to limit dumping complaints during the period.

Globalization pressures weighed heavily on the U.S. semiconductor industry during this policy episode. With the Japanese market the largest in the world, and Korean firms proficient DRAM producers, the U.S. industry demanded Japanese compliance with the 1986 STA. A billion dollars more in Japanese sales was seen to translate into important resources for U.S. firms' technological innovation and enhanced global competitiveness. The Bush administration's response to these pressures was mediated by the institutional context, which itself had been transformed by pressures associated with globalization. The newly created Super 301 process established the institutional framework for the policy debate and moved it toward an interventionist strategy. First, it required the USTR to respond to foreign trade practices that compromised U.S. interests and empowered the agency in relation to other elements of the administration. These rules helped to place unfair trade practices on the agenda and put the USTR at the center of debates by giving it lateral autonomy. Second, the trade legislation influenced the U.S. industry's strategies and demands. The SIA immediately capitalized on the institutional network in the 301 process to transmit its preferences to the USTR and work with the agency to address them. Over time, however, the institutional context, specifically the power of the USTR, led the industry to alter its strategy and demands. In this process, the USTR was not a passive register of the industry's preferences; instead, it took the lead in identifying a strategy that made sense in light of its objectives and developments in the U.S. relationship with Japan. Finally, as congressional reformers had hoped, the Super 301 process influenced the administration to adopt an activist trade strategy. While it is true that the Bush administration rejected the industry's Super 301 petitions, the administration did not reject the validity of its claims. In this respect, the Super 301 process reflected the increasing salience in the national arena of the belief that unfair foreign trade practices harmed U.S. industry and that the government should help to resolve them. As a consequence, this institutional context offered U.S. semiconductor manufacturers not only a high profile mechanism for a public review of the standing of the 1986 agreement, but more significantly helped to legitimate the industry's claims regarding unfulfilled market access promises and the appropriateness of a strategy to redress the unfair trade practices involved. The Super 301 process then put in place an institutional framework that created incentives for the Bush administration to use an industrial policy to offset the costs the globalization of competition entailed for the U.S. semiconductor industry.

Sematech: Another Five Years?

With Sematech up and running, policy debates involving the industry did not subside. Discussions included increasing federal funding and continuing the consortium for a second five-year period. This episode shows that increasing globalization did not dictate a liberal U.S. response; instead, the most significant causal factors were lodged within the national arena. Foremost, the Type III institutional context helped to determine the roles and influence of state and societal actors in the policy process. The presence of multiple institutional networks provided industry representatives with a privileged role in the policy process; they enjoyed access to key policymakers in the administration and Congress. But with the dispersion of decision-making authority across these two branches of government, the industry's preferences did not translate automatically or completely into policy outcomes. Similarly, this structure brought multiple government officials into the policy debate, many of whom disagreed on the merits of federal funding for the consortium. The eventual policy choice reflected the heterogeneity of the numerous state units involved in the policy process: although Sematech's funding was renewed, the program was pushed in several new directions, including a new focus on environmental issues.

Institutional Context

The DoD occupied a central role in the decision to renew Sematech. Public sector funding for Sematech came from the DoD's budget, and the program was administered by the Defense Advanced Research Projects Agency (DARPA). That should not be interpreted to mean, however, that other executive agencies did not play a role in the Bush administration's decision-making process regarding defense-oriented technology policy. Some of the advisory committees discussed below included representatives from Energy, Commerce, and OSTP. Representatives from other agencies, such as OMB and CEA, were able to weigh in on technology policy debates by virtue of their role in developing the administration's general economic policy.

Members of Congress also assumed a role in budgetary battles. Given the separation of powers system, Congress appropriates funds to executive branch agencies and can earmark funds to programs when the executive does not request them. As noted previously, defense-related technology spending programs fall under the purview of two congressional committees, the House and Senate Armed Services Committees. Executive agency budgets are ultimately determined by the House and Senate Appropriations Committees and approved by a vote of the full Congress and the president. As a consequence, the structure of decision-making authority that emerges in this episode reflects a division of responsibilities within both the executive branch and the Congress, and between them.

Government officials did not operate independently of interested industry officials. Thanks to several institutional networks, industry representatives assumed semiofficial status in the policymaking process. Foremost in this regard were the decision rules associated with the Sematech consortium. In particular, DARPA was charged with overseeing the consortium and was made one of its members. As a consequence, DARPA officials and industry representatives were able to interact on an ongoing basis concerning the scope and value of the consortium. This relationship proved important in enabling officials from both spheres to exchange information in an effort to influence the direction of the consortium. This interaction also led DARPA officials to serve as the consortium's advocate in policy debates, a role that would loom large in an administration generally unsupportive of interventionist strategies.

The NACS, the other primary recommendation of the DSB task force, was established by Congress in the Omnibus Trade and Competitiveness Act of 1988. It was expected to assist Congress and the president in devising a national semiconductor strategy to complement Sematech. The NACS comprised eight leading industry representatives and high-ranking officials from Defense, Commerce, Energy, OSTP, and the NSF. The committee's creation reflected congressional concerns about the costs globalization imposed on the country's semiconductor industry, but it also reflected a desire to establish a policymaking institution that would bring together government and industry representatives to suggest ways to gain "greater efficiency in the application of both public and private funds for semiconductor research and development." In doing so, the NACS was "to identify technical areas where the industry is deficient relative to international competition, identify new or emerging technologies that will impact national defense and commercial competitiveness, or both, and develop strategies, tactics, and plans to enhance U.S. semiconductor leadership" (*Cong. Rec.* 1988). While the NACS enjoyed a far-reaching mandate, its policymaking capacity was limited, since Congress and the Bush administration were not required to implement or act on the committee's proposals.

Other important networks included Sematech's governing board and the Advisory Council on Federal Participation in Sematech (ACFPS). The latter, established by the National Defense Authorization Act for fiscal years 1988 and 1989, comprised industry representatives and officials from Defense, Energy, NSF, and Commerce.[7] It reported directly to the secretary of defense. This body provided annual assessments of the consortium's progress and value.

Globalization, Industry Competitiveness, and Preferences

Sematech was established to increase the technological competitiveness of U.S. semiconductor firms. Its aim was to improve their manufacturing capability and regain world leadership in this capability by mid-1993. Soon after the consortium's start, its members realized that there was a more fundamental problem affecting the industry: the weakness of the 850 or so U.S. semiconductor equipment manufacturers. By 1988 the U.S. share of the $10 billion equipment sector had fallen to 49.5% from 66% four years earlier; during the same period, Japan's share rose to 39.3% from 25.8% (Mayer 1990, 9; NACS 1992, fig. 6). More tellingly, perhaps, whereas in 1980 the top ten semiconductor equipment firms had been American, by 1988 only one of the top five was; the rest were Japanese. Indications were that the decline of U.S. firms would continue, especially at the leading edge of the sector. First, Sematech's members noted that they planned to buy "more than 60% of their processing equipment for the next two generations of semiconductor products from Japanese suppliers" (Mayer 1990, 10). Second, Japanese firms held a dominant share of this sector's most advanced machines, lithography systems (also known as steppers). American firms supplied just 22% of world demand for these $2 million machines in 1988, and the future was not bright, given questions about U.S. firms' ability to meet rising R&D and production costs in light of their small size and turnovers.

Not surprisingly, U.S. chip makers found that they were increasingly turning to Japanese firms for the equipment they needed. This relationship was seen as detrimental to U.S. chip producers, in that they were likely to be technologically dependent on Japanese firms, who thanks to their *keiretsu* ties, tended to have close relationships with Japanese chip producers. Fearing that American firms would not be shipped equipment as rapidly as their Japanese competitors, Sematech shifted focus and sought to increase the technological competence of the American semiconductor equipment industry and to build vertical linkages between American equipment suppliers and users. These twin goals were to be accomplished through funding equipment R&D and signing purchase agreements between member firms and equipment suppliers.

By 1991 the performance of the U.S. industry appeared to be improving. Many attributed this to Sematech's positive impact. First, American companies captured 39.8% of the $50 billion world semiconductor market in 1990, up from 37.3% in 1989. Simultaneously, the Japanese share fell from 50.4% to 47.1%. By contrast, in 1979 U.S. firms had 57.9% of the world market and Japanese 25.8%. Second, in April 1992 VLSI Research, a leading market research firm, reported that for the first time in a decade American semiconductor equipment manufacturers had regained global market share. American firms captured 40.8% of the market for semiconductor equipment in 1991, up from 38% from the previous year.[8] Some observers suggested that the increase in market share was partly attributable to U.S. firms outselling their Japanese counterparts in Korea, whose semiconductor producers had become the largest suppliers of DRAMs to the American market. Third, Sematech reported in late 1992 that it would soon demonstrate the capability using only U.S.-supplied equipment to produce semiconductor devices with next generation 0.35 micron line-widths, achieving parity with Japanese firms.

The members, along with equipment manufacturers, found the consortium to be valuable. For example, Frank Squires, a Sematech official, stated that continued government support was required, because the United States is "competing with global regions that are using cooperative investments of public and private funds."

> This is nowhere more apparent than in Europe. JESSI, which is the European counterpart to Sematech, plans to spend $4 billion of public funds over the next five years in the area of semiconductor research. In the same time period, we estimate that the Japanese semiconductor manufacturers are planning to invest $15 billion more in plant and equipment and R&D than we will in the United States if nothing changes. Other Pacific Rim nations also have recognized the importance and potential of semiconductors. . . . The nature of international competition has changed. . . . Alliances among industry and government determine the terms of trade. . . . Unless we adapt, we will always be at a distinct disadvantage (Senate 1992a, 23).

As a consequence, prior to the expiration of the first five-year cycle of federal funding, the industry sought a renewal of federal support for Sematech at existing levels.

Policy Response

Debates regarding a possible renewal of Sematech began in November 1989 with the publication of the first NACS annual report. The NACS presented a dire picture of the industry's comparative position, pointing in particular to the widening gap in R&D spending between U.S. firms and their Japanese counterparts, and the absence of domestic semiconductor demand due to a weak U.S. consumer electronics industry. This report, which recommended increasing Sematech funding, received extensive media coverage and was discussed with interest at hearings before several congressional committees. The White House made no official response to the report, reflecting its preference for limited government intervention in the economy. This bias was associated with OMB Director Richard Darman, Chair of the Council of Economic Advisors Michael Boskin, and Chief of Staff John Sununu. These officials or their representatives, it should be noted, were not involved in the NACS process.

To compound matters, rumors flared in late 1989 that the Bush administration planned to cut funding for Sematech, among other programs.

This created much outcry on Capitol Hill.[9] Senator Al Gore (D-TN) expressed the growing congressional frustration with the administration: "The administration's posture has been to repeat a few proposals, such as the capital tax cut and antitrust changes. Some of these proposals may indeed be valuable. They are controversial, but some may be valuable. But whatever you feel about them, they certainly do not add up to a comprehensive or credible blueprint for keeping the United States competitive in the field of high technology. Our companies will not stay competitive if the government abandons them" (Senate 1990, 2).[10] Nevertheless, in May 1990 the administration took several steps to make certain that a Sematech-like exercise would not emerge for another sector. It removed Craig Fields from his position as director of DARPA under the pretense that he was venturing too far into the realm of industrial policy, disbanded DARPA's manufacturing division, requested a major cut in DARPA's budget, and decided not to provide federal support for HDTV.

It was in this context that the industry officially requested in late fall of 1991 a renewal of Sematech for a second five years. DARPA officials encouraged the consortium members to refocus their objectives for the second funding phase to include computer-aided manufacturing (Pollack 1991). As this was a precompetitive area for research, renewal would be more palatable to the administration, which had pressured the DoD to restrict its budget to areas explicitly connected to the military or precompetitive generic technology development. The consortium added this focus to its second five-year plan. Similarly, the NACS reports' hearings had raised a second potential objection to renewal: Sematech's requirement that firms developing products through the consortium hold back the product from nonmembers for a year. Some in Congress were concerned that this reduced the value of federal funding to the U.S. taxpayer and benefits to the industrial base.[11] As a consequence, in early 1992, Sematech's Board of Directors decided to make manufacturing equipment developed through the consortium available to nonmembers (and thus to firms that did not pay dues) and to shorten the testing and qualification process for new equipment.

These changes did not completely protect Sematech from the administration's desire to reduce federal funding for commercial research in light of its preference for free-market principles. In keeping with this desire, in January the Bush administration's initial Defense budget for fiscal year 1993 requested $80 million for Sematech. By the spring, high-ranking administration officials sought to curtail all funding for the consortium. DARPA officials were able to persuade the administration of the need to continue to provide support to the consortium and semiconductor manufacturing technology (Pope 1992). But to do so, they needed to craft a compromise position that appealed to the administration's fundamental goal of shifting the financing burden to the industry participants. For the 1993 fiscal year, the administration would request $80 million for the sixth year of Sematech. For the following four years it would allocate $80 million per year to microelectronics manufacturing research, but this money would be distributed on a competitive basis among "Sematech, individual companies, or universities that best address DoD's needs for high-performance information systems" (GAO 1992, 22). The plan also took into account some new realities as far as DARPA was concerned. DARPA officials were of the opinion that Sematech would not need as much funding in the future as it had in the past, since it had been effective in linking the needs of semiconductor equipment and materials suppliers with chip manufacturers (Robinson 1992a). In this regard, the agency saw that the industry would be gaining the bulk of the consortium's future benefits and, thus, the industry should take on a steadily larger proportion of the initiative's funding over the course of the second five-years. This approach would have an added benefit for DARPA in light of the end of the Cold War and the likely reduction in future defense spending. As the director of the agency's Microelectronics Office explained, "for DARPA, the future lies in optimizing distribution of limited funds across the range of information technology research" (Ibid., 1992a).

Industry officials lobbied Congress and, particularly, the House and Senate Armed Services Committees, to retain the consortium's funding at current levels. They argued that a reduction in federal support would force the consortium to scale back its plans over the next five years, thereby jeopardizing the success of the initiatives and the competitiveness of American firms.[12]

The industry received a receptive hearing from various quarters in Congress. This reflected the increasingly popular view that the government had a role to play in supporting industry. In early May the House Armed Services Committee voted 47 to 8 to fund Sematech at $100 million per year. It restored full funding, because it was "concerned that loss of one-fifth of the anticipated annual funding, will disincentivize [*sic*] and inject instabilities in a successful consortia that had not yet achieved the level of technical maturation in the industry due to both business dynamics and continued scientific discovery" (House 1992). In an indication that Sematech was not the only societal group able to access the decentralized decision-making process, the Committee also agreed to several environmental groups' demands and required that Sematech devote $10 million of its federal funds to the development of environmentally safe manufacturing processes.[13] Environmental critics had long charged the semiconductor industry as being among the nation's worst polluters, citing the fact that Silicon Valley has more Superfund sites than any other region due to groundwater contamination. These groups sought industry action to redress the harmful effects of the toxic chemicals used in semiconductor manufacturing for workers' health and safety and for groundwater contamination. The Armed Services Committee bill then intended to give Sematech a new mandate and require the consortium to work with the appropriate environmental organizations in developing pollution preventing manufacturing processes. The House Appropriations Committee soon agreed. The Senate Armed Services Committee voted to maintain funding at its existing level, however, noting that the consortium had "made significant progress in restoring American leadership in semiconductor manufacturing" (Senate 1992c, 146).

During the summer several industry actions seemed to confirm its opponents' position. Foremost, the increasing globalization of the industry resulted in some member firm actions that seemed to contradict the consortium's objective to enhance the American technology base. In July 1992, for example, Advanced Micro Devices and Fujitsu announced that they would build a $700 million factory in Japan to make advanced semiconductors. This followed several international joint ventures between Sematech members and Japanese firms to develop advanced 0.35-micron process technology, a technology the consortium hoped to demonstrate using only U.S. technology by year's end (McCausland 1992). U.S. manufacturers also linked up with their European rivals. IBM enlarged a previous relationship with Siemens to include Toshiba to develop 256-megabit DRAMs. In the spring, Motorola announced that it was forming a joint venture with Philips in a semiconductor design facility. Finally, two firms left the consortium in 1992, and a third notified the consortium that it was considering its options.[14] These departures led some to question the benefits of the federally supported program for the American industrial base. More generally, the continued globalization of the American industry raised the potential costs of an interventionist strategy.

These actions helped to make the Senate Appropriations Committee a formidable hurdle for renewal. Senator Daniel Inouye (D-HI), the chairman of its Defense Subcommittee, had earlier voiced concerns about Sematech's value to taxpayers. Senator Inouye requested that the GAO audit the consortium. Its report released in August (GAO 1992, 2) concluded that "Sematech appears to be on schedule for achieving, by the end of 1992, its overall objective of demonstrating the capability to manufacture state-of-the-art semiconductors using only U.S. equipment. However, according to Sematech and several of its members, this capability will enable the U.S. semiconductor industry just to reach parity with—but not surpass—its Japanese competition in terms of semiconductor manufacturing equipment at that time." Nevertheless, the committee lumped all Defense-sponsored technology projects into a single line item, totaling nearly $2 billion (Robinson 1992b). This would force all types of electronics and information technology firms to compete against each other for federal funds, without any guarantee of receiving the funds. The committee's action outraged all the relevant industry associations and members of other committees. For example, Senator Max Baucus (D-MT) stated that "[c]utting Sematech's funding to $80 million per year, as the administration wishes to do is bad enough. But killing the program at a single stroke is simply not a realistic option" (*Cong. Rec.* 1992).

A Senate-House conference panel on Defense Appropriations for fiscal year 1993 ultimately rejected this Senate action. It restored Sematech funding to its $100 million annual level, but allocated $10 million for environmental protection. Following congressional approval of this bill, the Sematech consortium was on its way to another five years of support.[15]

By the late 1980s, the globalization of the semiconductor industry intensified. In response, the United States continued to advance an interventionist strategy. In fact, the Bush administration intervened in the sector for the benefit of firms headquartered in the United States, even as the major Sematech members were signing numerous joint ventures with Japanese and European firms—the very firms the consortium was designed to confront—on the eve of the consortium's renewal. The institutional context shaping the renewal of Sematech had a significant impact on this choice. It accounts for the multiplicity of actors and preferences involved in this policy episode and the difficulties each group faced in advancing its interests. It also explains why the final decision required compromises and mandated that some of the federal funds be directed to other pursuits.

These elements aside, it is still surprising that Sematech supporters were as successful as they were in the decentralized institutional context. Several explanations appear plausible. First, the industry enjoyed privileged access to many of the relevant authoritative officials thanks to the presence of several institutional networks. This context enabled the industry to work with these officials to alter its position in a way that would gain others' acceptance. The modification of the industry's objectives for the consortium reflect this effort to build consensus for its renewal among officials in the executive branch and Congress. Two other noninstitutional factors provide additional insight into the general willingness of the Congress to go along with the consortium. First, the debate played out during the 1992 presidential campaign, and both candidates actively courted the high tech vote but from differing perspectives. Whereas President Bush was associated with the position that government should leave industry to its own devices, the Clinton candidacy became more closely associated with activist government and close government-industry relations. As the election approached, laissez faire came to be associated with an increasingly unpopular administration. Second, the U.S. economy entered an economic decline in 1990, lapsed into recession in July, and then showed anemic growth in 1991. Increasing unemployment accompanied this downturn, hitting a seven-year high in March 1992. There was an increasing belief among Democrats and Republicans in Congress that Sematech had been a success and that the administration needed to take further action along these lines to rejuvenate the lagging economy and industrial competitiveness in particular. As the 1993 fiscal year Defense budget worked its way through Congress, the U.S. economy improved only marginally, and President Bush's approval rating and his position in the presidential polls steadily declined. Taken together, the political and economic background helped to reduce congressional resistance to continued funding of Sematech.

Conclusion

This chapter illustrates that the institutional context affects the roles and capacity of state and societal actors in policymaking and, by doing so, the policy ultimately advanced. In particular, the two cases indicate that the presence of institutional networks enabled U.S. semiconductor firms to place their preferences squarely on the Bush administration's agenda. This was a significant asset, since the administration was generally unsupportive of interventionist strategies. Nevertheless, the Super 301 process created a policy process that gave priority to the identification of unfair foreign trade practices and the use of interventionist strategies to remove them. The creators of NACS hoped that it would lead to an overarching strategy to raise the industry's competitiveness. This advisory committee fell short of intentions, since it was not fully integrated into the administration's policy process. Its reports nonetheless did trigger several congressional hearings, which helped to place the industry's desire for the renewal of the Sematech consortium squarely on Congress's agenda.

The presence of these institutional networks, however, did not lead the industry to translate its preferences directly or completely into policy outcomes. Obstacles emerged largely due to the organization of decision-making authority. In the first case, the agency with lateral autonomy, the USTR, did not support the industry's desire to redress the failure of the 1986 trade agreement through a Super 301 case. The USTR saw such an action as conflicting with the agency's other trade priorities and unnecessary given the authority granted under Section 301. For the industry to achieve its goal of greater access to the Japanese market, it had to reorient its demands in line with the USTR's preferred strategy. In the debate surrounding the renewal of Sematech, the decentralized structure of decision-making authority increased the number of state units involved in policymaking, reducing the industry's capacity to achieve its preferences completely. This structure also enabled other groups with different priorities to access the policy process. To be successful the industry had to modify its plans for the consortium in a way that would make it more palatable to those raising objections or advancing alternatives. The industry's need to modify its plans and accept some conditions on its use of public funds support the expectation that lowest common denominator strategies will emerge from this context. Nevertheless, some constraints associated with a decentralized structure were reduced, as the fast approaching presidential election and the economic downturn led many in Congress to favor continued support for Sematech. The division among the multiple state units involved was not as great as otherwise might have been expected, which helps to account for the scale of the support emerging from this decision-making structure.

Institutions mattered in a second way. Both debates were structured by institutional innovations advanced during the Reagan administration. These included the Super 301 process and the NACS. These two institutional changes were triggered by pressures emanating from globalization, largely the apparent decline in American industrial competitiveness. Both innovations sought to remedy perceived liabilities in existing institutions, whether the executive's unwillingness to take strong action on trade or the absence of a statutory advisory committee to contribute to national semiconductor strategy. In this regard, the institutional restructuring reflected the distinctive characteristics of existing U.S. institutions in light of the pressures globalization created. This finding reinforces the view that existing institutions structure the direction of institutional reform, suggesting that the relationship between globalization and institutional reform is contingent on the specific institutions involved and their perceived costs.

Finally, these policies indicate that governments may be able to use interventionist strategies effectively in the face of globalization. Although it is difficult to isolate the effects of any single policy, Sematech and the STA improved the U.S. industry's competitiveness.[16] By the beginning of 1993, the U.S. industry regained some of the market share it had lost during the 1980s, eventually surpassing Japanese firms to reclaim the largest share of the global semiconductor industry. In 1994, moreover, the industry announced it would forgo government funding of Sematech when the second five-year program ended in 1997 and in 1996 established its own agreement with its Japanese counterparts to collect and monitor data on semiconductor trade. By the mid-1990s, the Bush and Reagan strategies enabled the U.S. industry to reestablish its market dominance, leading government and industry officials to see no need for further government support for the industry when the policies ran their course. Although liberalism currently characterizes U.S. strategy toward the industry, this outcome was made possible by ten years of large-scale government intervention.

Part Three

Britain

Chapter Six

Emerging Globalization and Intervention: 1970–1980

Britain's experience with the emerging globalization of the semiconductor industry in the 1970s is one of constant industry distress and government response. U.S. and European manufacturers located production facilities in the country in the 1960s and soon came to dominate the British market, creating intense competitive pressures on the smaller, national firms. This chapter investigates four policy episodes covering the 1970s. The episodes, institutional contexts, and policy choices are delineated in Table 6.1. During this period, both Conservative and Labour governments advanced industrial policies, which often involved massive support to national manufacturers and only those foreign firms with extensive operations in Britain. In effect, the industry's emerging globalization did not lead the country to adopt liberal policies.

This chapter shows that the institutional context provided representatives of the major semiconductor firms with privileged access to the policymaking process, which often was characterized by the lateral autonomy of the state unit responsible for industrial development. These institutions enabled government and industry officials to develop together strategies to respond to the growing globalization of the country's market and to the concomitant competitive decline of the industry. Even when the organization of decision-making authority became more decentralized during the early stages of the liberal-leaning Thatcher government, the

Table 6.1
Policy Episodes, Institutional Contexts, and Policy Choices

| Cases | Institutional Context | | | Nature of the Policy-making Process | Outcome |
	Institutional Networks	Decison-making Structure	Type		
Micro-electronics Support Scheme (1973)	Present	Lateral autonomy	V	Agency-industry cooperation	Industrial policy
Micro-electronics Industry Support Program (1978)	Present	Lateral autonomy	V	Agency-industry cooperation	Industrial policy
Inmos Start-up (1978)	Present	Lateral autonomy	V	Agency-industry cooperation	Industrial policy
Inmos Investment (1980)	Present	Decentralized	III	Industry access and intra-governmental divisions	Industrial policy with multiple objectives

industry's preferences remained on the government's agenda, providing the government with a way to quiet the opposition's concerns about growing unemployment.

Emerging Globalization and the Microelectronics Support Scheme

As early as the 1960s, British semiconductor manufacturers experienced competitive pressures from foreign firms. In the 1960s and early 1970s, European and American firms were the source. By the late 1970s and continuing into the 1980s, Japanese firms created intense competitive pressure for British manufacturers. In both cases, however, British firms confronted an uphill battle just to stay even with their foreign competitors.

Beginning in the mid-1960s, U.S. firms sought to increase their European sales of semiconductor devices. To protect domestic manufacturers, the Labour government applied a 30% import duty on foreign devices in November 1966 (Hills 1984, 198). This policy was intended to insulate the three major British manufacturers, GEC, Plessey, and Ferranti, which during the mid-1960s together accounted for about 10% of the £4.5 million British semiconductor market (Microelectronics 1967, 807). These firms were not among the top five European firms (even excluding American firms' European operations) in output or in technological capacity, consumed much of their semiconductor output in their own products, and focused on specialized devices for their defense or telecommunications interests (Sciberras 1980, 285–88; Dosi 1983, 218–20; Malerba 1985, chap. 5). The duty would have the unintended consequence, however, of encouraging U.S. firms to invest in Britain to avoid the adverse price effects of the tariff. Given the size of the British market, these new manufacturers increased competition dramatically.

On assuming power in June 1970, Prime Minister Edward Heath's Conservative government inherited an indigenous semiconductor industry that was not only just beginning to produce integrated circuits, but also was in the throes of severe competitive pressures. Principally, the country's semiconductor manufacturers found themselves at a disadvantage vis-à-vis their U.S. counterparts. This was thought to be a function of two factors.

First, British and European firms in general "tended from the beginning to follow a pattern of technological imitation, with significant time lags, of up to three to four years, against the United States in first commercial production. . . . The innovation process tends to be cumulative, in the sense that the probability of advance is likely to be proportional to the [position] already occupied *vis-à-vis* the technological frontier. This has reinforced the relative stability of European lags" (Dosi 1983, 217–18). Second, there was much downward pressure on semiconductor devices' prices, making it difficult for the British firms to remain profitable and plough revenues into future innovations. American firms were able to discount the prices of their semiconductor devices in the British market, thanks in large part to the significant subsidies provided by the U.S. Defense Department. Another factor increased the price advantage enjoyed by U.S. firms; in August 1971 President Nixon ended the Bretton Woods system of fixed exchange rates. This decision intentionally increased the competitiveness of U.S. firms in foreign markets; a year later, the dollar's value fell 17.5% below its 1970 level (Middlemas 1990, 334). Britain recorded a £17 million trade deficit in semiconductor devices for 1971.

These two factors had a direct impact on the British semiconductor industry's competitive position. By 1970 the leading position in the British market was held by two foreign multinational producers, Mullard and Texas Instruments. Mullard, a subsidiary of the Dutch firm Philips, was Europe's leading manufacturer; Texas Instruments was the first U.S. firm to set up a British-based production facility (Sciberras 1980, 284). GEC and Ferranti soon found it impossible to cover the high costs of development and commercialization associated with mass-produced, standardized integrated circuits. By the middle of 1971, both firms decided to withdraw from the production of these leading-edge devices (Microcircuits 1971; Hills 1984, 202). Instead, the firms opted, as Plessey, to focus on the production of application-specific integrated circuits (ASICs).

In the face of U.S. manufacturers' greater resources and price-cutting practices, British semiconductor manufacturers called on the government to help them to meet the U.S. competitive challenge. They requested two types of support: financial assistance for the escalating capital and R&D expenses associated with the development and fabrication of semiconductor devices; and some form of nontariff barrier to offset the advantage enjoyed by U.S. firms. The need for such support reflected the opinion of many in the industry that existing public sector schemes were inadequate. At this time, the government defrayed semiconductor manufacturers' production costs through the use of loans that the firm was required to pay back with interest. As the managing director of Ferranti Electronics stated, "[t]here are very few German, Japanese or American companies who could afford to pay back their government subsidies and remain profitable. We are no different" (McCarthy 1978a). The inadequacy of the existing public sector support programs led Ferranti's chairman to observe that "[t]here are growing disincentives to . . . innovation and discovery. On the whole [British] governments do not support risk innovations . . ." (Owen 1974). This indictment seemed to be confirmed by statistics regarding the investment rates for British industries more generally; between 1970 and 1973 the level of investment by industry fell from 6.2% to 3.6% of industrial production, even though interest rates fell from 7% to 5% by September 1971 (Newton and Porter 1988, 165, 162).

In contrast to existing government programs, the industry preferred policies that would match its own spending on R&D through nonrepayable investment grants. Such "front-end" support schemes were perceived as pivotal, because they would counterbalance the huge sums the U.S. Department of Defense was then channeling to the U.S. semiconductor industry. According to a report published by the Electronics Economic Development Committee undertaken during the previous Labour government, such a change was needed, if British semiconductor manufacturers were to remain competitive. The report (NEDC 1970, 46, 47, 50) noted that "it is clear that ways and means must be found to augment the resources that industry is currently devoting in this key area. . . . If Britain is to compete successfully in the application of semiconductors, larger resources than those currently made available hitherto for the development of semiconductors in this country will be needed. . . . Government policies can help by directly supplementing the cash resources that companies have available to plough back into investment, innovation and sales and marketing efforts."

Semiconductor manufacturers also lobbied for the implementation of import controls or some other form of nontariff barrier that would provide them with a guaranteed share of the British market (How the High Technology 1970; European Glut 1970). Without such an initiative, industry representatives warned, the country risked losing an indigenous capacity to manufacture integrated circuits. As Sir Arnold Weinstock, the chairman of GEC, explained, a situation had then developed "where you can buy in British markets, devices for one quarter of the manufacturing cost of the device. You clearly have to have some government intervention or you will have no industry. If you are not prepared to put government money behind these sorts of projects you will not have industrial participation in those fields."[1] In advocating such action at this time, GEC and the other British semiconductor manufacturers were not calling on the government to impose tariffs. Instead, the nontariff barriers the industry envisioned involved the government, the Ministry of Defense at the very least, playing a larger role in supporting the industry either by purchasing a specified amount of its components each year or by imposing import quotas on U.S.-made integrated circuits (How the High Technology 1970; Microcircuits 1971; Hills 1984, 202). Mullard, Philips's British-based subsidiary, also sought the imposition of quotas (How the High Technology 1970).

Institutional Context

On assuming office in 1970, the Conservative victors did away with several institutional innovations advanced by their Labour predecessors. The Heath government merged the Ministry of Technology (MinTech) and the Board of Trade (BoT) into a newly created Department of Trade and Industry (DTI). The DTI became the focal point for industrial development and enjoyed considerable lateral autonomy in this area.

Several other state units, however, were able to impinge on the DTI's independence. In particular, the Treasury limited the DTI's ability to extend financial support. Colin Thain and Maurice Wright (1995, 505) note that this constraint should not be overstated. The relationship between the Treasury and other departments

> is not a relationship of principal and agent, in which the former has authority to direct and impose decisions on compliant and complaisant departments. . . . While the Treasury is held responsible for the control of public expenditure, through the 'power of the purse,' in practice it is normally unable and unwilling to dictate either a predetermined total or allocations to spending departments which collectively comprise a loose federation of autonomous 'states'. . . . [T]he exercise of the Treasury's control is negotiated in a highly centralized and closed and stable network, within a set of interdependent relationships in which resources of authority, money, information, and expertise are shared and exchanged.

The Foreign Office also played a significant role when tariffs, market opening, or other foreign economic initiatives were discussed. In addition, the prime minister could become involved in the development of these policies, since he had final say over any policy and could also place any issue on the agenda.[2] Keith Middlemas (1990, 302) notes, however, that the DTI's lateral autonomy was minimally reduced by these other departments, since "Heath's [government] was unusual in the degree of freedom ministers in the new super ministries enjoyed. . . ."

Ministers of Parliament, it should be noted, have no direct role in the formulation of policies affecting industry. Although Parliamentary Select Committees such as that on Science and Technology provide occasions where aspects of policy are publicly examined, a Select Committee has the power only to inquire, monitor, report, and recommend. Parliament's role is limited at best to influencing the government's agenda.[3]

The National Economic Development Council (NEDC) also participated in the policy process at this time. Established in 1962, the NEDC brings together representatives from the government, the Confederation of British Industry (CBI), and the Trades Union Congress (TUC) to discuss the country's economic situation (Middlemas 1983, 195). The NEDC, then, is not an authoritative decision-making body but an institutional network. It serves as a forum in which the larger macroeconomic issues facing Britain are discussed among policymakers and the leaders of the country's two main peak associations, the CBI and the TUC.

A more specialized system of advisory bodies, the sectoral Economic Development Committees (EDCs), operated under the auspices of the NEDC. Each of the twenty-one EDCs comprised representatives from different industries within the sector, relevant trade unions, and officials from the Treasury or DTI. At this time, the Electronics EDC was most relevant for the semiconductor industry. Middlemas (1990, 336) notes that interaction with the EDCs provided the DTI with "more accurate information about the performance and weakness of manufacturing industry . . . than had been available to government at any point since the Second World War."

Several conventional institutional networks offered industry representatives additional avenues to influence policy formation. "Sponsorship" is perhaps the most significant of these conventional networks. It represents a standard procedure in the bureaucracy "for keeping in touch with industry and keeping track of aid to particular companies" (Wilks 1984, 191). Within the DTI and, for example, the Departments of Agriculture and Energy, certain departmental divisions enjoyed sponsorship responsibilities for specific sectors or industries. "The sponsorship divisions," Wyn Grant (1982, 30) writes, "offer a point of contact for the industries within government; the divisions act, to some extent, as spokesmen for the industries within government; and they also explain government policies to the industries." Over time, the central task of the sponsoring division has been "to ensure that its sector's interests were not overlooked and indeed were if possible forwarded . . . in the extensive consultations that were often a feature of the policy formation process within the British administration. . . . However, sponsorship did not mean the formulation of strategy for sectors; rather sponsoring divisions dealt with problems as they arose" (Cawson et al. 1990, 51). Nevertheless, another observer notes that during this period officials "had in practice to rely on [industry]. . . . [T]he growing complexity of industrial policy was to show that institutional adaptation and greater specialization within the Civil Service were not enough, because there were jobs that had to be done which civil servants had not the skills to deal with" (Young 1974, 172).

Policy Response

Thanks to the Type V institutional context, industry representatives enjoyed access to those DTI officials who could help the industry cope with the emerging globalization of the sector and the British market. Jill Hills (1984, 202–3) reports that the DTI considered several specific options for the semiconductor sector during the early part of the Heath government's tenure. Nevertheless, she concludes that "the Department seems to have worked on the basis that for several years, whilst the price of integrated circuits remained so low, there was not much that could be done for the industry." This initial response had much to do with the Conservative government's predilections regarding the appropriate relationship between the government and industry. The Heath government's "general policy for industry was to be one of disengagement, preferring the forces of the market-place rather than direct government to achieve rationalization" (Campbell-Kelly 1989, 284). Specifically, the government intended "to resolve the problem of modernization through strengthening Britain's integration into the international economy rather than through state-led national planning" (Newton and Porter 1988, 160–61). Membership into the European Economic Community (EEC) was to be a central element of this strategy.

As a demonstration of its commitment to a market-oriented approach, the government advanced several institutional and policy innovations. First, the new DTI would be based on the functions of the more liberal-inclined BoT rather than the more interventionist MinTech. In addition, the department's permanent secretary came from the BoT, and the department's most significant junior ministers "were all members of the [Conservative] party's right who had long wanted aid to industry reduced . . ." (Middlemas 1990, 310; Radcliffe 1991, 129). Second, the government repealed the Labour government's Industrial Expansion Act and abolished the Industrial Reorganization Corporation (IRC), both of which offered a broad writ for intervention (Young 1974, 40, 137). Together with MinTech, the IRC had played a direct role in rationalizing the electronic components sector through three significant mergers.[4] Third, the government entered office proposing to reduce spending on industry by 50% (Smith 1993, 155). During its initial period in office, the government refrained from assisting several sectors; it refused to join the Airbus project, or to support a nuclear merchant vessel and several programs for machine tools (Young 1974, 163).

The government's ideological proclivities made the newly appointed DTI officials resistant to an interventionist strategy for the sector. In fact, little government concern seems to have been raised when GEC decided to close two domestic standard integrated circuit manufacturing facilities in 1971 (Microcircuits 1971). Two years into the Heath government's tenure, a change in thinking regarding the merits of government support for the industry appeared to be in the offing. For example, the testimony of DTI officials to the House of Commons Select Committee on Science and Technology in August 1972 reveals that the department was no longer ruling out intervention. In response to the Select Committee's questions about the nature and scope of existing government policies toward the semiconductor industry, Christopher Chataway, the DTI's minister for industrial development, stated that "[a]s far as microelectronics are concerned . . . we are still looking at certain proposals in relation to [standard] integrated circuits and specialized integrated circuits particularly" (Commons 1972, 7). By December, Chataway informed the House of Commons that the government had decided to match the three firms' spending on R&D up to £10 million over the next six or so years. This strategy specifically "intended to encourage the development of integrated circuits specially designed for particular applications by British semiconductor manufacturers" (£10m State Aid 1972). This program, known as the 1973 Microelectronics Support Scheme, was available only to the three British-owned producers of specialized semiconductor chips, thus discriminating against foreign manufacturers then operating in Britain.[5] The government intended, moreover, to fund only those projects designed for specific end users and had substantial market potential. One report on the aid package concluded that "it is tailored to significant projects and markets rather than to the general aim of helping the industry" (Owen 1972). This report also noted that "[t]he new scheme is the result of submissions from the industry which began some two years ago." The industry, however, did not persuade the department to provide the aid in the form of a grant; the loans were expected to be repaid over time. That being said, the industry was able to persuade the government to support commercially viable applications of its research and discriminate against foreign firms, an outcome unexpected in light of the government's liberal predilections.

The globalization of economic competition affecting the British economy at this time helped to make the Heath government more willing to adopt this industrial policy. For many, 1972 represents the year in which the government jettisoned its liberal leanings and embraced intervention. Fearing large-scale unemployment due to the competitive pressures facing several British industries, the government approved costly rescues of Rolls Royce and Upper Clyde Shipbuilders, and it codified its altered philosophy in the 1972 Industry Act (Lee 1996, 46–48). Section 8 of this act provided the DTI with powers to make grants for regional development and to give assistance to "any firm, on more or less any pretext, so long as the minister could define it as benefiting the British economy." Middlemas (1990, 338) concludes that the origins of Section 8 "lay in the DTI, where officials had been arguing that world trading conditions were becoming disruptive and that British industries needed safeguards for their continued independence if they were to avoid potential American or European takeovers." Globalization then made these officials more, rather than less, willing to adopt interventionist strategies.

British semiconductor manufacturers eventually convinced the Conservative government to help them cope with the emerging globalization of the sector. Two factors loom large in producing this outcome. The government, which had come to office with strong liberal predilections, became more inclined to adopt interventionist strategies as the costs, both political and economic, associated with intensified international competition rose. Second, the institutional context created its own set of opportunities for interventionist strategies. Institutional networks enabled the industry to access the policy process and to play a continuous role in policy formation at the DTI. The ongoing interaction pattern that emerged between industry representatives and DTI officials, and that agency's lateral autonomy, led to a strategy to support the commercial applications of British-owned firms' products.

The Microelectronics Industry Support Program

One of the Labour Party's first initiatives on assuming power in February 1974 was to separate the DTI into autonomous departments of Trade (DoT) and Industry (DoI). By splitting the DTI into its two components, Harold Wilson, the new Labour prime minister, hoped to narrow the domain of each department. One department would focus exclusively on commercial policy, whereas the other would be responsible for industrial development and investment.[6] Coupled with the powers granted to it by the 1972 Industry Act, the DoI enjoyed lateral autonomy.

The industry secretary was not completely autonomous, however. First, the secretary of state for industry served at the pleasure of the prime minister. In other words, the prime minister exercised ultimate authority over the DoI and could limit the DoI's autonomy in at least two concrete ways: by firing the secretary of state for industry; or by deciding that any specific DoI initiative was a matter for the cabinet as a whole to decide. In fact, Wilson removed Tony Benn from his position as industry secretary in June 1975, due to what Wilson believed was Benn's excessive use of the 1972 Industry Act to support British industries (Middlemas 1991, 79–84).

Second, the Treasury, as previously noted, has responsibility for the government's budget. The Treasury's technical capacity to supervise the DoI's expenditures was enhanced by what Stephen Wilks (1984, 20) terms "one of the most important institutional changes in the field of economic policy to take place under the Labour government." This restructuring concerned the reorganization of the Treasury into four sections, one of which was the "Domestic Economy Group." The first official charged with directing this group explained that the change "organized the Treasury so that it could give greater weight to industrial policy and perhaps make a rather greater input into industrial policy and industrial strategy objectives" (Wilks 1984, 20). It seems that the Treasury was able to establish a "working partnership" with the DoI during the lifetime of the Labour government (Middlemas 1991, chaps. 3, 4). To what extent this change meant that the Treasury was a coequal in the formulation of industrial policy is unclear. Middlemas concludes that Treasury Secretary Denis Healey helped to formulate the government's industrial strategy, so that it would be "acceptable to both the Cabinet and industrial and labor representation and seems to have been content to leave it as a marker for [Industry Secretary] Eric Varley and the DoI" (Ibid., 89).

The Labour government also altered the prevailing structure of state-societal linkages. In 1976 the government established the Advisory Committee on Applied Research and Development (ACARD) as a means to provide ministers with more information regarding R&D and its applications. More importantly, the government reformulated and redeployed the system of advisory committees attached to the National Economic Development Office. Believing that the EDCs were too general, it replaced the twenty-one EDCs with thirty-nine sector working parties (SWPs). Some of the SWPs "were to be wholly new, some were existing EDCs, and others were created out of former, larger EDCs. . . ." The SWPs, in contrast to the EDCs, were "better tailored to specific industries. . . . The sectors were chosen, not because they were areas of desperate need, or ones characterized by great disparity of performance between companies, but because they were predicted to grow quickly in home as well as export markets" (Middlemas 1983, 94, 95).

The decision to revise the EDCs and institutionalize industrialists into the policy process can be attributed to the severity of the economic crisis that was then afflicting Britain.[7] According to Middlemas (1983, 93), "senior Treasury, Industry and Trade officials in 1974 found the country confronting a very serious recession, associated shortages of demand, and a demoralized business community, in conditions where the old apparatus and instruments of demand-management policy seemed otiose or inadequate." In its place, the Labour government intended to rejuvenate the British economy by regenerating British industry. The actions needed to improve industrial performance would be developed on the basis of detailed "tripartite" discussions among representatives from industry, unions, and government. Out of these discussions, the government hoped "to reorientate its overall policymaking and expenditure priorities toward industry . . ." (Elliot 1978) so as to "provide an improved climate for industry" (U.K. Chancellor 1976, 3). The establishment of an improved climate did not imply that the government intended to pursue strategies that were to be tailored to the specific needs of the thirty-nine different sector working parties. On the contrary, the Labour government revised the EDCs to pursue macroeconomic policies that would be attuned to the competitive pressures affecting British industries (Chancellor 1978, 2). In addition, the government planned to use the SWPs to identify "areas of industrial activity which can profitably be expanded to generate additional, self-sustaining and well paid employment in the years immediately ahead" (Chancellor 1976, 6).

Previously, the interests of British semiconductor manufacturers had been represented by the Electronics EDC and its microelectronics working group. In early 1976 this EDC was divided into several different SWPs. Among these working parties, the Electronic Components SWP (ECSWP) represented the interests of British semiconductor manufacturers. The ECSWP served as an institutional network. Middlemas (1983, 114) notes that the SWPs provided industry with a means to influence the policy process, because the working party process locked the government "and the civil service into accepting interdependence and the need to discuss industry's requirements, not cosmetically, at a late stage of a pre-ordained plan, but from the beginning." This conclusion was confirmed by both industry and government officials. For example, Kenneth Corn-field, the chairman of Standard Telephones and Cables (STC), at the time a major producer of telecommunications equipment and semiconductors, commented, "[t]hose of us who see at first hand the working of this in-dependent interface between industry, trade unions and the government are convinced that it offers the real prospect of furthering the country's industrial prosperity by ensuring that government intervention is increas-ingly informed and effective" (Corina 1976). In a White Paper (Chancel-lor 1978, 1) written in response to the first round of suggestions put forward by the thirty-nine SWPs, the Treasury and DoI wrote that the quality of the SWPs' work obligated it to "put to good use what the SWPs have so far produced and build on it for the future."

Policy Response

Upon taking office in 1974, Labour inherited a semiconductor industry lagging its foreign competitors, especially U.S. producers. Although the British semiconductor market (measured in terms of production plus im-ports minus exports) had grown from £62 million in 1971 to £180 mil-lion by 1976 (Scibberas 1980, 284), the bulk of this growth reflected the activities of foreign firms. The top seven firms in the market were U.S. and the Dutch subsidiary, Mullard. Several of these U.S. firms, including Motorola and National Semiconductor, recently established British pro-duction facilities. At the same time, the trade deficit rose to £60 million in 1976 from £17 million in 1971 (Ibid.). Imports increased even though the EEC maintained the highest tariff on semiconductors among the industri-alized countries (17% in comparison to 10% in Japan and 6% in the United States) and it imposed rules of origin that raised the cost of im-ported semiconductors in products destined for export to other commu-nity members.

By 1977 the viability of an independent British industry once again seemed to be in jeopardy. This perception was compounded by the rapid growth of the Japanese semiconductor industry and by Japan's establish-ment of its VLSI program in 1976. Three Japanese firms were now among the top ten firms in the world market while no British firm was among the top ten in the European market. With the Japanese apparently targeting the semiconductor industry, British manufacturers were uncer-tain about their capacity to meet the Japanese challenge in addition to the competition they already encountered from U.S. firms. Under the aus-pices of the ECSWP, representatives of the British semiconductor industry sought to convince the Labour government that it needed to assume a greater role in promoting domestic manufacturers. In particular, industry representatives asked the DoI, as they had during Heath's government, to increase the subsidies and grants available to the industry. Industry representatives emphasized that the integrated circuit was fast becoming the foundation of the electronic, telecommunications, and computer industries. Moreover, by opening up new markets, the microchip would become one of the more influential technologies of the twentieth century. Industry officials pointed out, however, that the prognosis for Britain's capacity to take advantage of the fruits of this device was not good. At present, the British market was increasingly dependent on foreign sources for the supply of leading-edge microelectronic products. In the short term, the working party (ECSWP 1979a, 1) observed, the country's reliance on foreign suppliers negatively affected Britain's balance of payments and employment opportunities. "In the longer term," due to the microchip's potentially wide-ranging applications, "Britain's success as a technologically advanced industrial society could be threatened."

The effects of the Type V institutional context on the government's strategy soon became apparent. The government hoped to revitalize the economy in part by using a selective, microeconomic policy, seeing that "Britain's problem was . . . of adjustment undertaken inadequately and too late" (Middlemas 1991, 87). Thanks to the close interaction pattern that emerged between government officials and industry representatives, DoI officials soon linked an improvement in the country's economic performance with that of its semiconductor industry.

In January 1977 the industry secretary proposed a £20 million program intended to increase investments in the manufacture and development of microelectronic devices. It was reported that this proposal resulted from "a year's deliberations, with representatives from such companies as Mullard, Plessey, and ITT" and the members of the sector working party (Corina 1977).[8] By December continued discussions between the industry and DoI officials led to the revision of this proposal (Microelectronics 1977). The evolution of the DoI's thinking illuminates the influence the industry wielded during this policy episode. At the outset, in a confidential paper to the ECSWP, the DoI stated that "the minimum essential five-year objective for the United Kingdom is to develop [a] microelectronics industry [that is] . . . self-sustaining . . ." (Owen 1978a). The department rejected the idea of trying to compete with U.S. and Japanese firms in the market for mass-produced, standard memory circuits.[9] Mass-produced memory circuits include DRAMs, the type of integrated circuits in which the United States and Japan were competing fiercely at this time, and were believed to be pivotal to ensuring a firm's technological advancement. The establishment of a competitive presence in this end of the microelectronic industry was estimated to require nearly £400 million, a sum thought to be beyond the country's means. Instead, the department decided that at least £80 million should be allocated over a five-year period to development of "application-specific microcircuits." Mullard and ITT, British subsidiaries of foreign-owned companies and members of the ECSWP, would be eligible for government assistance, since they developed new products in Britain. Other multinationals would not be supported.

The ECSWP responded to the DoI's proposal with its own paper (ECSWP 1979a; Poole 1978a; Owen 1978b). The working party, enthusiastic about the DoI's desire to support the industry, contended that the department had misunderstood the issues at stake. To be fair, the DoI was operating with information supplied to it by the industry, and the industry's preferences had changed over the course of four years. The working party now maintained that British firms needed to manufacture both application-specific and standard integrated circuits. The industry pointed out that due to the technological sophistication of standard circuits, British manufacturers were disadvantaged by their dependence on U.S. firms for the supply of such devices. Because standard circuits have a fairly simple design and are produced in high volumes, they serve as a testing ground for designers who seek to pack more circuits on smaller pieces of silicon, and for manufacturers trying to perfect delicate manufacturing processes. The production and development of standard circuits were thought to lead to the greatest number of technological innovations. In the working party's opinion, the technological development of British manufacturers would continue to lag behind U.S. and other foreign-owned companies, so long as Britain did not produce leading-edge devices. As a result, the government needed to create a program to assist British firms to manufacture standard circuits. The working party suggested that three types of ventures should be eligible for investment subsidies: 1) a British joint venture with a foreign partner; 2) a British-owned start-up; or 3) an existing British firm expanding into the production of standard circuits (Owen 1978b).

Second, the working party maintained that a DoI support program must also strive to increase the use of microelectronics in other British industries. At that time, only 15% of all integrated circuits produced in Britain were destined for the British market (Poole 1978b). Supporting British industries' use of microelectronics was critical, the working party argued (ECSWP 1979b, 5), because the future of Britain's microelectronics industry "lies largely in the speed and effectiveness with which the new technology can be made available and adopted throughout industry." Accordingly, the DoI was asked to make funds available to accelerate the applications of microelectronics throughout British industry.

In response to the industry's recommendations, the DoI announced the creation of two programs that mirrored the industry's suggestions: the Microprocessor Application Project (MAP) and the Microelectronics Industry Support Program (MISP). The MAP was designed to help British industry figure out how to apply microelectronic devices to its manufacturing processes and to its products. In allocating £55 million to this scheme, Industry Secretary Varley stated that "[t]he terms of support under this scheme will take account of weaknesses in United Kingdom industry which are clearly emerging from discussions [with industry] on the government's industrial strategy" (Owen 1978c).[10] The MISP allocated £70 million over a five-year period to augment the development or manufacture of integrated circuits in Britain. MISP had two main objectives: to encourage foreign manufacturers to produce standard circuits in Britain in partnership with British manufacturers; and to provide British manufacturers with the capacity to increase their innovation rates with respect to integrated circuit development. According to Varley, MISP would reduce Britain's dependence on foreign companies for its microelectronics needs by stimulating new investments in standard circuit development and/or production (McCarthy 1978b). This was a critical task, an Industry Department paper (Elliot and Lloyd 1978; see also, Government Responds 1978) stated, because "as a trading nation we have only one option . . . to catch up with our industrial competitors and to adopt and develop [microelectronics] at least as fast and comprehensively as they do. To opt out will lead to the very worst fears being realized." Secretary Varley added, "I don't want to see Britain become the pensioners of other peoples' manufacturing or technology" (McCarthy 1978a). Varley's perspective illustrates the extent to which the DoI had sought to reorient its proposal in accordance with the working party's recommendations. In fact, Varley did not try to conceal the industry's influence; as he stated, MISP was "in line with the recommendations on a strategy for the industry recently published by the NEDC's Electronic Components Sector Working Party" (Owen 1978d). Plessey soon announced that thanks to this aid, it would begin "producing bubble memories in commercial volume" (Hills 1984, 210). GEC also announced that thanks to this program, it had decided to enter into a joint venture with the U.S. firm Fairchild for the production of standard integrated circuits. The government contributed £7 million to the construction of a new production facility in northern England, but the joint venture was disbanded in 1980 when Fairchild was purchased by the French firm Schlumberger. By 1984, more than £50 million had been provided to more than forty companies for the manufacture and design of semiconductors.

The Labour government ultimately identified one means to regenerate a troubled national economy with significant public sector support for the country's semiconductor firms, including some foreign-owned firms. This decision emerged from opportunities created by the Type V institutional context structuring the policy process.[11] The presence of an institutional network, in this case the ECSWP, linked industry representatives to DoI officials, who saw interventionist strategies as a viable option, and who enjoyed the lateral autonomy to act on the industry's recommendations.

Inmos: Labour's Next Step

On assuming power in 1974, Labour also instituted a centralized structure for public sector support of venture capital. Although the DoI provided selective finance through its use of loans and grants, Labour believed that there was a need for a separate government institution that focused exclusively on the supply of forward-looking equity finance for industry. Consequently, the Labour government created a public sector venture capitalist (or state holding company), the National Enterprise Board (NEB).[12] It enjoyed lateral autonomy and was capitalized with £1 billion for direct investment and the purchase of shareholdings over a five-year period ending in April 1980.

The 1975 Industry Act stipulated that the board's investments should be confined to three broad purposes: "the development or assistance of the economy of the United Kingdom or any part of the United Kingdom"; "the promotion in the United Kingdom of industrial efficiency and international competitiveness"; and "the provision, maintenance, or safeguarding of productive employment in any part of the United Kingdom" (Kramer 1988, 9–10). In serving these purposes, the board was expected to achieve a return on its investments amounting to at least 15%. Consequently, as the first chairman of the NEB stated, these guidelines did not include "prop[ping] up non-viable companies simply to maintain jobs." Instead, the guidelines implied that the board should "take a wider view of the national benefits and opportunities that flow from any investment" (Grant 1982, 106).

In attempting to fulfill these objectives, the board's lateral autonomy was only minimally circumscribed by other government departments. As Kevin Theakston (1996, 177) notes, "[t]o operate successfully the NEB was held to require considerable autonomy in its day-to-day commercial decision-making. But holding ministers at arm's length also meant holding Parliament at arm's length. MPs could not question the industry minister in detail about the NEB's activities, including its expenditure of large sums of money." Some degree of accountability nevertheless was established. The secretary of state for industry had the authority to determine the board's financial duties and functions, and appoint the board's members. The secretary of state, however, could not "intervene in the day-to-day affairs of the NEB" thereby "insulating the Board from political intervention" and creating a "quasi-autonomous body" (Mitchell 1982, 57, 58–59, 63–64). The industry secretary's approval still was necessary for any investment that enabled "the NEB to control more than 30% of the votes at the" company's "general meeting or if the transaction" amounted to "more than £10 million" (Kramer 1988, 10–11).

Given the structure of decision-making authority created by the Labour government, the NEB and the DoI could both independently allocate public sector funds for industries to help them to modernize and adjust to international economic developments. As such, the NEB could pursue policies of which the DoI was unaware. This possibility was compounded, since the NEB, in contrast to the DoI, did not have an institutionalized relationship with the SWPs. Instead, the NEB was connected to societal actors by another institutional network.

Although a government body, the NEB actually bridged the divide between the private and public sectors, thanks to the manner by which the NEB was staffed during the two Labour governments.[13] Of the nine board members, four were always from industry (Kramer 1988, 12–13). In addition, a majority of the fifty-plus staff members who provided the board with detailed industrial analyses were drawn on short-term contracts from British industry and banking. The movement of staff members between the NEB and British industry provided the NEB with insight into not only the investment needs of British industry, but also those investments that might prove potentially rewarding. In addition, those British industrialists who worked for the NEB could not only influence the NEB's investment patterns, but also gain firsthand knowledge of the board's areas of interest. Consequently, the staffing practices of the NEB created an institutional network through which industry representatives could influence the government's investment practices.

Industry Distress

By the early 1970s, British manufacturers had exited the market for standard circuits. They lacked the financial resources required to cover the R&D and capital expenses needed to develop these devices. The customized circuits that British manufacturers produced were not as technologically advanced as the standard memory circuits produced by U.S. and Japanese firms. The absence of a British manufacturer of standard circuits disadvantaged both British manufacturers and users of semiconductor devices vis-à-vis their Japanese and U.S. competitors. On the one hand, British semiconductor manufacturers lagged behind their competitors in developing the latest semiconductor technologies and, thus, in innovating and entering new markets. On the other hand, British users of standard circuits were dependent on foreign suppliers, consequently contributing to the country's growing trade deficit in semiconductor products. Because there was believed to be a great deal of synergy between producers and users of semiconductors, many observers saw the lack of an indigenous standard circuit producer as detracting from Britain's ability to exploit market opportunities in the increasingly lucrative electronics and information technology industries.

Policy Response

The NEB employed industrialists as consultants to identify rewarding investments. Iann Barron, a British computer designer and director of a minicomputer company, had worked for the NEB in this capacity on several occasions. Most recently, he had "produced a report for the NEB examining the minicomputer industry" in the spring of 1977 (McLean and Rowland 1985, 30). This report warned against investing in minicomputers and, instead, argued that the NEB should support semiconductor manufacture or word processing. In response, NEB officials asked Barron to investigate how the board might support semiconductor manufacturing, especially standard circuit production in Britain. Barron concluded that the board should provide established British producers with finance capital rather than investing in a start-up venture. In other words, Barron advised the board not to invest public sector funds in a British start-up venture that intended to manufacture standard integrated circuits. Pursuant to Barron's advice, the NEB entered into discussions with Plessey concerning potential investment opportunities in its semiconductor operations.[14]

In the summer of 1977, Barron became convinced that the NEB could successfully back a British-based start-up. His shift was due to an invitation to join two established American semiconductor designers in starting a new semiconductor firm: Richard Petritz, an American semiconductor chip developer, who had worked for Texas Instruments and established Mostek, an American producer of integrated circuits; and Paul Schroeder, an American designer of integrated circuits for Mostek. This firm's objective was to leapfrog the next generation of standard circuits, the 16K DRAM, to produce 64K dynamic and static random access memory integrated circuits (SRAMs). Believed to be at least three years away from production in 1977, the 64K chip was expected to be the single most important semiconductor product (Wilkinson 1979b). As Barron explains, "[w]ithout transfer of technology from the United States no amount of investment would have sufficed. And until I met Petritz I did not know how the technology could have been imported" (McLean and Rowland 1985, 31). This firm, which would become known as Inmos, would overcome this problem—in the same manner as such previously successful U.S. start-ups as Intel and Mostek had—by luring established American VLSI designers away from their current employers.

Due to Barron's earlier work for the NEB, he knew that the board was interested in funding a venture in semiconductor technology. Consequently, after devising a preliminary blue-print for a standard circuit manufacturer, Petritz and Barron approached the NEB in November 1977 (Ibid., 30–33). Between November and March 1978, the Inmos team and NEB officials worked out a mutually acceptable business plan for their joint venture. This plan called for the NEB to invest £50 million in Inmos, the British-based and majority-owned manufacturer of high-volume, standard integrated circuits. Although some production facilities would be located in the United States, all R&D facilities were to be headquartered in the United Kingdom. In exchange for its investment, the NEB gained control of 76% of the company's shares.[15]

Since the NEB's investment was more than £10 million, and the investment enabled the NEB to control more than 30% of the votes at a shareholders' meeting, the board's investment had to be approved by the industry secretary. With little delay the industry secretary approved the NEB's proposed venture in early May 1978. The DoI, although in the midst of preparing the MISP and MAP programs, favored the NEB's venture, because of the information it had gleaned from discussions with other elements of the industry thanks to the SWPs. However, members of the ECSWP were not involved in formulating this initiative. Among the members of this working party, only Mullard and ITT, the two British-based foreign subsidiaries, were against the Inmos venture, seeing the start-up as a direct threat, in terms of both markets and technical personnel (see Wilkinson 1979a; Brown 1978).

On learning of the NEB's investment, Treasury officials tried to get the cabinet to stop it (Barnett 1982, 152). Although the Treasury was able to control the NEB's budgetary allocation, it possessed little sway over what the NEB did with the funds it was allocated; the Inmos investment was well within the board's £1 billion budget. The only other member of the cabinet that did have the authority to override the NEB's investment was the prime minister. Prime Minister Callaghan had become an enthusiastic convert to the link between a healthy microelectronics industry and Britain's economic future (Blackstone and Plowden 1988, 145–46). By late May 1978, the prime minister authorized the NEB's investment in Inmos.

A Type V institutional structure affected this policy episode and helped to make the Inmos decision possible. The presence of an institutional network enabled Inmos's founders to transmit their ideas to relevant government officials. Having worked for the NEB, Barron consequently possessed a special relationship with the board's staff members. This relationship provided Barron with the knowledge that the NEB would be interested in investing in a project such as Inmos, and the board's officials with a sense of the venture's viability. Due to the NEB's lateral autonomy, other state units played a secondary role in the policy process. As a consequence, the investment scheme that was worked out for Inmos between the industrialists and NEB officials ultimately became policy.

The Second Inmos Debate: The Conservatives' Turn

The terms of the NEB's 1978 agreement with Inmos called for the board's funding to be made in two stages: initially and in 1980, if the board was satisfied with the firm's progress. By the time Prime Minister Thatcher assumed power in May 1979, Inmos had not received its second installment of funding, nor had it chosen where in Britain to locate its production facilities. Inmos's R&D center was located in Bristol, in the prosperous Cotswolds. The firm hoped to set up its production facilities in Bristol, since many U.S. firms had found it beneficial to locate their production and R&D facilities in close proximity. Not only would an integrated design and production complex reduce overhead costs, but the proximity of the two facilities would enable design and production personnel to interact with and, thus, learn from each other. These two issues were soon to prove troublesome for Inmos in light of the Conservatives' ascent to office and their decision to reduce the NEB's autonomy; the new government replaced the Type V context with a Type III context, one which decentralized decision-making authority.

Unlike the previous Labour government, Thatcher's Conservative government viewed the principle of government support for industry unfavorably. In fact, the Conservatives generally believed that an industry's investment decisions should be left to the market to decide, no matter the industry. As Prime Minister Thatcher said in March 1980, "[w]e should not expect the state to appear in the guise of an extravagant good fairy at every christening, a loquacious companion at every stage of life's journey, the unknown mourner at every funeral" (quoted in Young 1989a, 147). Regeneration of British industry instead was to be accomplished through macroeconomic measures. As a DTI document explained: "Of overriding importance is the objective of controlling inflation. . . . [T]his will make a more substantial and lasting contribution to the improvement of industry's international competitiveness than fine-tuning by the instruments of industrial policy and the major means to that end is the determined control of monetary growth and public expenditure" (Morgan and Sayer 1988, 248). Accordingly, the Conservatives had been quite hostile to the NEB and its activities while in opposition; during the 1979 campaign, Thatcher had promised "to strip it of practically all its power to buy companies and to force it to hive off its existing stock" (Kramer 1988, 19). Others within the Conservative Party focused specifically on the NEB's investments, maintaining that Inmos, in particular, "should either be wound up or sold off to private sector investors" (Redwood 1984, 65).

Soon after taking office in 1979, the Conservative government enacted several guidelines for the NEB, each of which curtailed its lateral autonomy. Foremost, the industry minister had to approve all NEB investments above £5 million, the board had to dispose of £100 million within the 1979–1980 fiscal year, its total spending limit was reduced to £750 million, a figure its current holdings surpassed, it was to invest only when "adequate returns" could be reaped in "a reasonable period of time," and the industry minister could no longer direct the NEB to grant selective aid under Section 7 and 8 of the 1972 Industry Act (Kramer 1988, 18–23). Sir Keith Joseph, the Conservative government's industry minister until September 1981, indicated how he would react to the NEB's investment activities when he stated, "[b]asically, I'm averse to seeing public money invested in manners which open up pressures for money to be put into things that shouldn't survive—one's seen too much of that in the past twenty-five years" (quoted in Redwood 1984, 66). The political controversy surrounding the NEB's actions led the prime minister and the cabinet to play a more hands-on role in scrutinizing the NEB's investments; as a result, every cabinet minister was afforded an opportunity to influence not only the way in which the board's investments were to be made, but if in fact they should be made at all. The NEB's lateral autonomy, therefore, was eliminated, and a once-centralized structure had now become extremely decentralized.

The Conservatives did not alter the structure of the NEB itself. As such, industrialists continued to staff the NEB and, thus, an institutional network continued to exist. This institutional network did not play the same role in the second Inmos debate as it did in the first one. The firms' preferences already were placed directly on the government's policy agenda, thanks to the decision to make its investments in two stages. As a consequence, a policy debate ensued, which most observers would have considered unlikely for the Thatcher government to join: whether to discuss, let alone to approve, an additional £25 million public subsidy to help a high technology firm enter an intensely competitive market with no guarantee that the firm would be profitable in the short or long term.

Policy Response

By December 1979 the NEB was satisfied with Inmos's progress and asked the industry secretary to approve a second £25 million allocation to Inmos.[16] Soon thereafter Joseph endorsed the NEB's recommendation. This action was surprising given Joseph's noted aversion to public sector support for industry. Some have speculated that by virtue of his position as the head of the DoI, he became influenced by the department's institutional bias to support industry (Richards and Smith 2002).

When in early 1980 the cabinet took up the issue of Inmos's second funding installment, its discussion concerned neither Inmos's technological progress nor whether public funds should be used to provide Britain with an indigenous productive capacity in the leading edge of semiconductor technology. Instead, due to the decentralized decision-making structure, the cabinet found itself concerned with how Inmos's future Bristol production facility would adversely impact several departments' preexisting interests. For example, the Ministry of Agriculture was against the Inmos venture, because its Bristol factory would be located on a site previously designated for agricultural purposes (Redwood 1984, 77). By contrast, the Scottish and Welsh ministers were in favor of giving Inmos its second installment of funds, only if the firm would relocate its production facilities in an area of high unemployment in one of their constituencies (McLean and Rowland 1985, 83). With the debate still brewing, the Treasury had the opportunity to object to the venture on grounds similar to those their predecessors invoked in 1978 (Hills 1984, 215). Due to these differing perspectives, the cabinet was unable to rule on the question of whether to give Inmos its second installment of funds. Instead, the issue became more complex, as the Conservative government split into three factions: those ministers who did not want Inmos to receive any further government aid; those who wanted to provide Inmos with the second funding installment; and those who were willing to fund Inmos, but only if the firm located its production facilities in an area of high unemployment. The cabinet debated the Inmos funding issue during the first half of 1980 and found itself deadlocked twice (McLean and Rowland 1985, 85).

By July the government's overall economic strategy had come under intense attack in the House of Commons. The Labour opposition claimed that the government's economic strategy accelerated the country's already high level of unemployment.[17] This criticism provided Welsh Secretary Nicholas Edwards with the opportunity to force the cabinet's hand. Edwards believed that funding Inmos could quiet the Labour opposition, if the firm were to locate its production facilities in an area of high unemployment. Although government financial support for Inmos contradicted the Conservatives' desire to reinforce the free play of market forces, "Edwards argued that funding Inmos could be justified on ideological grounds if it meant creating a source of employment in job-hungry Wales"—the nearest area of high unemployment to Inmos's existing R&D complex (McLean and Rowland 1985, 84). By the middle of July, the cabinet, sensing the political wisdom of Edwards's arguments, agreed to allow the NEB to transfer funds to Inmos. On July 30, 1980, Prime Minister Thatcher told Parliament that the government "[is] prepared to help the transition to higher productivity and to more jobs" (Rawstorne 1980). As evidence of the government's determination, the prime minister stated that £25 million was to be made available to Inmos to create two thousand jobs over the next three to four years in Wales, an area of high unemployment. In announcing the government's decision to Parliament, the prime minister made no mention of the role the £25 million would play in fostering Inmos's technological development. In fact, the division within the government over the funding issue forced Inmos to postpone the start of SRAM production, thus delaying the firm's entrance into a market characterized by significant first-mover advantages.

The Conservative government's decision to attach conditions to Inmos's second funding installment reflected the impact of the decentralization of decision-making authority. Multiple state units were able to weigh in on the merits of the NEB's support for Inmos, a discussion set in motion by the terms of the NEB's initial decision to provide funds to the firm. Many were unsupportive of interventionist strategies generally and were concerned with how the investment might affect their own departmental concerns and objectives. As a consequence, the policy debate elevated these issues, in the process subordinating the technological concerns that had led the NEB to identify Inmos as an investment candidate in the first place. In the end, the cabinet saw the investment as one way to lower unemployment in one of the country's more depressed regions, thus dampening the opposition's criticisms.

Conclusion

The British semiconductor industry experienced intense competitive pressures throughout the 1970s due to the emerging globalization of the semiconductor industry and, in particular, the British market, which had become a base for U.S. and European manufacturers. British firms soon found that they lagged behind their foreign counterparts for the technologically most advanced products, leading some national firms to exit certain product areas. This chapter shows that the institutional context affecting policy debates in the Heath, Wilson, and Callaghan governments fostered close interactions between industry representatives and largely autonomous government officials responsible for industry-related issues. This context enabled industry representatives to work with government officials, who were not equally favorable to intervention as a remedy for the industry's competitive difficulties, to develop industrial policies to confront its competitive problems. When the institutional context changed following the Conservative Party's victory in 1979, so too did the policy process and the policy advanced. This new context decentralized authority, empowering multiple ministers' interests in the policy debate. With Inmos's preferences squarely on the agenda, the government provided the British start-up of advanced memory chips with its second funding installment, but did so in a manner that advanced the government's regional and employment objectives rather than the firm's competitive needs. Across the mid- to late 1970s, then, British governments adopted interventionist rather than liberal strategies in response to the pressures associated with the globalization of the industry.

The chapter also indicates that private sector access to the policy process does not by definition equal influence over policy. The industry's ability to achieve its preferences also hinged on whether government officials were favorable to them. Two variations of this dynamic are illustrated by the cases involving the Conservative governments. In the case involving the Thatcher government, for example, the Inmos team's demands were squarely on the agenda. However, the decentralized decision-making structure reduced the team's influence over policy choice, since it brought multiple state units into the policy process that did not share the preferences of the Inmos team, the NEB, and the industry secretary. The case involving the Heath government suggests a second dynamic: in structures characterized by lateral autonomy, private sector actors still may find it difficult to achieve their preferences, if government officials are not open to them. The Heath government came to office with strong liberal predilections and created a DTI that sought to replicate them; at the same time, the industry enjoyed a privileged position in the policy process and advanced strong preferences for interventionist actions. The industry, however, did not succeed in persuading DTI officials, until their preferences shifted in response to growing national economic dislocations. Once these officials came to favor a new strategy, the institutional context provided industry representatives with the opportunity to persuade DTI officials of the merits of developing an interventionist strategy to their benefit.

The institutional context experienced several transformations during the period examined here. Institutions structuring government-industry and intragovernmental relations were both subject to reform. Two reforms were advanced in response to the globalization of competition the British economy encountered. Both changes—the creation of the SWPs and the

1972 Industry Act—increased the capacity of the state to intervene in the economy. Other institutional changes—such as the creation and reform of the NEB or the formation and division of the DTI—were driven by national-level dynamics rather than globalization. Whether these reforms amounted to an increase or decrease in the capacity of the state varied due to the ideological predilections of newly elected government officials. The contrasting ideology of the Labour and Conservative governments regarding the appropriate role of the government in the economy also often led them to undo each others' institutional reforms, suggesting that ideology is likely to shape how government officials view the benefits and costs of different institutions. However, the Heath government's experience suggests that liberal predilections may prove less constraining, when globalization pressures turn intensely negative; that government opted for institutional transformations that increased the state's capacity to intervene, when several sectors appeared on the verge of succumbing to foreign competitors.

By the end of the 1970s, British semiconductor firms were struggling to maintain their presence in the industry. The policies examined here sought to redress this situation by making available more than £200 million of public sector funds to support the development and use of microelectronics in Britain. This money supported programs that had diverse objectives. For example, the Microelectronics Support Scheme funded national firms producing ASICs, whereas the MISP subsequently provided funds for joint ventures between national and foreign firms to produce standard integrated circuits. A third policy provided support for the use of microelectronics in other sectors. Finally, the government's funding of Inmos sought to establish a national manufacturer of mass-produced standard integrated circuits. As the 1980s approached, it was too early to determine whether these strategies would succeed in helping British firms to increase their competitive position in the global semiconductor industry. One conclusion was becoming clearer, however. The challenges facing British firms would multiply during the next decade as the cost of product development escalated, Japanese firms became more proficient innovators, and Prime Minister Thatcher sought to advance her neoliberal agenda.

Chapter Seven

Intervention, Disengagement, and State Transformation: The Conservatives' Turn

The Thatcher government inherited a British semiconductor industry continuing to experience severe competitive pressures, even though it had received considerable government support during the previous decade. British firms found survival in their home market difficult due to the large presence of U.S., European, and soon Japanese firms, which were setting up manufacturing plants in Britain and exporting from them to Europe and other destinations. The globalization of the industry provided opportunities and obstacles for British firms. These pressures set the stage for continued policy debates regarding how the country should confront the pressures, whether in terms of making the economy more accessible to foreign firms or promoting a national capability in semiconductors and information technology (IT) more generally.

This chapter examines three policy episodes spanning the 1980 to 1996 period. Table 7.1 indicates that the governments' policy choices varied across the three episodes, corresponding to differences in the institutional context. The two industrial policies, for example, emerge from a Type V context, one in which industry representatives were accorded access to those policymakers responsible for industrial development and who enjoyed the lateral autonomy to act authoritatively. The liberal strategy, by contrast, is developed in a Type II context that enabled Prime

Table 7.1
Policy Episodes, Institutional Contexts, and Policy Choices

| | Institutional Context | | | | |
| | Institutional Networks | Decison-making Structure | Type | Nature of the Policy-making Process | Outcome |
Cases					
Alvey Program (1983)	Present	Lateral autonomy	V	Agency-industry cooperation	Industrial policy
Post-1983 Thatcher	Absent	Executive-centered	II	Executive autonomy	Liberal strategy
Foresight Program (1993)	Present	Lateral autonomy	V	Agency-industry cooperation	Industrial policy

Minister Thatcher to operate autonomously from those industry and state officials who saw the need for interventionist strategies.

Institutional change influenced each policy episode and the variations in policy choice across them. Different dynamics trigger change in each case, but the proponents of reform generally saw existing institutions as ill-suited to confront the pressures facing the country. In the first case, for example, Prime Minister Thatcher's government created a minister of industry for information technology and a new advisory committee in recognition of the significance of the sector and the need to help British manufacturers cope with the competitive challenges they faced. While these reforms reinforced the nature of the existing institutional context, the second and third cases modify it and, ultimately, the policies previously advanced. Thatcher saw her overwhelming victory in the 1983 elections as empowering her preferences for liberal strategies and providing her with the opportunity to consolidate authority in her own hands. Believing that the existing context had fostered the ill-advised use of interventionist strategies, Thatcher reformed the context so as to pursue a liberal strategy, one she believed to be more appropriate. Following John Major's victory in the 1992 elections, his Conservative government embraced the opposition's promise to create a minister of science and provided the Office of Science and Technology with lateral autonomy over the country's academic science research budget. This reform soon triggered the creation of new institutional networks and targeted support for commercially applicable research. This chapter reinforces the book's central contention that the institutional context creates its own set of opportunities and constraints, thereby influencing the ways globalization shapes state policy.

The 1983 Alvey Strategic Computing Program: Growing Globalization and Continued Competitive Distress

On taking office in 1979 the Conservatives intended to leave market forces to their own devices. The government pruned back the activities of the state, most particularly public spending. These cutbacks affected the MISP, which was scaled back by £25 million, and the MAP, which was terminated. Secretary of State for Industry Patrick Jenkin justified these actions in terms that reflected the government's guiding neoliberal philosophy: "If companies do not have the prime responsibility for their own research and development and their own market strategy, surely we will simply perpetuate that comfy over-dependence of the industry on government patronage which many see as one of the sources of our problems" (de Jonquieres 1982).[1]

When the Conservatives assumed office in 1979, they did not modify the powers accorded to the Department of Industry. Under the 1972 Industry Act, the DoI was given primary responsibility and the resources to assist British industries' investment needs. In effect, it enjoyed lateral autonomy. The government did advance at this time one institutional reform affecting the DoI; reflecting the greater economic and technological importance of the IT sector, the government created a minister of industry for information technology in November 1980. This minister was responsible for developing and coordinating government initiatives affecting such technologies as computing, telecommunications, electronics, and microelectronics. The creation of this ministerial position centralized policy development within the DoI for initiatives concerned with the IT industries.

At this time the semiconductor industry was linked to the DoI's policy process by virtue of several institutional networks. These included such formal networks as the ECSWP and informal networks such as sponsorship. Although these networks provided the industry with a privileged role in policy development, the IT sector's declining competitiveness soon led to the establishment of another institutional network. As discussed below, this institutional network provided industry representatives with an even more influential position in the DoI's policymaking process than existing networks provided.

In January 1981 Kenneth Baker was appointed minister for information technology. In one of his first initiatives, Baker sent a group of DoI officials to Japan to investigate the possibility of having British industries and universities collaborate with Japanese industries in some aspects of Japan's recently announced Fifth Generation Computer Program.[2] The charge of Baker's mission was to investigate the possibilities of trading British scientific excellence for Japanese excellence in developing commercial applications; through such an exchange it was believed that the competitiveness of Britain's IT industry could be improved, thus increasing the country's share of the world market. During their fact-finding trip to Japan in October 1981, however, it became clear to the DoI officials that Britain's level of technological development in basic information technologies such as standard VLSI circuits was severely lacking. In addition, DoI officials realized that because of the technological edge of the Japanese industries, "[t]he exchange of information between [Japanese and British] researchers would in no way inhibit Japanese industry from competing actively with British industry. On the contrary such information would swiftly be turned to competitive advantage" (Oakley and Owen 1989, 23). As one official in the DoI's IT division concluded, "[i]t seems a whole series of miracles is called for if our research is to be fully exploited to our own commercial benefit" (Ibid., 21).

As a result of the visit to Japan, these DoI officials ruled out British collaboration with Japan. These officials did see merits in the overall Japanese approach employed in the Fifth Generation Program: an approach characterized by a concentration of financial resources on key technologies in key industrial sectors. Baker responded to his subordinates' reading of the British IT industry's relative weakness by forming an investigative committee in April 1982, under the direction of John Alvey, then senior director for technology at British Telecom. The Alvey Committee included civil servants and high-ranking representatives from the country's leading semiconductor, computer, electronics, and telecommunications manufacturers. The committee was charged to consult widely with IT manufacturers and users to figure out how the sector might overcome its competitive disadvantages and, in particular, whether a response paralleling Japan's Fifth Generation Program was appropriate for Britain. The Alvey Committee then served as an institutional network through which representatives from the IT sector would be able to interact with those policymakers who were not only poised to respond to the sector's lagging competitiveness, but who also possessed the lateral autonomy to act on their preferences.

After deliberating for five months, the Alvey Committee forwarded its recommendations to Baker in November 1982. The committee urged that a five-year, £350 million, national collaborative research program be initiated to increase Britain's expertise in four technologies that were perceived as being critical to the future development of the IT industry (U.K. Alvey Committee 1983). These enabling technologies included: VLSI circuits, software engineering, information processing systems, and man-machine interface. The primary goals of the collaborative program were to make certain that within the next five years Britain would gain access to internationally competitive VLSI technology and that the country's computer and electronics industries would not be overwhelmed by the Japanese and U.S. industries. As the committee wrote: "The issue before us is stark. We can either seek to be at the leading edge of these technologies; or we can aim to rely on imported technology; or we can get out of the race. The latter we do not regard as a valid option. Nor is the reliance on imported technology practical as a general strategy, though we cannot be completely self-sufficient either. . . . The only sensible option . . . is to share in the future growth and development of the world IT sector . . . in specific targeted priority areas" (Alvey Committee 1983, 14). While the proposal was nationalist in tone, it did not seek to exclude foreign multinationals, so long as the results of their involvement in the program would be shared with British firms, and they did not leak valuable technical information out of the United Kingdom. With regard to the program's funding, the committee called on the government to contribute £250 million and participating firms £100 million. More specifically, the report called on the government to cover 100% of university research, 90% of those projects where the wide dissemination of results was likely, and 50% for all other projects.

The substance of these recommendations largely reflected the preferences of the committee's industry members. In October 1981 Britain's leading semiconductor firms, all of which were members of the Alvey Committee, recommended that the Conservative government adopt a more interventionist approach (ECSWP 1981, 1, 8). In an April 1982 report, the country's electronics firms urged the government to initiate a collaborative research and development program that would concentrate the country's resources on specific IT-related technologies. This report stated that "firms and the state should collectively concentrate resources in order to achieve and sustain competitiveness in world markets." Among the selected areas was the enabling technology of microelectronics (EEDC 1983, 6). The similarity between the sector's previous proposals and those of the Alvey Committee reflected the fact that this committee offered the IT sector a direct and privileged role in the DoI's formulation of a response to the sector's growing competition. In effect, this institutional network advantaged the sector's interests during this stage of policy development.

Policy Response

Following the release of the Alvey Committee's proposals, the DoI recommended that a program based on the committee's report be established immediately. Sir Brian Hayes, the DoI permanent secretary, stated that such a program was necessary "because we are competing with countries in Europe, Japan and the United States which are doing precisely [the same thing]. We cannot afford to sit back and say we'll leave it entirely to market forces to decide what happens" (quoted in Samuel 1984, 89). The DoI's acceptance of this strategy is hardly surprising, given the fact that by virtue of its participation in the Alvey Committee's discussions, DoI officials had helped to develop what came to be the committee's proposals. Moreover, the department's minister for information technology had created the Alvey Committee and initiated its investigation in response to his subordinates' dire conclusions regarding the competitiveness of the country's IT sector. What is surprising, however, is Industry Secretary Jenkin's acceptance of the committee's recommendations, given his opposition to state intervention in the economy. His about-face can be attributed to the institutional network, which enabled the industry to provide Jenkin with information that convinced him that public sector support was required, if Britain were to have a technologically competitive IT industry. The industry's participation in the Alvey Committee's investigation also enabled it to help design a strategy that would bear on those areas of the IT sector where the industry perceived its prospects to be brightest and where it was willing to invest its own resources. These characteristics coincided with those Jenkin had earlier delineated as being necessary for him to approve a larger role for the state in industrial development. As Jenkin explained in June 1982, "[i]t is for the industry itself to decide where the prospects are brightest and how to concentrate its efforts. . . . [A] selective strategy can only succeed if the industry is motivated to make it succeed" (Jenkin 1982, 4).

Jenkin's decision to press ahead with this interventionist initiative encountered only minimal scrutiny and resistance from the rest of the cabinet, an equally surprising development, given the Conservative government's intention to reduce state intervention in the economy. One reason for this result is that the other departments capable of playing a role in policy development, particularly the Treasury, lacked the technical capacity to assess the Alvey Committee's recommendations and, thus, to undermine the DoI's support for them (Keliher 1990, 68–69). Moreover, those that had the technical expertise were already involved in the development of the proposals. For example, the prime minister's advisory body on IT issues, the Information Technology Advisory Panel, comprised several industrialists who had submitted supporting recommendations to the

Alvey Committee and one who was a member of that committee (Oakley and Owen 1989, 53).

Cabinet scrutiny did fall, however, on the program's funding scheme. Baker and Jenkin unintentionally unleashed this debate with their decision to revise downward the committee's recommendation that the government fund 90% of research that would be widely disseminated. Treasury officials subsequently maintained that the government's contribution should be limited to 60% for such projects. Apparently the prime minister got involved at this stage and decided that the ceiling for all projects should be 50% (Cane 1983; Keliher 1990, 72). Additionally, Treasury officials made it clear that they supported the program, only so long as it did not require the government either to allocate new funds or to appoint new civil servants to run it. Nonetheless, the DoI possessed—together with pledges from the Department of Education and Sciences and the Ministry of Defense—the necessary resources to fund the program out of its current budgetary allocation. Beyond these issues, the available records suggest that the DoI's autonomy was only minimally circumscribed. As such, the DoI's jurisdictional independence was reinforced by its monopoly over technical expertise and its budgetary resources.

The Conservative government's strategy for the IT industry did not conform to its ideological predilection to let market forces determine the fate of British industry. Instead, as Wilks explains, the Alvey Program "amounts to state-led, inter-firm collaboration on the Japanese model, working to a long-term strategic objective. It indicates a substantial government commitment to technological innovation which goes well beyond setting the climate or even providing incentives" (Wilks 1985, 136). Jenkin's speech to the House of Commons (Jenkin 1983) announcing the government's decision to provide £200 million to what would become the Alvey Program illustrates the magnitude of the Conservatives' policy shift: "After detailed consultation with industry I am now able to announce . . . that we shall be embarking on a collaborative research project. . . . Industry, academic researchers and government will be coming together to achieve major advances in technology which none could achieve on their own. . . . [T]his programme will ensure for British industry access to the new technology and to the products and processes on which our future prosperity depends." In effect, the government had decided it was necessary to manipulate market forces to benefit British industry and the national interest more generally. The institutional conditions shaping the policy debate played a pivotal role in leading the Conservative government to pursue this interventionist response. The Type V context enabled industry representatives to interact with those policymakers who had the capacity to respond to the competitive pressures the industry faced. Out of this interaction, a consensus emerged concerning the need for the Thatcher government to intervene. Not surprisingly, nearly all the program's budget was used up within the first three years by 192 collaborative projects (Wren 1996, 161).

The Post–1983 Period: A Neoliberal Regime Ascends

In the June 1983 general election, Thatcher's Conservative Party increased its majority in the House of Commons by nearly 100 seats. This was one of the most one-sided results in Britain during the twentieth century, and the first time during this period that a prime minister had won a second term after a full term in office. Thatcher capitalized on this victory to fortify her capacity and that of her supporters to move forward with her neoliberal program. In particular, the prime minister completed a process of institutional innovations she had pursued incrementally since assuming office in 1979: consolidating decision-making authority in her own hands and reducing the role of interest groups in policymaking (Burch 1983; Jenkins 1988; Young 1989b). In seeking to alter that structure of decision-making authority, Thatcher was determined to break with the long-standing tradition that "the British executive is collective and the prime minister's power is exercised *in* and *with* the Cabinet" (Kavanagh 1990, 245). In place of cabinet government, Prime Minister Thatcher sought to create an executive-centered structure, so that she could control policymaking and determine the direction of policy (Pym 1984, 17–18; Doherty 1988, 63; Holmes 1989). In effect, the prime minister sought to create a Type II structure, one in which decision-making authority was concentrated in her own hands and her government disengaged from the network of linkages connecting government to interest groups.[3]

Thatcher relied on three tactics to increase her influence over decision making. First, she used her powers of appointment to make certain that only like-minded officials held key cabinet positions. The 1983 electoral victory allowed Thatcher to remove the remaining "wets" (those less supportive of her agenda) from her cabinet. More unusually, the prime minister employed these powers with respect to senior civil servants. Breaking with tradition regarding the apolitical nature of the senior civil service, Thatcher sought to ensure that only officials sympathetic to her policy beliefs were appointed to key posts. Through both sets of appointments, the prime minister strategically placed a network of ideologues in key positions in various departments.[4]

Second, Thatcher tended to decide matters outside the formal cabinet, bypassing it through the use of informal, small decision-making bodies (see Lawson 1992, 125–29). As Thatcher selected which officials would participate in these ad hoc bodies, she not only circumvented those who might oppose her, but also made certain that only she and her supporters were involved in policy decisions.

Third, the prime minister relied on an independent group of advisors and policy experts located in Downing Street for advice and policy initiative (Thatcher 1993). One means by which Thatcher undermined the traditional pattern of policy formulation was to strengthen the Policy Unit that Prime Minister Harold Wilson had established in 1974 to assist him, most particularly, with economic policy (Willetts 1987, 443–44). Consisting of about eight advisers responsible only to the prime minister, the Policy Unit assumed a more significant role in policy formation during the later period of Thatcher's tenure. Principally, Thatcher's reliance on the Policy Unit for policy direction offered her an additional mechanism by which to incorporate her ideologues into policy development and exclude those less supportive of her views.

The prime minister took several actions that directly undermined the DoI's autonomy and initiative. Soon after the 1983 election, she merged the DoI with the Department of Trade to form an integrated Department of Trade and Industry (DTI). Thatcher hoped that the more liberal Department of Trade might dampen the DoI's interventionist culture, and the conventions and customs that had emerged with it. More immediately, the prime minister reduced the new department's functional authorities. In contrast to previous reorganizations involving this department, the prime minister made it difficult for DTI officials to advance interventionist strategies or even to play a role in industrial development by "further prun[ing] back [the DTI] to a core of functions with little resemblance to a Ministry of Industry" (Middlemas 1991, 369). Its administration of regional development grants was moved to the Scottish and Welsh offices in December 1984, and in September 1985 the DTI's responsibility for small firms was moved to the Department of Employment. Moreover, when the department's policy planning unit insisted on an interventionist strategy, the unit was abolished.

Second, between 1983 and 1990 eight different people held the position of secretary of state for trade and industry, suggesting that this was a portfolio over which the prime minister kept a careful watch. One could interpret the rapid turnover of ministers as an indication that Thatcher had learned from Keith Joseph's experience and would not provide any subsequent minister with the opportunity to become influenced by the DoI's cultural bias toward intervention. Joseph, industry secretary from 1979 to 1981, had been an outspoken champion of the need to do away with industrial support and the DoI itself. Yet, he soon found himself supporting subsidies to several industries and providing financing to start Inmos.

In altering the structure of decision-making authority, Thatcher indirectly affected a second institution, government-industry linkages. Though such networks as the Economic Development Committees (the resurrected name for some SWPs) and sponsorship continued to link industry representatives to the policy process, they did so under a different context. Now, they linked the industry to officials at the DTI who wielded only nominal influence over the government's strategy toward industry. Thatcher also directly affected the structure of these linkages. Through a process of circumventing, downgrading, and eventually eliminating the prevailing institutional networks, Thatcher parted with the traditional British practice of including relevant private sector interests in policy formation (Moon 1995, 8–9; Painter 1989). This process culminated with the decision in 1987 to abolish sponsorship and twenty-one of the EDCs, including the IT EDC. These actions reflected Thatcher's hostility to the principle of tripartism, the process of collective decision making among government, industry, and unions, and her belief that it was partly responsible for the country's economic difficulties. As a DTI White Paper explained, "[t]he ability of the economy to change and adapt was hampered by the combination of corporatism and powerful unions. Corporatism limited competition and the birth of new firms, whilst, at the same time, encouraging protections and restrictions designed to help existing firms" (DTI 1988, 1). Richard Rose (1989, 241) concludes that "the Thatcher philosophy is [best] described as *state distancing*, for the institutions of the Crown are not meant to be mixed up in the everyday activities of the marketplace, such as bargaining about wages or making investment decisions."

These institutional changes and procedural innovations amounted to a change in the institutional context affecting industry. Now, this area was shaped by a Type II structure, one characterized by an executive-centered decision-making structure and the absence of institutional networks. This context strengthened Thatcher's capacity to make certain that her government adhered to a liberal strategy to foster the competitiveness of British industry. The central component of this strategy comprised the reduction of public sector support to industry, whether regulatory or financial, as well as the encouragement of foreign direct investment. Not unexpectedly, the IT sector spent the post-1983 period seeking to reverse this strategy. Nevertheless, the absence of institutional networks and the executive-centered decision-making structure meant that Thatcher could advance an industrial strategy opposed by the IT industry and some members of her government, two groups empowered by the former Type V institutional context.

Competitive Pressures Continue

By the spring of 1983, the IT sector's competitiveness continued to decline. Between 1981 and 1984 import penetration in the sector increased from 45% to 61%, and the country's trade deficit in IT products nearly doubled from £480 million in 1982 to £950 million by the end of 1984 (McCalman 1988, 45, table 3.1). During the same period, the British share of the world market fell from 5% to 4% (Ibid.). These difficulties were most pronounced in the semiconductor industry. The deficit in semiconductor devices increased by nearly $160 million between 1983 and 1984, as Britain's share of the world semiconductor market fell to 2% (Bird and Park 1987; Plodding 1985). Similarly, the total output of British semiconductor manufacturers was less than £150 million compared to a world market that topped £10 billion (Manners 1984). Although such British manufacturers as Ferranti and Plessey were world leaders in semicustom chips, and Inmos was becoming a leader in the manufacture of 16K and 64K SRAMs, the country's major manufacturers—Inmos, Plessey, Ferranti, GEC, and STC—were small players in global markets in 1984. In fact, not one of these firms was among the world's top thirty producers. Plessey, the country's leading semiconductor producer at the time, was the sixth largest European firm, accounting for just one-tenth the sales of Philips, Europe's premier firm and number ten in the world. Perhaps more indicative of the position of the indigenous firms, they manufactured less than half of the semiconductors produced in Britain. "The bulk of these chips were made by Philips and Texas Instruments in England and by National Semiconductor Corp., NEC, and Motorola in Scotland" (Rise and Fall 1988, 41).

There was growing concern in the mid-1980s that the technological competency of British manufacturers was close to the threshold below which an independent, British semiconductor industry was no longer viable. In particular, some feared that the country might soon be forced to depend not only on imported integrated circuits, but also on the technology to develop, design, and apply integrated circuits to the wide range of products incorporating them. According to the *Times* (Manners 1984, 18), the weakness of the British semiconductor industry had proven disadvantageous to other British industries: "The British have lost significance in world computer, telecommunications, and consumer markets through lacking a strong, continuous, technically aggressive presence in chip-making." The status of these technologies was further weakened, as the British semiconductor industry's position continued to deteriorate. By 1988 British firms accounted for just 21.7% of the European market, a decrease of 4% since 1983 (Rosenbaum 1989; Eustace 1984). Given this development, a widely publicized 1985 report by Cambridge Econometrics forecast that imported electronics products would increase by at least another 10% to "account for 70% of the UK market by 1993" (de Jonquieres 1985a, 4). Previous British policies had done little to increase the position of national firms in the global market.

Policy Response

Following the Conservative Party's success in the 1983 elections, Thatcher advanced a liberal strategy to foster the competitiveness of British industry and the economy. She hoped to create an "enterprise culture" in which free markets inspired individuals to innovate and create wealth.[5] A central element of this strategy was to encourage U.S. and Japanese semiconductor and IT producers to invest in Britain. Industry Secretary Jenkin (How Inward Investment 1982, 402–3) explained:

> The government is committed to maintaining and strengthening the operation of market forces in order to improve the country's economic performance and free flow of inward direct investment contributes to this central policy objective by introducing additional productive capacity to compete with established sources in the UK and with imports, as well as to raise exports. Such investment, often bringing new technological skills and managerial expertise, thus tends to increase both the quality and quantity of output and employment in this country. . . . The essence of the case for encouraging inward investment is that it helps to increase output and employment through establishing technically efficient and economically competitive production in the UK that would [otherwise] be carried out overseas (or, possibly, not at all).

In the government's view, inward investment by foreign firms was not, then, explicitly limited to improving the competitiveness of domestic industries. Rather, such a strategy would provide far-reaching benefits for the British economy as a whole: Inward investment would bring new technologies, management styles and attitudes, capital, jobs, and exports. The importance of this last goal to the government's strategy is well illustrated by the testimony of a DTI official to a House of Lords Select Committee in 1985 (Lords 1985, 284–85):[6]

> Mr. Duguid: [T]hrough the process of inward investment, local manufacturing is substituting for imports.
>
> Lord Ezra: So we are being told there could be some improvement in the [balance of payments] position as a result of American and Japanese multinationals establishing themselves over here?
>
> Mr. Duguid: That is correct, my Lord, yes.

Lord Ezra: Not due to British firms catching up?

Mr. Duguid: I did not wish to imply that. . . . I expect an improvement as a result of two processes: 1) multinationals—and we have got some evidence of it beginning to happen already, and 2) the improved performance of our indigenous companies. I think the latter will be, frankly, an uphill struggle, because there are always problems in trying to compete with these well-established, large companies.

Although previous British governments had welcomed and fostered inward investment, they had placed conditions on the incentives granted to foreign investors. Prior to 1979, for example, to receive government investment grants and tax rebates foreign investors had to show that their investments would provide net UK benefits and would not result in the displacement of indigenous production capabilities. However, "after 1979 new inward investments that were associated with greater efficiency or more successful management than existing British establishments were allowed to over-ride the displacement hurdle, as were mostly mobile investments which another member of the European Community might allow in" (Dunford 1989, 111). Additional guidelines on foreign investment, including making certain that the investment did not create over-capacity, were also compromised. In some cases, moreover, the government offered large subsidies to foreign investors to attract them to Britain and subsequently allowed these firms to take advantage of government support programs without conditions to ensure that the results derived from them benefited British firms.[7] Coupled with the government's removal of exchange controls and other deregulatory efforts, these initiatives sought to reduce the transaction costs foreign investors assumed in using Britain as a manufacturing site to benefit from the creation of the single European market.

Not surprisingly, the indigenous British IT industry opposed Thatcher's reliance on inward investment to spur its competitiveness. British manufacturers wanted the government to scrutinize the inward flow of investments to make certain that domestic manufacturers were not being harmed.[8] The possibility that indigenous manufacturers could be displaced by foreign manufacturers was not, however, viewed negatively by the government. In fact, as one DTI document observed, the government was fully prepared to accept the loss of a national semiconductor manufacturer or other IT-related industry: "A corollary of introducing a competitive spur is acceptance of the risk of displacing some of the output and jobs provided by existing IT companies" (quoted in Morgan and Sayer 1988, 255).

National IT manufacturers were critical of the government's inward investment strategy not simply because of the risks it implied for them, but also because that was the only way in which the government sought to increase the sector's competitiveness. After 1983 the Thatcher government resisted using public sector funds to enhance the national firms' competitiveness. National producers maintained that such support was pivotal, because British manufacturers continued to lag behind other countries not only in developing IT innovations, but also in applying semiconductor technology.

The industry's appeal for public sector support came from many directions. In a 1983 report, for example, the Electronics EDC acknowledged that the survival of the British IT industry depended on a healthy semiconductor industry. As a result, the EDC called on the government "to create a Ministry of Communications with powers to promote the development of a national semiconductor industry . . ." (de Jonquieres 1983, 8). The Information Technology Economic Development Committee (ITEDC) offered another proposal in its 1984 report. It (1984, 2) noted that the British IT industry accounted for only 5% of the world market. "[British manufacturers could] no longer continue to invest adequately in product development, in marketing or in production facilities. . . . On present trends the UK will not have an independent broad-based IT industry by the end of the decade. . . . We believe that new policies are needed, on the part of industry and of government, to attempt to reverse the decline before it's too late." The ITEDC proposed that another initiative along the lines of the Alvey Program be established. If Britain did not exploit IT "as urgently or as effectively as other advanced nations," the EDC warned, the country "shall continue its decline to third world status" (Ibid., 5).

A similar picture was painted by the Electronic Components SWP. This group advised the government that the country's microelectronics industry was continuing to find survival a struggle. To improve the industry's competitiveness, the Electronic Components Working Party called on the government to increase its R&D support. To justify the need for such action, the SWP pointed out that in 1984 the government's level of support was just 53% of the German government's contribution and only 28% of the French contribution. It noted that by 1985 Britain was "the only large EEC country not providing direct state support to an indigenous volume chip manufacturer" (de Jonquieres 1985b). In a letter to the House of Lords Select Committee on Science and Technology (Lords 1986, 109–10), the industry's trade association, the Electronic Components Industry Federation (ECIF), sought to publicize the competitive pressures the country's semiconductor manufacturers faced and their preferred remedy:

> [In the past it has been] national policy that the UK should have an effective and healthy microelectronics industry because of its fundamental role as a key enabling technology. [But] structural factors and massive direct and indirect intervention by governments of competitor nations greatly distort market forces and mean that Britain will no longer be able to sustain such an industry—unless sustained and countervailing action is taken by the British government. Such action is needed on a number of fronts; but continuing R&D support, and even more importantly financial support of investment in microelectronics production on a scale more comparable with that provided in competitor nations are major concerns. . . .

These consultative bodies appear to have provided industry representatives with a channel through which to persuade DTI officials of the need to augment the department's funding of the industry's R&D. Even though the government was committed to market-oriented strategies, the DTI members of these consultative bodies supported an interventionist approach to enhance the competitiveness of the British IT industry. Due to the prime minister's consolidation of authority, however, these DTI officials were unable to determine the government's industrial strategy. In contrast to the recommendations of the consultative bodies, the Conservative government slashed public expenditure on trade and industry by 38.2% and more specifically reduced spending on scientific and technological assistance by 47% between 1979–1980 and 1989–1990 (Lawson 1992, 301). The cut in public expenditure was most drastic between 1984–1985 and 1989–1990; it was cut 48.5%, whereas it actually grew 16.4% between 1979–1980 and 1984–1985 (Johnson 1991, 287). Colin Wren (1996, 197) calculates "that the fall in expenditure on industrial subsidies over the 1980s has been dramatic, from about £5 billion in grant equivalent terms in 1979 to a little over £300 million in 1990 (1980 prices)." These cutbacks reflect a fundamental change in the focus of the DTI during this period; its interventionist role was scaled down, if not eliminated, and it became a regulatory and advisory enterprise department (Thain and Wright 1995, 157).

The industry soon recognized the inadequacy of its traditional channels of influence. Accordingly, with the Alvey Program's budgetary allocation set to expire in 1988, the IT industry utilized alternative avenues to convince the Conservative government to adopt an interventionist strategy. First, the industry sought to force the government's hand by publicizing its displeasure with the government's general industrial strategy at hearings held before the House of Lords Select Committee on Overseas Trade in the spring of 1985 (Lords 1985). Hugo Young (1989a, 362) contends that these hearings were "the most carefully orchestrated attack made by industry on the entire thrust of the government's economic policy. . . . Numerous ennobled company chairmen past and present testified before [the] Select Committee to the effect that, owing to the decline in manufacturing industry, the country faced disaster. . . . The [Committee's] report, doomladen in its pessimism, was scathingly rejected by the Government [as] a mixture of special pleading dressed up as analysis and assertion masquerading as evidence."

Second, industry representatives organized the IT 86 Committee, or Bide Committee, to develop and promote a successor to Alvey. The need for such an additional public sector effort was confirmed by the civil servant the prime minister appointed to oversee the Alvey Program; Brian Oakley predicted that many of the program's research projects would be jeopardized, if they were to rely exclusively on funds supplied by the participating firms. In contrast to the Alvey Committee, this second investigation consisted solely of industry and university officials who were not directly incorporated in any department's policy formation process (see Oakley and Owen 1989, chap. 14).

The Bide Committee's report, released in November 1986, echoed the opinions representatives of the sector had expressed throughout the post-1983 period (IT 1986). "Information technology is a discipline which is developing so fast that a laissez faire approach will not suffice" (13). "More effective development and use of IT will improve the competitiveness of industry in general. Failure to respond fully and swiftly to the opportunities it offers would seriously damage that competitiveness" (6). The report called on the government to help accelerate the translation of existing research results into commercially exploitable spin-offs by contributing £425 million over the next five years to a follow-up to the Alvey Program. These funds were to be earmarked for partnerships between IT users and suppliers, collaborative research on future applications, and continued participation in European programs, such as the second phase of ESPRIT.

Since the committee did not participate in the policy process, its report did not affect the prime minister's agenda. When the government finally responded in January 1988, its answer was shrouded in the last chapter of a White Paper (DTI 1988) delineating the DTI's revised mission to create an enterprise culture. The White Paper reported (36) that the government saw no reason to "provide a specific program of support for applications in IT." "The responsibility of the government is [instead] to create the right climate so that markets work better . . ." (iii). In the prime minister's opinion, her government already created such a climate by spurring the free play of market forces (Parliament 1987).

This White Paper acknowledged that the government was contributing to the second five-year phase of the EC's ESPRIT program and "this provides very substantial support for collaborative research in IT" (DTI 1988, 36). Thatcher's government had been under pressure from the IT sector to support this EC program, which all other members had approved. Britain became the lone holdout, seeking a reduction in the program's funding and requesting that the EC withhold some funding, until the program demonstrated effectiveness. In delaying the program, other EC members viewed Britain as jeopardizing the competitive advantage European firms might attain from the collaborative research. The EC threatened to establish a program without Britain and pressured the Thatcher government to go along. It was only after the Conservatives' election victory in 1987 that the government agreed to the program. The precise reasons for this decision are unclear, but they seem not to reflect an interest in the collaborative program itself. In this respect, following the election victory, the prime minister also did not reappoint a minister for information technology. Moreover, British firms ultimately found it difficult to participate in this EC program, since the government was not willing in practice to make the large public sector contributions necessary for British firms to collaborate with their European counterparts.

One consequence of Thatcher's neoliberalism was that market forces were largely allowed to determine the fate of British semiconductor firms during the second half of the decade. Given their small size and specialized technology, the fully integrated indigenous producers found it difficult to match their larger foreign rivals and ultimately became attractive takeover targets. By the mid-1980s, Plessey became one of the world leaders in the market for application-specific integrated circuits, and Inmos's technologies were some of the most advanced in the world. In 1984 Thorn-EMI purchased Inmos, only to sell it in 1988 to SGS-Thomson, a French-Italian firm. Plessey, which had acquired Ferranti in 1987, was itself acquired in 1989 by a combined bid from GEC and the German firm Siemens. In 1986 STC pulled out of the competitive semiconductor market and relied on its American partner, LSI Logic, for the supply of semiconductor technology. In addition, STC, which had acquired the country's leading computer firm, ICL, sold it to Fujitsu in 1990. By the end of the 1980s, GEC-Plessey was the sole British semiconductor firm that designed and produced chips in mass quantities, and most of its devices were oriented toward niche markets, such as the telecommunication, aerospace, and military spheres.

During the post-1983 period, Prime Minister Thatcher's government advanced a strategy toward the competitive challenges faced by the country's semiconductor industry that diverged from that of previous governments. It opted not to extend further public sector subsidies and, instead, adopted a liberal strategy, which reduced the barriers to foreign investment in Britain so as to increase competition and innovation in the

British market. The Type II institutional context shaped this choice of strategies in two key respects. First, the executive-centered structure of decision-making authority enabled Prime Minister Thatcher to make certain that her government advanced industrial strategies in line with her neoliberal preferences. Second, the absence of institutional networks linking industry to the locus of policymaking authority limited its representatives' influence on policy. Given these institutions, the prime minister enjoyed the autonomy to reject the use of subsidies and to support the sector through inward investment, a key component of her government's liberal strategy to regenerate the British economy.

Technology Foresight:
A New Strategy for a Globalized Economy

By 1990, 700,000 people were employed in the IT sector in Britain, and it accounted for 5 to 6% of the country's GDP. Britain became the fifth largest electronics producer in the world and accounted for 20% of European production of semiconductors, second only to Germany (U.K. Foresight 1995). At this time, GEC-Plessey Semiconductors (GPS) was the only remaining British-based large-scale producer of standard integrated circuits. There were numerous other British-based producers and designers of specialized circuits and process technology, but these firms were small in size and turnover, and focused on niche markets. In fact, no British companies were among the world's top fifty electronics firms. As a consequence, foreign multinationals from Asia and the United States accounted for the bulk of activity in the sector. This development characterized other high technology sectors in the British economy, since by "1990 foreign-owned companies accounted for 22% of manufactured output in Britain" (Lee 1996, 185). In this regard, the Conservatives' liberal strategy enabled Britain to become a central production site within the globalized economy. Some of these multinationals, particularly American and Japanese firms, were using Britain as their main European R&D site.

When John Major succeeded Margaret Thatcher as prime minister on her resignation in November 1990, he inherited the Type II institutional context she created. During his first year in office, Major continued his predecessor's emphasis on attracting inward investment and deregulating the economy as the primary means to increase industrial competitiveness. Membership in the EU's single market and completion of the GATT talks were additional ways the government identified to rejuvenate the manufacturing base. To encourage British-based firms to capitalize on the global economy, the government provided additional export credits, which would underwrite bank loans on foreign governments' purchases of British products. Major's liberal strategy had a direct impact on GPS, which assumed a minimal role (and sometimes none at all) in JESSI and other EC collaborative programs, due to the unwillingness of the Conservative government to help it amass the necessary funds to participate in the research programs.[9]

The government's strategy quickly came under attack from several quarters. The ECIF, the primary trade association representing 140 national and foreign producers of integrated circuits among other types of components, criticized the government's inward investment strategy: "It is relatively easy to set up an assembly plant, but unless there is enough intellectual property development around that, all you actually own is a little assembly plant that can be written off in three years. . . . [M]ore pressure should be brought to bear on inward investors to establish a properly balanced contribution to our industrial well-being, not something that can be removed overnight after three or four years" (Lords 1991b, 327). The most sustained criticism was leveled by the House of Lords Select Committee on Science and Technology, which during 1990 held hearings on the state of British manufacturing industry, innovation, and other factors affecting the country's declining industrial competitiveness more generally. After sifting through the evidence, the Committee's report *Innovation in Manufacturing Industry* (the Caldecote Report) drew rather pessimistic conclusions: "The failure of British manufacturing industry to remain competitive has had serious consequences. Our manufacturing base has declined. Our home market is increasingly penetrated by imports. Our share of world markets in manufactured goods is too small. The implications for our future prosperity are grave" (Lords 1991a, 29). Its recommended response included not simply a shift in national attitudes towards industry, but also a shift away from the current liberal policy: "If market forces alone are to determine the course of events it is conceivable that we will end up with no significant British-owned manufacturing industry in the United Kingdom. Government has a legitimate role in identifying and promoting generic technologies and industrial sectors of key importance for the future. We are not suggesting that the government should 'pick winners' but that they should take a strategic view of those areas in which we could or should have competitive advantage in the 1990s and beyond" (Ibid., 38). The Major government not surprisingly disagreed with the committee's conclusions and recommendations. It pointed out that Britain's share of world trade had recently increased (thanks in large part to the activities of inward investors), reflecting the government's creation of "a framework in which enterprise and initiative have been able to flourish, not by intervention or subsidy" (Parliament 1991, 3). Thanks to the institutional context, the government's opponents were excluded from the policy process, and its industrial strategy remained focused on attracting inward investment and creating a stable macroeconomic setting. Once this context was altered, however, government officials and industry representatives were empowered who agreed with the Select Committee's evaluation, and the government ultimately oversaw a shift in strategy along the lines the Select Committee suggested.

Institutional Context

After leading the Conservative Party to victory in the 1992 elections, Prime Minister Major launched several personnel and institutional changes. Among the former, he appointed Michael Heseltine as secretary of state for trade and industry, a move unfathomable during Thatcher's tenure, due to his well-known interventionist proclivities. Given that the Conservative government held just a twenty-one-seat majority following the 1992 election, Heseltine enjoyed some bargaining leverage in relation to the prime minister. Heseltine reestablished links with industry through the creation of several institutional networks. He reorganized the DTI to include a Competitiveness Division comprising a mixed public-private sector team, reinstated sponsorship of industry, and relied on seconded industry officials to help the DTI's civil servants better understand specific sectors.

These changes suggest that Heseltine hoped to bring the DTI back to its former structure; but in 1992 Heseltine's DTI lacked the lateral autonomy or the resources to act as it had in the past. With regard to trade issues, Heseltine shared jurisdiction with a number of departments, not to mention the European Commission, which played the key role in developing the negotiating stance for the Uruguay Round. As for the industry side of the department, Heseltine's independence was constrained by several other changes instituted after the 1992 election. First, the government's new Industrial Policy Committee was headed by another cabinet minister, the Lord Privy Seal, who had no direct jurisdiction or organizational resources for the area. Second, a new cabinet committee was instituted to limit public spending. This "EDX," chaired by the chancellor, provided the Treasury with an additional means to make certain that departments would stay within agreed limits (Major 2000, 666). Third, Major created an Office of Science and Technology (OST), elevating its head, the science minister, to the rank of cabinet minister. The government's £1.1 billion annual budget for basic research was transferred from the Department of Education and Science, where it had been the smallest budgetary component, to the OST, where it became the focus. The science minister did not control the government's entire £5 billion annual expenditure on civilian and military R&D, about two-thirds of which is earmarked for military and agriculture pursuits. This minister, nevertheless, was endowed, both in terms of decision-making authority and budgetary resources, with the lateral autonomy to oversee the government's strategy toward academic science research.

The rationale behind these changes is not completely clear. The first two changes appear geared to limiting Heseltine's lateral autonomy at the DTI and to continue the liberal strategy rather than herald a return to intervention. The prime minister (Major 1993) suggested as much soon after appointing Heseltine: The country "need[s] a strong, competitive manufacturing base. Private enterprise, not government will create that. Unlike our political opponents, I do not want to go back to a failed past of subsidies and state control." The reason for the creation of the OST and the science minister is less clear, but nonetheless suggests that domestic dynamics can create pressures to transform extant institutions in ways that do not support globalists' expectation for a reduction in state capacities. During the 1992 elections, the Labour Party, reflecting the interests of the science community, argued that there should be a cabinet minister in charge of the science budget, while the Conservatives had opposed it (Cookson 1992). Following the elections, the prime minister nevertheless adopted the idea. The civil servant who drew up the reorganization plans explained that "the prime minister had a conviction that science and technology would be important to us if we were going to continue as a strong Group of Seven nation" (Ibid., 34). Beyond this point, it is not clear that the prime minister, let alone the newly appointed science minister, identified a specific strategy that the reform would make possible.

Toward a New Strategy

Heseltine's establishment of a Competitiveness Unit and reinstatement of sponsorship in early 1992 suggest that he hoped to change the direction of the government's strategy toward industry and might do so in the direction identified by the government's critics. One vehicle toward a policy shift was the creation of annual competitiveness reports (Parliament 1994; 1995). According to Heseltine (2000, 421), the purpose of these reports was "to change attitudes. We had to replace the traditional (and insular) British and government view that 'we are doing fine' with a realistic appraisal of the nation's strengths, weaknesses and relative performance against others." Identifying fiercer global competition as the central challenge facing the country, the reports, nonetheless, reflected the government's strategy to get the macroeconomic environment right by reducing the role of government in it. As the first competitiveness report (Parliament 1994, 15) noted: "Businesses—not governments—create wealth. The primary responsibility for improving competitiveness must lie with firms. The Government's role is to create the conditions in which firms throughout the economy can improve competitiveness." The reports' policy recommendations largely reinforced the importance of inward investment, identified additional deregulatory initiatives, repackaged existing policies, and reallocated existing expenditures. One reason for this status quo orientation was the participation of several other departments in writing the competitiveness reports and the influence of the Treasury and Cabinet Office (Bowen 1994).[10] The prime minister, in particular, remained committed to a strategy that focused on getting the macroeconomic climate right, by reducing inflation, maintaining a highly competitive exchange rate, and increasing the skill level of the population (Major 1993).

Eventually, the government's strategy strayed from its neoliberal bent. This resulted from opportunities associated with the institutional changes affecting science and technology policy Major advanced following the 1992 election. In particular, the Type V institutional context provided the new science minister with the possibility to modify and redirect existing policy.

Almost immediately after assuming office, the new science minister, William Waldegrave, sought to draw upon the collective wisdom of industry, academics, and scientists to evaluate the country's science and technology strategy, as it affected the country's capacity for wealth creation. In effect, the OST devised an institutional network, a consultative process in this case, linking the affected constituency with the authoritative policymaker (Parliament 1993, 3). A central theme emerging from this year-long review was the country's difficulty in translating innovations into commercial products. This perspective framed the department's White Paper, *Realising our Potential*, which (Ibid., 8) proposed a significant break with existing Conservative science and technology strategies: "... a closer partnership and better diffusion of ideas between the science and engineering communities, industry, the financial sector and Government are needed as part of the crucial effort to improve our national competitiveness and quality of life." The White Paper (Ibid., 4) noted that: "[T]he United Kingdom's competitive position rests increasingly on our capacity to trade in goods and services incorporating or produced by the latest science and technology. This applies as much, for example, to trade in financial services as it does to manufactured goods and to both small and large enterprises. There are no captive or protected markets on which we can rely; and every year increasingly fierce competition is joined by new entrants from the Pacific rim and elsewhere. The United Kingdom has no room for complacency if our present excellence is to be developed as well as it must be to match competitors, old and new."

A core proposal of the White Paper was the creation of a "technology foresight program," modeled on a Japanese strategy, which would seek "to produce a better match between publicly-funded strategic research and the needs of industry and other users of research outputs" (Ibid., 17). Toward this end, "[s]cientists, engineers, economists, financiers, businessmen, industrialists, and civil servants will develop a shared appreciation of technological opportunities and industrial possibilities" (18). "The aim is to achieve a key cultural change: better communication, interaction and mutual understanding between the scientific community, industry, and Government Departments" (5). To advance this strategy, the OST consolidated and absorbed several state entities that award grants for science research, and established a new Council for Science and Technology with representatives from industry and universities. A steering group, headed by the science minister and including academics, industry officials, and representatives from the DTI, MoD, and the OST, soon identified fifteen priority sectors in the belief that "[t]o maintain and increase wealth creation, the UK requires a strong manufacturing base, efficient service industries and an effective research and development capability. Public funding can be focused on areas of existing and emerging national commercial advantage, often attracting additional investment in R&D from the private sector" (OST 1995). Put otherwise, the steering group concluded that the most appropriate strategy for the country would be one that targets emerging technologies that are likely to have wide-ranging commercial applications. One report at the time (Brown 1993, 4) noted that the proposal amounted to a repudiation of Thatcher's neoliberalism, as that strategy now would be replaced by government support for industrial research having specific commercial value. The OST soon aligned the science and technology budget under its purview with the steering group's recommendations, earmarking more than $100 million of the 1995 research budget for such targeted, near-market spending (Williams 1995). One component of this funding included a £40 million "Foresight Challenge," for which business and academia were invited to make proposals for collaborative R&D initiatives in the fifteen targeted sectors. The government matched contributions from industry as a means to make certain that the research had a clear commercial focus.

IT and electronics comprised one of the fifteen targeted sectors. As with each of the sectors, an institutional network was created to represent the interests of the sector. The Information Technology and Electronics Panel (ITEP) linked the sector to the steering group, which reported to the science minister. The globalization of the British industry infused the panel's perspective and recommendations. It (U.K. Foresight 1995, sec. 2) noted that "what matters is the level of economic activity in the UK, the contribution to taxation and balance of trade and to employment, rather than 'UK ownership' of businesses and companies, however defined."[11] This perspective reflected the facts of the sector: the top ten revenue-earning firms in the sector were inward investors, and the continued attraction of such firms would be integral to the future growth of small and medium national firms in the sector. The panel recommended for priority action the promotion of "key attractors for investment by both overseas and UK investors, such as a highly educated workforce, first class research and access to leading edge technology in displays and silicon." It proposed more specifically that collaborative, jointly funded centers of excellence in semiconductor and display technologies be established; these were to bring together experts from government, industry, and academia. When appropriate, foreign collaborators were to be involved. It also proposed that the government develop a coherent strategy for "the information superhighway."

Given the panel's integration in the policy process, its recommendations led to some concrete policies. First, the Foresight Challenge provided £1.5 million to investigate options for forming commercial alliances with foreign firms to exploit new technologies for displays; a similar grant was awarded for telecommunications research. Second, an Information Society Initiative was started in early 1996. This program, which included £35 million of new money over four years, sought to "combine within a single coherent package existing as well as new support programmes, and aims to: raise awareness of the opportunities; encourage technology transfer within and between supplier sectors (for example IT, telecommunications, broadcasting and publishing); promote the development of competitive sources of key underpinning technologies; and spread best practice in the use of information highways and multimedia services" (Parliament 1995, 142).

Third, the ITEP (Foresight 1995) noted that Britain had been successful in attracting inward investment in the semiconductor industry, but that this might not continue in the future, unless actions were taken to make certain that Britain remained an attractive location for such investment. This conclusion reflected the panel's belief (Ibid., annex 10) that "in order to be a major player in the substantial silicon fabrication business and have the best opportunity to design systems with embedded electronics, it is essential that the level of inward investment in silicon fabrication facilities is maintained or grown and the current and new fabrication facilities are backed by local design and development centres." In this light, a "National Microelectronics Institute" should be created to overcome skill shortages in the British population, "insufficient resource focus and levels in the R&D community" and facilitate the creation of local technical and equipment suppliers in the sector, all steps that were expected to help Britain remain attractive to foreign investors in the sector. The panel recommended that the cost of such an institute be funded jointly by academia, government, and industry. While "a state-of-the-art fabrication facility would cost up to £500 million," the panel maintained that a facility able to achieve its recommendations could be established at a fraction of that cost. Such an institute was formed in July 1996, headquartered on the campus of Heriot-Watt University in Edinburgh, Scotland, and used existing manufacturing facilities and equipment. The DTI contributed some of the Institute's nominal start-up costs and nine firms, including GPS and the U.S., European, and Japanese firms producing in the country in the sector, eventually agreed to participate and cover its ongoing costs.

The Foresight Program was envisioned to be an ongoing process to identify the technologies and capabilities that would increase Britain's competitiveness in the global economy. By the end of 1996, the government had awarded nearly £30 million to projects in the fifteen targeted sectors, and industry had contributed an additional £62 million to them. These were modest sums by comparison to previous initiatives involving the semiconductor industry, perhaps indicative of the OST's primary responsibility for academic science research (Sharp and Walker 1994, 417). In this regard, a more significant element of the strategy may have been its implicit recognition that the government should support basic research with a specific industrial focus. Upon taking office in the spring of 1997, the new Labour government subjected the program to a comprehensive review. Following extensive consultations with representatives from the private sector, the government decided in December 1998 to continue the program, albeit with some modifications to take into account lessons from the first round (see Shortcomings 1998). Prime Minister Tony Blair (Parliament 1998, foreword) explained that his government launched a new Foresight round, because "we must promote creative partnerships which help companies: to collaborate for competitive advantage; to promote a long term vision in a world of short term pressures; to benchmark their performance against the best in the world; and to forge alliances with other businesses and with employees."

The Foresight Program is unexpected in light of the Major government's avowed neoliberal philosophy. The selection of this strategy targeting priority areas for government funding reflects the opportunities offered by the Type V institutional context, one characterized by a government department enjoying lateral autonomy and the presence of institutional networks providing industry representatives access to this state unit. This context created a close collaboration between the newly created science minister and the research community, enabling them to work together to identify the problems in existing wealth-creation strategies and to devise a revised science and technology strategy to improve the country's ability to commercialize innovations and help it to remain attractive to foreign investors.

Conclusion

This chapter examines three policy episodes occurring during the tenure of the Thatcher and Major Conservative governments. These governments entered office convinced that a liberal strategy would help the country to respond to globalization. While this strategy became a core component of the Thatcher and Major governments' initiatives toward industry, both governments also adopted an interventionist approach, whether they directed massive amounts of state support to the IT sector, or whether they sought to redesign the way the government funded and approached science and technology innovation. That is, the Major and Thatcher governments did not advance just liberal strategies in response to the globalization of the semiconductor industry. The variation in the governments' responses reflects the impact of the institutional context.

The two industrial policies emerged from policy debates shaped by a Type V institutional context. This context provided industry representatives with a privileged role in policymaking; in particular, it accorded them access to those policymakers who could act relatively autonomously from other departments' input and who were receptive to a new strategy in light of the globalization of competition. A contrasting strategy emerged from the policy debate transpiring in a Type II institutional context. Here, industry representatives found themselves unable to access authoritative policymakers; instead, the prime minister enjoyed the autonomy to pursue her preference for a liberal strategy. Prime Minister Thatcher rejected a strategy involving new subsidies for the sector and, instead, viewed the sector as benefiting from the use of a liberal strategy to spur the country's economic growth.

The variation across these institutions is significant for what it indicates about a country's capacity to respond to such international pressures as globalization. All three cases were affected in important ways by institutional changes, whether through the creation of new institutions or the elimination of existing ones. The contrasts across these changes, moreover, suggest that domestic dynamics shape the direction of state restructuring advanced in response to global pressures. That being said, the three cases indicate that globalization may encourage more rather than less state capacity. In each case the institutional innovation involved the creation of new capacities for government officials and industry representatives that fundamentally affected the course of policymaking and the policy ultimately adopted. The episodes examining the Alvey and Foresight programs, for example, identify institutional changes that created new policymaking capabilities for government and industry officials through the centralization of authorities and the creation of new institutional networks. These capacities enabled both government and industry representatives to interact with each other to address the challenges the sector faced and to translate them into concrete policies. In the other case, by contrast, Thatcher sought to advance a liberal strategy. To do so, she first consolidated her position within the state, so as to increase her capacity to operate autonomously from other government officials and societal actors. In contrast to some globalist arguments, this case indicates that a liberal strategy may be correlated with a strong rather than a weak state (Clark 1999, 94, 97; Held et al. 1999, 4–5). Such a state may uniquely afford policymakers the capacity to advance such strategies, since it provides officials the autonomy to advance their preferences and, concurrently, limits the influence of those groups most likely to confront increased competition.

Finally, the evidence suggests that the country's membership in the EC did not limit its governments' autonomy to advance initiatives best thought to harness globalization to Britain's advantage. The EC's increasing control over trade policy since the late 1970s may provide one explanation for the lack of such initiatives discussed here. Even with the supranational institution's capacity in this realm, both the Thatcher and Major governments were able to chart their own course. In this regard, both advanced inward investment strategies that sought to capitalize on EC policies to benefit Britain. The emerging single market, together with generous benefits from the Conservative governments, helped to lead the largest proportion of foreign firms to locate their European plants in Britain. In some respects, the existence of the EC and its panoply of collaborative R&D strategies helped to empower Thatcher and Major in their efforts to deflect the demands of those national firms seeking greater government support. In responding to the Bide report, for example, Thatcher noted that there was no need for another national program, given the existence of an European initiative. Of course, her government's reluctance to fund that program hampered British firms' participation in the European programs. On a second front, the Major government maintained some room for maneuver in the face of EC regulations on national industrial support. With the approaching completion of the Single Market, the European Commission announced several initiatives to tighten its capacity under Articles 92 and 93 of the Treaty of Rome to control and limit members' use of industrial policy.[12] The Foresight Program, launched as the Commission was increasing its control of assistance schemes, indicates that the EC's creeping purview did not limit the Conservative government's ability to advance interventionist strategies in response to globalization.[13]

In sum, this chapter indicates that globalization does not happen apart from the state. The state, even when retreating from the economy, plays a significant role in determining how globalization impacts the country. Moreover, globalization does not appear to have made it impossible for a state, previously exhibiting a diminished role, to adopt a more engaged role. The Major government's science and technology policy indicates that even in a country possessing a highly globalized economy, the state can reconstitute itself and adopt a more assertive role toward globalization.

Part Four

Conclusion

Chapter Eight

Globalization and Domestic Institutions: Conclusions

Since the 1970s the United States and Britain have encountered intense competitive challenges in the semiconductor industry and responded with a series of strategies, both interventionist and liberal. I draw on the insights of historical institutionalism to account for U.S. and British responses to the globalization of competition in the semiconductor industry. Two domestic-level institutions influence a country's choice of strategies: the organization of decision-making authority and the structure of state-societal relations, particularly the linkages between government officials and industry representatives. The argument developed in chapter 2 focuses on how these two institutions shape the pattern of intragovernmental and government-industry relations during policymaking. These institutions, in particular, affect the roles and strategies of government officials and firms in the policy process, creating constraints and opportunities for the development of different types of policies. A focus on the domestic institutional context indicates that the two institutions often create conditions that can lead a country to adopt strategies that are inconsistent with globalist expectations for liberal strategies. The empirical evidence, moreover, shows that the two countries' strategies converged on similarly interventionist strategies as a consequence of similar domestic institutional incentives. The institutional context also influenced their selection of liberal strategies, making it difficult to correlate these choices with the constraints thought to emerge from globalization.

This chapter begins by providing an overview of the book's empirical findings and theoretical implications in light of the expectations of the globalist perspective. The second part considers the plausibility and explanatory strengths of other approaches. A third section examines the sources and consequences of institutional change. The chapter concludes by evaluating the effectiveness of several U.S. and British strategies examined in previous chapters.

Empirical Findings

Throughout the three decades examined here, Britain and the United States responded to pressures associated with the globalization of the semiconductor industry, experimenting with liberal strategies and industrial policies. Britain advanced industrial policies in the three policy episodes taking place in the 1970s and the two debates in the early 1980s. These were followed by a commitment to neoliberalism until the mid-1990s, when Britain again adopted an industrial policy. At this time, the Major government launched a series of initiatives to support the commercialization of research and promote the competitiveness of workers employed and the supplier base used by foreign direct investors in the sector. The United States adopted two liberal initiatives in the late 1970s and early 1980s. After 1985 the Reagan administration advanced industrial policies in both the trade and investment areas. These initiatives were continued through the 1990s. The role of the state receded later in the decade, but only after the U.S. industry regained its global primacy.

As the globalists expect, the two countries did advance liberal strategies in response to pressures associated with the globalization of competition in the industry. While Thatcher's strategy comes closest in supporting globalist expectations regarding the logic of attracting mobile investors, the pressures globalists associate with the open global economy did not loom large in the other two examples of such strategies. In fact, the initial goal in the cases involving the Carter and Reagan administrations was to develop more interventionist strategies. The evidence indicates that proponents of such initiatives were thwarted due to the decentralized structure of decision-making authority shaping the two policy episodes. Even Thatcher's experience runs counter to elements of globalist arguments, since it indicates that the type of liberal strategy globalists expect may necessitate a strong rather than a weak state (Clark 1999, 94, 97; Held et al. 1999, 4–5). Such a state may uniquely afford policymakers the capacity to advance such strategies, since it enables officials to remain insulated from the groups most likely to experience deleterious pressures associated with increased competition.

When the globalization of production and competition seemed to reach new heights, moreover, governments in both countries advanced interventionist strategies. For example, the Reagan administration advanced two industrial policies in the mid-1980s, as production increasingly shifted toward Asia. These were not exceptional experiments, as the next administration reinforced them. Similarly, the Heath government abandoned its liberal ideology in the face of stiffening competition in its market from U.S. and European firms. More recently, as the industry has become more globalized, the Major government developed a strategy targeting emerging technologies with commercial applications and sought to make Britain an attractive location for foreign investors in industries using the technologies.

Throughout the period examined here, firms and officials in both countries demanded interventionist strategies. The homogeneity of these demands is striking with respect to the two countries' industries. Once the industries experienced costs from the globalization of competition, they sought government support to offset the advantages their foreign competitors were thought to enjoy. In the United States, an internationally oriented industry generally sought interventionist and discriminatory initiatives to compensate for the advantages of Japanese firms, its primary global competitor. Sematech represents an extreme example of this tendency. In Britain, the major firms sought government support for their R&D and, with one exception, generally did not seek the exclusion of those foreign firms that developed products in Britain. One explanation for this contrast may reflect the fact that the U.S. industry is less reliant on foreign producers for technology. Nevertheless, the preference of the two industries for intervention suggests that the globalist assumption that firms prefer liberalism may not be the case for all sectors, particularly those in which cheap factor inputs are viewed as less significant determinants of competitive success (Campbell 2003, 257–58) and foreign firms are perceived to enjoy a competitive edge. More generally, the actions of the two industries indicate that they continue to identify themselves as national entities and operate basically as "national firms with international operations" (see Held et al. 1999, chap. 5). Their national identity, which loomed large in the policy episodes as the costs associated with the global economy increased, became significant resources for the firms as they sought government strategies to promote their competitiveness. In this respect, the sector's globalization has not diminished the salience of viewing international economic relations as being premised on competing nations.

Government officials in both countries exhibited more heterogeneity in their preferences. In this respect, officials were far from uniform in their belief in the efficacy of industrial policies in general or the need to develop such strategies for this particular sector. That is, the sector's technological significance did not compel all officials across both countries to see the merits of intervening. Generally, those officials with responsibility for trade or industry policy had the strongest preferences for interventionist initiatives. Other officials in both countries evidenced strong support for liberalism, particularly those in Conservative governments and Republican administrations. These officials often came to office strongly committed to liberal beliefs and persuaded by their efficacy. These governments nevertheless often advanced strategies that contradicted their apparent ideological convictions.

One reason for this outcome reflects the fact that some state units such as the Defense Department enjoyed the lateral autonomy to advance their preferences for interventionist strategies. A second more frequent reason reflects actions advanced by the Reagan administration and the Heath, Thatcher, and Major governments. Each modified the existing institutional context to cope with pressures associated with globalization, often for reasons unrelated to developments in the semiconductor industry. In doing so, such reforms as the strike force or the ministers of science or information technology led to a new institutional context and empowered officials who preferred an alternative approach to confront the challenges national manufacturers faced in light of the globalization of production. In these examples and in others, the institutional transformations were consequential for policy choice because they altered intragovernmental and state-societal relations and, thus, created new opportunities for policymaking. And in this respect, without such institutional reforms, the empirical evidence suggests that these governments would not have pursued such interventionist policies as the STA, Alvey, or Foresight programs.

Additionally, foreign-based firms operating in both countries did not pursue exit strategies in response to the governments' use of interventionist strategies. While Japanese firms, for example, were excluded from Sematech, they did not seek to leave the U.S. market or curtail their strategic alliances with several U.S. firms involved in the project. In fact, the two countries' use of interventionist strategies may have helped to make them more attractive locations. Tyson (1993, 143) reports that one unintended consequence of the STA was an increase in Japanese producers' FDI in the United States. Several of the British industrial policies, such as MISP and Foresight, were open to foreign-based manufacturers, which may have increased the interest of these firms in the British market. Even those initiatives that were restricted to British-owned firms, however, may have had a similar result, since they too helped to increase the technological capacity of British firms and workers. On several occasions, foreign-based firms, such as Philips and ITT, lent their support to greater intervention on the part of British governments to nurture technological development. These reactions do not confirm globalist expectations regarding the likely mobility of international firms; although it is possible that this outcome may reflect factors contingent to the sector in question or the countries' markets, it is consistent with others' (see Garrett 1998, 800–801) arguments, suggesting that further investigation into this expectation is in order.

Many globalists maintain that globalization has emerged due to factors beyond the control of the state, including such systemic forces as capitalism, technological innovation, and international organizations. The state often is relegated to a secondary role, significant only in terms of an agent of privatization and deregulation (Scholte 2000, chap. 4; Held and McGrew 1998). The cases examined here suggest a different picture: state actions, including interventionist ones, deserve more consideration as facilitators of globalization. Often overlooked, the 1986 United States-Japan Semiconductor Trade Agreement called on the Japanese government to set up an administrative entity "to provide sales assistance for foreign semiconductor producers as they attempt to penetrate the Japanese market."[1] This led MITI to assume a key role in managing the Japanese market. MITI, among other steps, formed the International Semiconductor Cooperation Center to facilitate dialogue between U.S.-based suppliers and Japan-based users of semiconductors. Out of this action Japanese firms created several industry-wide user associations to facilitate design-in linkages with U.S. firms (see SIA 1990, 8–10). Over the next several years cooperation between the SIA and the Electronic Industries Association of Japan's Users' Committee of Foreign Semiconductors became institutionalized to such an extent that the renewal of the STA in 1996 largely comprised a market data agreement between the two industry groups.[2] Ceding governance of the sector to the industry associations was possible thanks to ten years of interventionist actions on the part of both governments, which altered Japanese firms' sourcing patterns and the competitive position of the U.S. industry.

British governments were equally important in facilitating the globalization of the country's market. An early industrial policy, the 1978 MISP, was open to those foreign multinationals that set up production facilities in Britain. Perhaps more significantly, thanks to the Thatcher and Major governments' efforts to deregulate the British economy, Britain soon became the most popular European location for foreign multinational corporations. Even when the Major government opted for an industrial policy in the mid-1990s, it too helped to reinforce globalization; one aim was to promote the skill level of British firms and workers in the sector in the hope of continuing to attract foreign firms to Britain in the future. One element of this strategy was the establishment of the National Microelectronics Institute. This government-industry-university collaborative effort comprised nine firms, whose home bases included Britain,

Asia, the United States, and other parts of Europe. These strategies were successful; the pace of foreign direct investment in Britain continued to be strong, helping the country remain the top European market for foreign direct investment (Croft 1999).

The findings also suggest that international institutions were less significant entities than some globalists maintain. The WTO and its predecessor the GATT, the institutions most likely to impinge on states' responses to the globalization of competition in this sector, did not become central decision-making entities or significant constraints on the states' options. One reason for this outcome is that the international trade institution, particularly its Agreement on Subsidies and Countervailing Measures, does not rule out subsidies and, in some cases, permits them (see WTO 1994; Amsden and Hikino 2000). Among the latter are subsidies for industrial research and development, including targeted ones, such as those the U.S. and Britain advanced. While both countries generally adhered to GATT trade rules, the United States bypassed the institution with respect to the two semiconductor trade agreements it negotiated with Japan. The United States unilaterally determined that Japan's trade practices were unfair and aggressively sought benefits for national firms. The STA and its renewal were triggered, ironically, by the actions of U.S. firms and government officials who saw the liberal tenets of the GATT as a means to advance their desire for the Reagan and Bush administrations to become more involved in the industry. The emergence of the WTO in 1995, however, is likely to limit the nationalist orientation of such market-opening initiatives. Following the Uruguay Round, the United States modified Section 301, noting that retaliation would be forthcoming against WTO members only when authorized by the findings of the WTO's dispute settlement system. Yet, WTO rules do not make it impossible for the United States to use other strategies to help its industries cope with globalization. In this regard, as Alice Amsden and Takashi Hikino (2000, 105) write, "[i]n the name of science and technology, countries in a position to exploit the WTO's rules can continue to support their own industries, to target national champions for government assistance, and to advance the general cause of their national competitiveness."

Another set of international institutions assumed a more significant role in British policy debates. Britain's membership in the European Union and that institution's movement toward a single European market constrained, but did not eliminate the autonomy of British governments to promote national industries. During Prime Minister Heath's tenure, the British-owned firms sought import restraints against their U.S. competitors. The investment strategy ultimately adopted discriminated against all foreign-owned firms. Henceforth, however, these firms did not seek to limit access to the British market, perhaps reflecting the complexity of the trade policy process following Britain's ascension to the common market and the growing importance of European firms in the domestic economy. Britain's membership, in contrast, more often increased the policy instruments available to British governments to achieve nationally generated objectives. The Conservative governments, for example, sought to capitalize on the regional agreement to attract new investments into Britain, which may not have been as numerous without membership in the Single Market. The panoply of collaborative R&D strategies helped to empower Thatcher in her efforts to deflect the demands of those national firms seeking greater government support; in this regard, the case could be made that there was no need for a national program when one existed at the European level. Finally, the emergence of the EU did not curtail British interventionist initiatives to increase national competitiveness in the mid-1990s. Others (Lavdas and Mendrinou 1999) have pointed out that the original EEC treaty leaves unclear many of the details regarding state aid limitations and the authorities delegated to the European Commission; even as the Commission has sought to fill these gaps, member states still possess room to maneuver, especially in such areas as research and development (see EC 1996).

Taken as a whole, the empirical findings show that neither Britain nor the United States was constrained to adopt liberal strategies in response to the globalization of the semiconductor industry. Moreover, both countries converged on interventionist strategies by the mid-1990s, as the industry's globalization intensified further. These findings indicate that while globalization has increased the economic challenges facing states, it does not limit states' policy options or reduce their significance in confronting the challenges. Although limited to two countries' responses to the globalization of a single industry, these findings suggest, at the least, that further research is warranted in other sectors and countries to evaluate globalist expectations.

Institutions and Other Explanations

Chapter 2 explains that the institutional context affects a country's policy choices by determining the roles and capacity of government officials and industry actors in the policy process. The institutional context will be most conducive to interventionist strategies, for example, when it enables an ongoing interaction pattern between firms and government officials who can operate relatively autonomously of other state units. Such policies become more difficult, as the number of state units involved in policymaking increases, or when institutions do not foster an interactive pattern of policymaking between firms and officials. Tables 8.1 and 8.2 illustrate the findings across the case studies; they show the institutions present in each case, the nature of the policymaking process, and the strategies advanced. The two tables show that the process and outcomes generally conform to the argument's expectations.

Table 8.1
Findings: U.S. Cases

| Cases | Institutional Context | | | Nature of the Policy-making Process | Outcome |
	Institutional Networks	Decison-making Structure	Type		
Innovation Initiatives (1979)	Present	Decentralized	III	Industry access and intra-governmental divisions	Liberal strategy
High Tech Working Group (1982)	Present	Decentralized	III	Industry access and intra-governmental divisions	Liberal strategy
U.S.-Japan Semiconductor Trade Agreement (1986)	Present	Lateral autonomy	V	Agency-industry cooperation	Industrial policy
Sematech (1987)	Present	Lateral autonomy	V	Agency-industry cooperation	Industrial policy
U.S.-Japan Semiconductor Trade Agreement (1991)	Present	Lateral autonomy	V	Agency-industry cooperation	Industrial policy
Sematech Renewal (1992)	Present	Decentralized	III	Industry access and intra-governmental divisions	Industrial policy with multiple objectives

Table 8.2
Findings: British Cases

Cases	Institutional Context			Nature of the Policy-making Process	Outcome
	Institutional Networks	Decison-making Structure	Type		
Micro-electronics Support Scheme (1973)	Present	Lateral autonomy	V	Agency-industry cooperation	Industrial policy
Micro-electronics Industry Support Program (1978)	Present	Lateral autonomy	V	Agency-industry cooperation	Industrial policy
Inmos Start-up (1978)	Present	Lateral autonomy	V	Agency-industry cooperation	Industrial policy
Inmos Investment (1980)	Present	Decentralized	III	Industry access and intra-governmental divisions	Industrial policy with multiple objectives
Alvey Program (1983)	Present	Lateral autonomy	V	Agency-industry cooperation	Industrial policy
Post-1983 Thatcher	Absent	Executive-centered	II	Executive autonomy	Liberal strategy
Foresight Program (1993)	Present	Lateral autonomy	V	Agency-industry cooperation	Industrial policy

Tables 8.1 and 8.2 also indicate that there are no cases in three of the six potential institutional contexts. This outcome arises because

the contexts are analytical possibilities and not meant to describe those prevailing in the United States and Britain. Wide variation in each country's institutional context, moreover, is unlikely in the twenty-five-year period examined here, given that existing institutions tend to structure the direction of change. My research design narrowed the array of contexts studied, but I selected the two countries for comparison because they should be an easy confirmation of the globalist view. The United States and Britain generally are thought to have a long-standing preference for liberal economic policies and possess weak state institutions. Different investigations could yield cases in the other institutional contexts, and further research is needed to explore fully the plausibility of the book's institutional argument. For example, research on several Western European and East Asian countries (Milner 1988; Okimoto 1989; Wade 1990; Weiss 1998) generally suggests that they share similar institutions to those studied here, but further, more nuanced research both at the issue area level and over time is needed to determine the structure and effect of their institutions. Recent work on institutions and industrial strategies more specifically suggests that a longitudinal investigation of China (Zhu 2003) would enable a comparison of the Type IV and VI contexts, and that Sweden approximates a Type IV context (Weiss 1998, chap. 4). Although largely cast at a national level, work on the former Soviet Union and post-Soviet Russia (Evangelista 1995; Brown 2001) indicates that this comparison may provide the opportunity to contrast Type I, II, and III structures.

This book focuses on the institutional constraints and opportunities that affect states' responses to globalization. Like other historical institutionalist approaches, I do not claim that institutions are "the sole 'cause' of outcomes" (Thelen and Steinmo 1992, 3). Instead, institutions mediate the effects of other factors on policymaking. An institutional approach, as Ikenberry (1994, 3) points out, "is limited in that it stresses the role of variables that ultimately must be combined with others to provide an explanation. Institutions tend to matter as part of a larger causal chain. . . ." To develop expectations of how institutions can affect the type of industrial strategies adopted, I assumed that challenges associated with globalization create discrete incentives for firms and officials to favor interventionist or liberal strategies. A more developed understanding of preferences is in order for this part of the argument, especially since state and societal actors' preferences help to initiate the policy debates that domestic institutions mediate.[3] In this respect, the policy episodes examined in chapters 3 through 7 were initiated by firms and officials who perceived that globalization created new vulnerabilities requiring greater government involvement. Such perceptions tended to reflect characteristics associated with the sector, particularly how increased competition impacted the industry's large R&D and production costs and its significant linkages to other industries. Certainly not all sectors will elicit such concerns and a different set of demands will emerge. That being said, dynamics associated with this industry helped to show how institutions mediate a country's response to globalization, specifically enabling and constraining interventionist responses.

More generally, four well-developed explanations in the comparative politics and international relations literatures identify factors that also loomed large in the policy debates examined here: state-centered, societal-centered, ideology-based, and realist explanations. In what follows, I review the plausibility of these perspectives, arguing that they identify factors that play a role in one or more policy episode, but that the institutional context conditions these factors' impact on policy choice.

State-centered (or statist) arguments focus on the actions (or nonactions) of the state, defined in terms of central decision makers, such as the president, prime minister, secretary of state, etc. They posit that a distinction can be made between the state and its society, and that government officials are an active and a largely independent participant in the policy process. The basic premise of these arguments (e.g., Johnson 1982; Lake 1988) is that policy outcomes derive from the preferences of government officials who arrive at conceptions of the national interest independent of, and immune from, societal groups' pressures or desires. Similarities (or differences) in the policies pursued within a country over time, or across countries, would be attributed to similarities (or differences) in the interests of the relevant policymakers within each country.

Proponents of a contrasting societal-centered approach (e.g., Milner 1988; Frieden 1988) contend that an explanation for a country's policy choice can be given when societal groups and their interests or organizational characteristics are understood. According to this perspective, a country's response to international economic competition reflects the demands and preferences of relevant private commercial interests. Generally, proponents of this approach argue that societal actors press for policies that further their material interests. Similarities (or differences) in policy choices cross- or intranationally are attributed to similarities (or differences) in societal groups' preferences.

The basic propositions of both of these approaches are essentially correct: similarities and differences across the policies reflect variations in the relative power of state or societal actors in the policy debate. That may be true, but neither approach helps us to understand a priori why their identified causal agent does or does not drive policy in all the cases. In this regard, the case studies indicate that the institutional context determines the role and impact of state and societal actors in policymaking. The autonomy of government officials was most pronounced in the Type II institutional context. As the case examining the post-1983 Thatcher government shows, the absence of an institutional network limited the British semiconductor and information technology industries' role in policy development. By contrast, the government's capacity, in this case that of the autonomous executive, the prime minister, to pursue a strategy in keeping with its own preferences was enhanced. As the evidence reveals, the prime minister's decision to rely on a strategy of attracting foreign investment was developed with little input from those British industries that would be most affected and ran counter to their preferences for policies supporting their development. Although this case confirms the statist argument, it is the only one that gives it unequivocal support.

When institutional networks were present, by contrast, industry representatives were able to translate their preferences into the policy process. Industry representatives enjoyed the most influence on policy choice when an institutional network linked them to a structure in which government officials enjoyed lateral autonomy (a Type V structure). Even in these structures, however, government officials remained significant actors. In some cases, such as the Sematech episode, the industry did not have to do much convincing to achieve its interests, since it interacted with like-minded officials; in others, such as the STA, the industry was beholden to its government allies to convince dissenters in the state apparatus. The renewal of the STA in 1991 similarly indicates the importance of government officials. USTR Carla Hills was willing to advance the industry's demands for further action to open Japan's market, but only when the industry's strategy reflected her own preferences. Moreover, in other cases, such as the debate surrounding the Alvey Program in 1983, the industry achieved its interests, thanks largely to the institutional capacity of its government allies relative to that of other state units. Finally, the case involving the Heath government indicates that even in structures characterized by lateral autonomy, private sector actors still may find it difficult to achieve their preferences, if the authoritative government officials are not favorable to them. Firms' ability to capitalize on an institutional network then may require these officials to be open to a new strategy.[4] Given that industry representatives ultimately found these contexts most empowering, the importance government officials played in the achievement of the industry's interests suggests that societal-centered explanations are likely to offer an incomplete and misleading understanding of the actual policy process.[5] These findings reinforce that of other research (Mansfield and Busch 1995), suggesting that these separate state and societal approaches may be more fruitfully viewed as complementary; the institutional explanation developed here provides one way to combine them.

Ideology is often seen as an important determinant of a country's response to international economic pressures. Such explanations can take various forms, often emphasizing the economic ideas that are considered legitimate in the national arena (see Hall 1989). Chapter 2 maintains that ideas of this nature, particularly those regarding the appropriate role for state and societal actors in economic policymaking, are embodied in the very structure of the institutional context. As a consequence, it is difficult to conceive of these ideas as completely separate from the institutions they help to create (see Goldstein 1993). Some (Weiss 1998) nonetheless see a country's historical traditions or orientations as shaping the types of strategies that a country is likely to embrace. It is often difficult to pinpoint the causal mechanisms of such approaches apart from the behavior in question. Nevertheless, this line of reasoning suggests that U.S. and British responses to globalization are influenced by their "historically formed regime predisposition hostile to government coordination and public-private cooperation" (Ibid., 20). This perspective then helps to explain why governments in both countries did not develop an overarching or systematic strategy for managing their industries. Indeed, such policies as Alvey and Sematech, for example, were reactions to specific problems, designed to terminate within a specified period. That being said, both countries' strategies and institutions suggest that they are not adverse to public-private cooperation to respond to international economic pressures. Yet, some might still view the lack of a systematic strategy as confirming the two countries' general hostility to intervention and the interventions themselves as a reflection of the countries' tendency to justify such actions in the national security and high technology realms. An ideological explanation remains insufficient, however, since there were variations across the multiple policy episodes. These differences tended to correspond to constraints and opportunities emerging from various institutional contexts, indicating that a focus on institutions also is necessary.

Some (e.g., Odell 1979) also associate ideas with the beliefs of specific governing elites. In this regard, several leaders in both countries came to power with very strong ideological convictions. Those governing elites who were strong exponents of liberalism, e.g., Margaret Thatcher, John Major, and Ronald Reagan, at times were able to pursue strategies consistent with their ideologies. The case studies suggest that Thatcher and Major enjoyed such an ability thanks to their positions within an executive-centered institutional context lacking institutional networks. The Type II context provided both prime ministers the room to pursue those policies they believed to be most appropriate. When the organization of decision-making authority provided others with power or lateral autonomy, however, the Thatcher and Major governments adopted strategies that were inconsistent with the prime ministers' ideological preferences. Reagan had a similar experience. His administration advanced a strategy in keeping with his ideology, only so long as the institutional context constrained those in his administration who preferred more interventionist strategies; once the institutional context, either through change or a shift in issue areas, empowered officials with competing preferences, the president found himself endorsing industrial policies. Finally, while both Thatcher and Reagan individually held strong liberal predilections, by the mid-1980s their strategies toward the sector diverged sharply, reflecting variations in the countries' institutions.

A fourth approach focuses on states' concern for their relative capabilities. Scholars working in the realist paradigm of international relations (e.g., Waltz 1979, chap. 6) point to the enduring impact of the anarchical nature of the international system and relative power. While some industries may be more expendable than others, these scholars would expect states to be concerned about the performance of their semiconductor industry, given the industry's role in underpinning industries critical to economic growth and national security. This approach (e.g., Mastanduno 1991) would expect the two countries to offset, through some type of interventionist strategy, their semiconductor industries' loss of market share to, or technological backwardness compared with, foreign manufacturers.

A focus on relative gains concerns offers a useful, albeit underdeveloped, first cut at why some government officials were amenable to industrial policies and why firms' demands gained significance in many of the policy episodes.[6] For example, the industry's declining performance, measured in terms of a deterioration in its market share, frequently prompted the policy debate and led some officials to favor an interventionist strategy. Even when this indicator was not salient, as in the cases examining the Carter administration or Major government, other competitiveness concerns, whether narrowly or broadly construed, had a similar impact. Yet, in other cases, such as in some of the Thatcher government's debates, these concerns assumed an indirect role at best.

The case material suggests that the institutional context played an important role in affecting whether these concerns were embodied in policy choices. For example, in the eight policy episodes taking place in a Type V institutional structure, policies were advanced that sought to promote the industry's competitiveness and, often, the country's relative position. The Type V structure fostered the development of such policies for one important reason: it empowered those government officials and industry representatives who believed that the declining competitiveness of the country's semiconductor manufacturers had negative implications. It is no wonder then that this context produced strategies that were the most interventionist in terms of the role the public sector played in relation to the industry. That being said, officials operating in these contexts exhibited variations in their views, indicating the limitations of a relative gains understanding of preferences. Some, such as American officials in the mid-1980s, drew an explicit link between the performance of the American industry and the country's relative power; others, such as those in the Heath government, were focused more explicitly on the viability and performance of the national industry in light of other economic dislocations. Finally, USTR Hills was less focused on the competitiveness of the industry than on fulfilling her institutional mission with respect to Japan's market commitments.

In three of the four cases affected by a Type III institutional structure—the Carter administration's innovation initiatives, Reagan's HTWG, and the second Inmos debate—the decentralized decision-making structure shifted the focus of the policy debate away from declining industrial competitiveness and toward the different preexisting interests of the executive departments and agencies that participated in each debate. As expected, the decentralized structure empowered multiple state units, many of which did not share the interventionist preferences of officials in Commerce, USTR, or DoI. The presence of such diverse interests largely accounts for the differences in the outcomes emerging from the Type III context; whereas the vast majority of officials in the Carter and Reagan administrations saw no need to veer from their commitment to liberalism, the Thatcher government identified an investment in Inmos as one means to address unemployment in an underdeveloped region and to enhance its electoral prospects. The experience of the post-1983 Thatcher government indicates that a Type II institutional structure also may militate against relative gains concerns coloring policy choices; the executive-centered decision-making structure and the absence of networks enable the primary government official to develop her strategies and preferences autonomously of those groups most likely to experience declining competitiveness. For Prime Minister Thatcher, autonomy empowered her use of actions consistent with her commitment to neoliberal tenets, regardless of the industry's competitive position.

In the fourth case shaped by a Type III institutional structure, the renewal of Sematech in 1992, the interventionist strategy suggests that relative gains concerns may have been instrumental in helping to temper the impact of the numerous state units involved in policymaking. Yet, such a conclusion may not be warranted. Certainly, some in Congress were focused on the industry's performance in relation to its foreign competitors and this helps to explain the industry's receptive hearing in that arena; so too were DARPA officials, who persuaded the administration that continued funding was essential to help the industry consortium meet the Japanese challenge and, thus, the administration meet its national defense goals. Yet, DARPA officials were less convinced that such concerns required five more years of funding for the consortium. Moreover, the relevant congressional committees ultimately endorsed a strategy that not only differed from DARPA's, but also mandated Sematech to pursue environmental goals even though it had yet to reach technological parity with its Japanese competitors. That outcome indicates other concerns at work. One explanation for general congressional support for continued Sematech funding reflects other national-level developments, especially the fast-approaching presidential election, the economic downturn, and the related scrutiny given to free-market strategies.

The four cases transpiring in a Type III context indicate a limitation of the institutional approach developed here. Across these cases, the decentralization of decision-making authority necessitated a lowest common denominator approach in response to firms' and/or officials' association of globalization with vulnerabilities. Yet, the consensus position varied across the four policy episodes; policymakers advanced initiatives to assist the industry, but these strategies differed in the extent to which they targeted the sector and the scope of their benefits. A more developed conception of the sources of officials' preferences then is needed to explore more completely the link between domestic institutions and policy choices. One way to understand which strategy diverse officials will find mutually acceptable when globalization is seen as costly is to focus on the intensity of globalization pressures as they manifest themselves in national economic performance and elections.

Both factors loomed large in Sematech's renewal, helping the participating state units to settle on an industrial policy with multiple objectives. Due to the intensity of these two concerns, other objectives only minimally diminished the industry-specific issues triggering the policy debate. The more limited intensity of either economic or electoral concerns may explain why the multiple state units involved in developing the Carter administration's innovation initiatives and the Reagan administration's HTWG strategy could agree only to nominal changes in the general economic environment affecting industrial activity. When only one of these two concerns was salient, the consensus position represented a midpoint between liberalism and an industrial policy. For example, when Prime Minister Thatcher's government decided to make a second investment in Inmos in 1980, it did so largely to quell concerns about rising unemployment in the country. That logic led the government to advance a strategy that gave priority to objectives related to the labor market rather than Inmos's technological needs. A similar outcome characterized the Reagan administration's response to the industry's Section 301 petition prior to the strike force's creation; in the face of the country's rising, unprecedented trade deficit, the multiple executive agencies authorized the USTR to begin negotiations with Japan to redress the claims, but did not grant the USTR the negotiating leverage to achieve a specific solution. Focusing on national economic performance and electoral concerns may be one indicator of the extent to which the diverse interests of functionally differentiated state units will constrain the type of policy advanced in a Type III context when globalization is perceived to portend vulnerabilities. However, further research is needed to explore the impact of these dynamics, especially whether similar economic and political factors apply when globalization offers opportunities.

In sum, these four theoretical perspectives identify causal factors that contribute to the policy choices studied here. The impact of these factors, however, is largely mediated by the institutional context shaping the policy debate. As a consequence, the institutional argument provides a foundation for what John Odell has termed "conditioning hypotheses." These hypotheses, Odell (1990, 165–66) writes, "specify the conditions under which other hypotheses are most likely to be useful or valid." The development of such hypotheses is a critical task in the international political economy literature, Odell maintains, because "we need to reduce complexity and theoretical proliferation . . . by encompassing rather than ignoring significant dimensions and results."

Institutions and Change

Globalists maintain that globalization triggers state transformation. No systematic explanation has been offered for how globalization causes institutional change. Implicit in some work, however, is the notion that the state apparatus will decrease in significance and size given the more limited role the government is expected to play in the economic sphere.[7] The empirical chapters find that the United States and Britain frequently transformed the two institutions examined here, the organization of decision-making authority and the presence or absence of institutional networks, in response to pressures arising from globalization. However, most changes sought to enhance the state's capacity to respond to these pressures, by centralizing decision-making authority or drawing societal representatives more closely into policymaking processes. Examples of such changes include the creation of the Reagan administration's trade policy strike force, Super 301, Britain's Economic Development Committees, and the minister of information technology. The examples of institutional change that most closely fit globalist expectations were those advanced during the later period of Thatcher's tenure. While these reforms sought to reduce the state's involvement in the economy and society, they also increased the capacity of the British state and its independence in the policymaking process. Even this case, then, is difficult to reconcile with globalist expectations, since Thatcher strengthened the state in an effort to extricate it from the economy.

More generally, it is likely to be difficult to pinpoint the direction or type of institutional reform arising from globalization.[8] At least three reasons can be offered for this conclusion. First, the evidence suggests that globalization is likely to transform national institutions when actors see costs in existing institutions and the policies that emerge from them. Each example of state transformation noted above was advanced because existing configurations were considered inadequate to deal with international pressures facing the country. This is the case regardless of whether reformers sought to increase the capabilities of a specialized element of the governmental apparatus, as the U.S. Congress did in creating the Super 301 process, or whether the reformer sought to decrease the capacity of other state units or domestic groups as Prime Minister Thatcher did. In this regard, the relationship between globalization pressures and the state's transformation is contingent on particular agents' understandings of the costs and benefits of different institutional forms. Given that the agents, pressures, and institutional contexts are likely to vary over time, pressures associated with globalization are unlikely to produce similar institutional changes across states or even within them over time.

Second, the existing institutional context affects the extent of change possible. It does so by creating opportunities for, or constraints on, reformers' capacity to achieve their preferences. In this regard, the argument advanced in chapter 2 regarding the institutional constraints on policy choice sheds light on how much institutional change is likely to occur. Most importantly, unless a reformer is able to operate autonomously during policymaking, the refashioning of an institution hinges on a coalition-building process among authoritative elites that makes change of any type difficult and, at the least, tempers its scope.

Contrasts in the organization of decision-making authority help to shed light on why institutional change tended to be incremental in the United States, whereas in Britain reforms often represented wholesale changes in the policy process, either by creating or eliminating decision-making centers or institutional networks. In Britain, the reformers tended to be prime ministers, who enjoy significant capacity to achieve their preferences (Pierson and Smith 1993). As Chris Painter (1989, 473) notes, "the reality of the British system is one of inadequate safeguards against arbitrary executive power. . . . The limitations of judicial review and supervision are compounded by the relative ineffectiveness of legislative institutions and parliamentary scrutiny, and the element of constitutional fiction that has crept into the conventions of individual and collective ministerial responsibility." Reformers in the United States did not enjoy a similar degree of independence, due to the country's separation of powers system. As chapter 5 indicates, proponents of trade reforms in the U.S. Senate were unable to achieve their desired institutional changes due to presidential veto threats. That is, the existing decentralization of authority blocked the possibility for reform. It was only after the Democrats recaptured the Senate in 1986 that institutional change was advanced; but their failure to gain a veto-proof majority led to less extensive changes than some proponents had originally desired. The organization of decision-making authority, then, mediates whether and to what extent reformers can advance their preferences for institutional change.

These two factors indicate that the existing structure of national institutions affects the impact of globalization on state transformation. In particular, the institutional context shapes the preferences and capacities of those involved in the transformation process. As a consequence, we should not be surprised to see the pace and direction of state restructuring vary across national contexts.

Third, other factors may contribute to the direction of institutional reform demanded. The case material indicates that domestic dynamics may loom large in this regard. For example, the demand for institutional change in Britain was often a by-product of the ideological divide separating the two major British parties, especially with regard to the merits of government intervention in the economy and its ability to respond to the pressures the country encountered.[9] A turnover in party control often led to a transformation in the name and capabilities of the industry department, with Labour increasing the department's capacity and Conservative governments reducing it. Institutional change in the United States often reflected executive-congressional jockeying for policymaking control. Reforms advanced by Congress, for example, sought to enhance the responsibilities of the trade representative's office, whereas the executive branch sought reforms that would maintain its autonomy. Additionally, it is possible that "domestic pressure may act as a counterweight to whatever global pressures there may be to" reduce institutions (Campbell 2003, 249). This dynamic is well illustrated by the Major government's decision to create a cabinet minister responsible for science and technology policy, an action reflecting national-level demands. The decision centralized policy authority and, subsequently, led to the creation of new state-societal linkages. This example of state transformation is especially noteworthy in that Major's predecessor had weakened these institutions in an effort to advance liberalism and Britain's immersion in the global economy. Institutional change then may be neither unidirectional nor irreversible.

Even though institutions are pliable, their mutability does not suggest their lack of causal significance. Even when altered, institutions continue to affect agents and outcomes in unanticipated ways. This is best illustrated by the experience of the strike force; President Reagan centralized the trade policy process in September 1985 to do little more than indicate his concern for unfair trade practices and the rising trade deficit and, hopefully, to silence his congressional critics. Yet, the newly centralized policy process empowered Commerce and USTR officials who capitalized on their new lateral autonomy to advance an interventionist strategy. This example illustrates that the institutional context does not bend at will to the preferences of agents. Once altered, this context exerts new constraints and/or opportunities on the role government officials and societal groups play in the policy process. In effect, although some reformers may seek to rein in the state in response to globalization, the impact of state restructuring ultimately hinges on the array and influence of the relevant public and private sector actors involved in the newly modified policy process.

This conclusion is reinforced by Thatcher's experience. She was largely able to achieve her goals in modifying British political institutions: the role of interest groups in policymaking was reduced, intervention in the economy was minimized and, in its place, a liberal strategy was advanced. What explained Thatcher's capacity to control the consequences of her institutional reforms? To date, institutionalists have focused on explaining unintended change and have largely neglected the conditions affecting the implications of change more generally.[10] This is not surprising, as Bo Rothstein (1996, 154) notes, because "understanding the implications of institutional change is probably one of the most challenging problems for political science." While further research on this issue is necessary, two institutional explanations can be suggested for Thatcher's capacity to control the consequences of institutional change. One focuses on the larger political system in which Thatcher operated; as the central decision point within the political system she could make certain that the changes and the outcomes she desired ensued.[11] In other words, Thatcher's position in the political system allowed her not simply to effect change, but also to control its consequences. A second explanation focuses on the type of change Thatcher advanced. In contrast to the other examples of change identified here, Thatcher's were exclusionary. The changes involved reducing the policy influence of other government officials and societal groups. In doing so, these innovations minimized what was found here and in other studies (Thelen and Steinmo 1992, 16) to be a common reason for institutional change to result in unintended consequences: the changes empowered other agents who used the new institutional context to advance preferences different from those of the reformer. This second explanation suggests that institutional change may produce its intended outcome when the change insulates and reinforces the position of its intended beneficiary. Further research into the conditions that afford some agents greater capacity to effect institutional change and to control the consequences of their actions is needed. This line of inquiry is central not only to a full understanding of the agent-structure relationship, but also to a more practical understanding of the utility of institutional changes designed to confront globalization.

Globalization and Policy Effectiveness

This concluding section considers the effectiveness of several of the U.S. and British policies examined here. Such an evaluation is in order given the degree to which both countries' governments sought to promote their semiconductor industries, and could claim some success, and the current positions of their industries in the global market. By the mid-1990s, for example, the U.S. industry had regained much of the market share it had lost during the 1980s, eventually surpassing Japanese firms to regain the status as the largest supplier of semiconductors in the world. In 1996, moreover, the industry welcomed a decidedly weakened extension of the trade agreement with Japan. In 1997 it opted to continue the Sematech program, but without government subsidy and welcomed memberships from European, Korean, and Taiwanese firms. By the late 1990s, then, the U.S. semiconductor industry regained its previous market dominance and perceived its prospects bright enough to forgo further government support.

By contrast, the status of the British semiconductor industry appears mixed. On the negative side, Plessey, which had acquired Ferranti in 1987, was itself acquired in 1989 in a combined bid from GEC and the German firm Siemens, giving rise to GEC-Plessey Semiconductors (GPS); in 1988 Inmos was acquired by the French-Italian consortium, SGS-Thomson; and in 1986 STC pulled out of the competitive semiconductor market and relied on its American partner, LSI Logic, for the supply of semiconductor technology. By the end of the 1980s, GPS was the only remaining large-scale British semiconductor producer, and most of its devices were oriented toward niche markets, such as the telecommunication, aerospace, and military spheres. Nevertheless, in 1998 the Canadian firm Mitel purchased GPS, effectively leaving Britain without a major indigenous manufacturer of integrated circuits.[12] On the positive side, Plessey became one of the world leaders in the market for application-specific integrated circuits, and Inmos's technologies were among the more advanced in the world. Equally important, Britain became the preferred European location for foreign investors by the mid-1980s. As a result, the country's trade deficit and productivity rates improved. The country now boasts the second largest semiconductor industry in Europe, albeit as a function of foreign direct investors.

Can any of these changes be attributed to the policies examined here? Although there is no question that these policies have had significant effects, an evaluation of their effectiveness, as F. Gerard Adams (1983,

406) writes, "is not a straightforward matter." At least three analytical difficulties are associated with such an investigation. First and most broadly, the criteria by which one determines the success or failure of any policy are not clear. For example, several recent evaluations of industrial policy effectiveness (Wade 1990; Vestal 1993; Callon 1995; Nolan and Peck 2003) employ different measures of success. Second, the effects of each policy cannot be isolated from other factors, such as changes in interest or exchange rates that may have simultaneously affected industrial competitiveness. This problem makes it especially difficult to assess the efficacy of both Sematech and the STA. The two programs not only ran concurrently, but they also operated during a period of large decline in the dollar's value, which some argue translated into greater profits and competitive gains for American firms. Third, a determination of policy effectiveness requires an investigation into whether the policy represents the most efficient use of a country's resources. That is, the analyst needs to determine such opportunity costs as: whether the strategy provides benefits as compared to either not having a policy at all or other possible policy alternatives; and whether the strategy entails any costs with regard to the functioning of other aspects of the country's economy.[13]

Recognizing the difficulties in exploring the latter two investigations, a rough evaluation can be made using three criteria: 1) whether the policy's intended objectives were fulfilled; 2) whether the policy's benefits outweighed its costs for the industry; and 3) the nature of the policy's spillovers for related industries and the country's relations with other countries. The first criterion captures a common source of policy failure: overly ambitious objectives. The last two allow for an examination of the strategies' impact on both a political and an economic level, and capture some of the opportunity costs associated with the policy.

The following offers a preliminary assessment of five policies discussed here: the Alvey Program, the Inmos venture, the Sematech initiative, the STA, and Thatcher's liberal strategy. These policies are examined largely because they are the more controversial of those examined in terms of the government's role and data are available to make an assessment. Britain's Alvey Program and the U.S. Sematech initiative are the most effective according to the three criteria. They met their initial objectives: increasing the technological capacity of the two countries' semiconductor or information technology industries. In fact, measured by the number of technological developments or improvements in existing manufacturing techniques that resulted from research carried out under the sponsorship of the Alvey Program and the Sematech initiative, British and U.S. observers (Wilkinson 1988; DTI 1991; Tyson 1993; Grindley, Mowery, and Silverman 1994) conclude that both programs were worthwhile investments. Moreover, both programs were credited with producing positive spillovers for equipment manufacturers and process technologies, as well as improving such intangibles as the degree of communication between users and suppliers, the knowledge base, and the level of interest in exploiting certain technologies.

This is not to suggest that the two programs were not without shortcomings or costs. For example, the Alvey Program's impact on the competitiveness of the British IT sector did not meet original expectations. The reasons for this outcome, a 1991 government-commissioned evaluation concludes, were two-fold. The program was precompetitive in orientation, and thus some of its commercial potential may have been oversold; the commercial exploitation of some of the research also was limited by firms' "strategic decisions, capital shortages, and management deficiencies." In effect, "[t]he Program did not achieve a number of its strategic targets but this was because it was beyond the scope of a collaborative R&D program to resolve all the problems of the IT sector" (DTI 1991, v).

Some might discount Sematech's success, since the consortium altered its objectives and, thus, did not succeed in fulfilling its original goal. Sematech was originally established to hone the manufacturing skills of U.S. integrated circuit producers, but soon shifted its focus to hone the skills of U.S. semiconductor equipment manufacturers. This objective change may not be a sign of failure, but rather recognition of where the consortium's resources and time could be best spent.[14] Nevertheless, it is true, as Peter Grindley, David Mowery, and Brian Silverman (1994, 736) note, that "[t]he consortium's ability to revise its goals and research agenda . . . creates difficulties of accountability and evaluation that cannot be ignored in a program that receives substantial public funds."

Thatcher's liberal strategies were in some respects quite effective. They achieved most of the prime minister's objectives. Foremost, Britain became the preferred European location for foreign investors by the mid-1980s, and the country's trade deficit and productivity rates improved. Nevertheless, there is some debate whether domestic firms registered increases in productivity and output due to the presence of the multinational firms; in fact, most observers (e.g., Morgan and Sayer 1988, 255–56; Lee 1997) conclude that the influx of inward investment had deleterious consequences for British firms.[15] In particular, this strategy proved costly for domestic firms, as all but GPS exited the market or were taken over by foreign manufacturers. By the end of Thatcher's tenure, Margaret Sharp and William Walker (1991, 323) report that foreign firms, such as Intel, Texas Instruments, and NEC, came to dominate the British market. "Looking back on the 1980s," they conclude, "it seems increasingly likely that historians will identify this as the period when Britain disengaged itself from high technology manufacture or at least from the development of advanced technology. With the possible exceptions of the chemical, pharmaceutical and aerospace industries—and even they seem precarious—Britain under Thatcher became a technological follower rather than a leader and not a particularly effective one at that."

Thatcher's liberal strategy was premised on the belief that an open, competitive domestic market would reverse Britain's industrial decline, since it would bring greater innovation, wealth creation and, thus, profits. Increased profitability was expected to provide a rise in private R&D spending, thereby replacing the loss of state subsidies. Private sector spending on R&D grew by only 10.8% over the 1980 to 1990 period, whereas government-financed R&D fell by nearly 14% between 1983 and 1988 (Lee 1997, 168; Davis, Flanders, and Star 1992, table 10). Without money for innovation, the competitiveness of British industry further eroded: "a manufacturing trade surplus of over £3 billion in 1980 had deteriorated into a deficit of over £8 billion in 1986" (Morgan and Sayer 1988, 260). More tellingly, British manufacturing contracted severely during the 1980s to just 20% of GDP by 1990, a decline of 8% from 1980 (Davis, Flanders, and Star 1992, 46). Accordingly, the liberal strategy failed to achieve its central objective and in the words of one House of Lords report (1991a, 29), posed "grave" implications for Britain's future prosperity, since it seemed to aggravate rather than reverse Britain's industrial decline.

In its technological impact, Britain's Inmos strategy was more successful. By 1984 Inmos had become one of the world's leading manufacturers of SRAMs, and its "transputer" was thought by some to be technically the best microprocessor in the world (Plodding 1985). Moreover, by 1988 the transputer had become a commercial success, as IBM decided to incorporate Inmos's microprocessor into its computers (Rise and Fall 1988).[16]

Inmos's technological success helped the Conservative government's efforts to privatize the firm. In fact, when the British electronics conglomerate Thorn-EMI purchased Inmos in 1984, the government was able to recoup much of its financial investment, thereby making the government's direct financial costs minimal. In addition, the investment produced positive externalities for Britain's regional development and employment efforts; the firm had located its production facilities in South Wales, which employed about 450 workers through mid-1993. Some might contend that the firm paid a high price in exchange for creating these jobs: its production schedule and its market entrance were delayed, thereby hindering Inmos's ability to earn profits, a disadvantage the firm could never overcome. However, the government's original objectives for providing Inmos with financial backing, to ensure a British source of mass-produced, leading-edge memory circuits, turned elusive due to the costs and intensity of competition in semiconductor manufacturing. Inmos exited the DRAM market in 1985 in favor of focusing on higher value, but lower volume SRAMs. Even so, Inmos's profits remained low, and Thorn sold Inmos in 1988 to the French-Italian conglomerate SGS-Thomson.[17] Based on the end result, then, the Inmos venture did not fulfill the government's original objectives, since SGS-Thomson, and not Britain, was the main beneficiary of Inmos's leading-edge technology.[18]

The STA was considerably more successful in fulfilling its objectives. The trade agreement and the Reagan administration's subsequent retaliatory tariffs did effectively stop Japanese firms from dumping their semiconductor devices in the U.S. market. But the agreement could not stop other foreign firms from dumping; in 1992 U.S. firms filed antidumping petitions against South Korean semiconductor firms. Additionally, U.S. firms did not reach the agreed-upon figure of 20% of the Japanese market within the stipulated five-year time frame. Nonetheless, the first agreement was partially successful on the market access score: C. Fred Bergsten and Marcus Noland (1993, 136) calculate that "the impact of the trade agreement was to nearly double U.S. semiconductor exports [to Japan] between 1987 and 1991." This progress was significant, as the SIA (1990, iii) calculated that in 1991 alone "U.S. sales . . . will be $1.16 billion higher than they would have been absent the Agreement." Under the auspices of a second agreement, U.S. firms eventually reached the 20% mark by the fourth quarter of 1992 and have done so consistently since the fourth quarter of 1993.

The STA had negative effects, however. First, it led to an increase in the price of semiconductor devices in the U.S. market.[19] This price increase adversely affected the competitiveness of American DRAM users, predominately electronics and computer firms (Flamm 1996, chap. 5). In doing so, divisions emerged within the U.S. electronics industry about the merits of the agreement and whether an extension should be sought. Mixed signals then were sent to the Bush administration regarding the most appropriate strategy for the sector. Second, the European Community considered itself to be disadvantaged by the STA, and subsequently, filed a complaint before the GATT, contending that the STA gave U.S. firms privileged access to the Japanese market and arbitrarily raised the prices of DRAMs in the European market. A GATT panel ruled in the EC's favor regarding the level of prices, and the EC subsequently signed its own semiconductor agreement with Japan. Third, while this strategy may have led to more openness in this Japanese market, it is based on bilateralism and retaliatory threats, which not only transgress the multilateralism of the GATT, but also heighten the level of confrontation and uncertainty in the international economy. Taken together, these three outcomes detract from the overall effectiveness of the strategy, since they produced negative externalities for U.S. computer and electronics firms, and the country's relations with its trading partners.

The five strategies then represent differing degrees of success. None was a total success, but the Alvey and Sematech programs score the highest marks across the three categories of success noted above: achieving the strategy's objectives; creating net benefits for the industry; and limiting negative externalities, whether political or economic. These two programs share three common features. First, they emerged from policy processes that enabled the affected firms to play an influential role. This feature suggests that industry representatives were able to provide information and ideas regarding which technologies were likely to be significant and which technological goals were possible. Second, the Sematech initiative and the Alvey Program are government-industry collaborative research efforts, funded jointly by both the government and their industry participants. This suggests that the programs targeted areas where the industry perceived its prospects to be brightest, or where it believed its investments would prove most beneficial. Third, the goal of the two programs was the improvement of indigenous manufacturing technologies rather than the development of a specific product or the promotion of an individual firm. The goals of these programs were not overly ambitious or specific; they sought to bring national capabilities in line with those of foreign competitors rather than push the limits of the technological frontier.

The three other policies lack these features. Their shortcomings can be understood by reference to the one feature they all had in common: overly ambitious objectives. The Inmos venture, for example, aimed to provide Britain with a competitive producer of integrated circuits, a tall order given the competitive nature of the industry, the difficulties experienced by GEC and Ferranti in staying competitive in this market, and the vast sums of money needed to enable Inmos to innovate continuously. In the case of the STA and Thatcher's liberal strategy, their success was contingent on an alteration in the behavior of foreign entities, targets controlled only indirectly by U.S. or British policymakers. Moreover, convincing foreign firms to buy another country's products or to tutor national firms are ambitious objectives, especially when doing so is likely to lead to a decline in the foreign firms' profits and competitive advantages. It is no wonder then that it took six years for Japanese firms to increase their purchases of American chips to the desired level, and why many observers contend that Thatcher's inward investment strategy resulted in little more than a "hollowing out" of Britain's manufacturing base.

Some speculation is in order regarding why Thatcher's liberal strategy may be the least successful of these five strategies. One explanation focuses on the limited role domestic manufacturers played in the policy's development. As recounted in chapter 7, industry representatives tried to convey that the strategy's objectives were unrealistic. Given the institutional structure shaping the policy episode, the industry found itself excluded from the policy process and, thus, unable to affect policy direction. A second explanation focuses on the organization of decision-making authority. Prime Minister Thatcher created an executive-centered process and, in doing so, she downgraded and weakened the agency traditionally associated with industrial policy, the DTI. As a consequence, the prime minister's priorities drove the government's industrial strategy and these were developed without much concern for or information about the specific problems or position of national industry in the global economy. These two institutional traits contrast with those characterizing the other policies; generally, these strategies were developed in an institutional context that brought together industry representatives and those government officials who possessed the technical expertise and functional mandate associated with a department of industry or more specialized subunit. In addition, these officials possessed the lateral autonomy to advance initiatives that were not beset with compromises due to the participation of other state units in policymaking. As the foregoing suggests, such an institutional context did not guarantee that the policy would be completely successful. It could not. The ideas advanced by the relevant government and industry officials played the important role in that regard. And on this score, the globalists are correct in noting the difficulty in successfully using industrial policies. However, the obstacles affecting these policies may not emerge from globalization. Instead, the policies examined here suggest that the biggest constraint was lodged within the states themselves; the private and public sector individuals involved in policy development often were overly optimistic about what could be accomplished if the government helped the industry cope with globalization pressures.

Thatcher's neoliberal strategy is instructive for an additional reason. This policy and the institutions producing it were advanced to help Britain to engage globalization effectively. Yet, the post-Thatcher period indicates that state reconfiguration and the policies flowing from it are not irreversible when the institutional context leads to policies that are seen as harming national industrial innovation and development. Upon winning the 1992 election, John Major oversaw a series of institutional reforms. Under the guidance of a newly empowered science minister, new institutional networks were created in an effort to help the government design a strategy to help Britain better capitalize on the global economy. This new context empowered industry and government officials who believed a more interventionist strategy was required. This outcome suggests that even in a country possessing an economy extensively immersed in the global economy, we should not rule out institutional and policy changes that increase the state's policy-making capacity, its linkages with societal groups, or its role in the economy.

Globalization matters. It creates new pressures for states to confront and reinforces longstanding ones. Globalization does not, however, determine how states will respond to those pressures. States' domestic institutions mediate their responses. These institutions create opportunities and constraints on state action, affect the likelihood that states will reconstitute themselves, and influence policy success. Significant differences among states in their institutional structures mean that in the future we should see considerable divergence among states' responses to globalization, including national strategies, institutional transformation, and degree of policy success.

Notes

Chapter 1: Globalization and Convergence?
The Domestic Impact of Globalization

1. For excellent overviews of this literature, see Held et al. (1999, chap. 1), Held and McGrew (2000a), and Guillén (2001b).

2. There are different labels for the perspective, another indication of the early stages of its development. Held et al. (1999) divide the globalist perspective into two camps, the hyperglobalists and the transformationalists; the former see globalization as spelling the end of the nation-state. Weiss (2003a) uses the label "constraints school" to refer to the transformationalists or moderate globalists.

3. A good example of this position is Scholte (1997). For an important exception, see Held et al. (1999).

4. This focus on institutions is shared by others (Berger 1996; Milner and Keohane 1996; Prakash and Hart 2000a; 2000b; Weiss ed. 2003) skeptical of the globalist perspective. These collective volumes often focus on the role of different institutions or, as the Weiss volume, explore a broader conception of institutions rather than, as I seek to do, specifying a priori which institutions matter, the forms they can take, and how they link to specific types of behavior.

5. For a lucid overview of the logic, see Rodrik (1997) and Drezner (2000).

6. See also Strange (1996, 75).

7. For a discussion of the varied perspectives on this point, see Held and McGrew (2000a).

8. Held and McGrew (1998, 232) and Scholte (2000, 146–48) include regional bodies in this contention.

9. Ikenberry (1988; 1994) and Thelen and Steinmo (1992) provide excellent overviews of this perspective.

10. The conventional wisdom is best articulated by Katzenstein (1978). For an insightful, early critique, see Zysman (1983, 347–49, n. 23).

11. For an overview of this literature, see Cortell and Peterson (2002).

12. It should be noted that there is no one set of measures or data used to demonstrate the existence of globalization. These measures represent a synthesis of globalist writings.

13. There are several types of semiconductors. The focus here is on integrated circuits, which represent the most technologically advanced segment of the industry and the largest and fastest growing segment. Integrated circuits include microprocessors, memories, and application-specific or custom chips (Malerba 1985, chap. 2). The policy episodes focus on standard and application-specific integrated circuits. The terms semiconductor, integrated circuit, chip, device, and microchip are used interchangeably throughout the book.

14. Author calculations from Department of Commerce (1979a; 1979b).

15. The U.S. Office of Technology Assessment (1993, 56, table 3.3) reports that nearly 50% of these workers were employed in Japanese affiliates.

16. A strategic industry is "one that is essential to the economic and national security interests of the state and one that engages in an activity that affects the national economy with critical forward and backward linkages through the existence of positive externalities" (Green 1996, 31).

17. This possibility represents one of the few areas of consensus in the globalization debate. For a useful discussion, see Held and McGrew (2000a).

Chapter 2: Globalization, Domestic Institutions, and Industrial Strategies

1. In this respect, I adhere most closely to the conception of institutions Ikenberry (1988, 226–29) advances. He identifies three institutional levels. The first one includes "the administrative, legislative, and regulatory rules that guide the adjudication of conflict." A second focuses on "the centralization and dispersion of authority within the state." The third includes the "norms that govern the relations between state and society."

2. Some refer to these policies, which blur the boundaries between trade policy and industrial policy, as strategic trade and investment policies (e.g., Hart and Prakash 1999). For excellent overviews of the literature exploring conditions justifying such strategies, see Tyson and Zysman (1983) and Hart and Prakash (1999).

3. Peter Hall (1986, 17) also employs the term "institutional network." He writes "that the institutional networks affecting state action extend well into society, in such a way as to expose the state again to societal influences. The state appears as a network of institutions, deeply embedded within a constellation of ancillary institutions associated with society and the economic system."

4. Harvey B. Feigenbaum (1985) suggests that in those cases in which elites can move between public and private sector employment, policymakers

might come to view an institutional network as a means by which to make certain that policies are pursued that do not offend a potential employer.

5. For an excellent overview of this literature, see the collection of essays in Marsh and Rhodes, eds. (1992).

6. This statement echoes Evans' (1997, 74) admonition that "[g]overnment-business relations cannot be interpreted without first specifying the internal structure of the state. The consequences of government-business ties depend fundamentally on the character of the state's internal organization." Evans offers a different understanding of the organization of the state structure than that emphasized here; he focuses on what he calls a Weberian bureaucracy. As Evans (1995, 12) writes, "[h]ighly selective meritocratic recruitment and long-term career rewards create commitment and a sense of corporate coherence. Corporate coherence gives these apparatuses a certain kind of 'autonomy.'" This attribute is seen to enable the state to resist capture from business or being distracted from the issue of industrial transformation.

7. Firms are then assumed to be interested in increasing their relative or competitive position.

8. Weiss (2003a, 28–29) makes a similar claim, positing that "domestic institutions, depending on their character, can hinder or enable states to respond to new challenges and accomplish new tasks, thus softening, neutralizing, or exaggerating the potentially constraining effects of global markets." For economic competition, Weiss (Ibid., 29) links "liberal-market contexts" to market-conforming strategies and "coordinated market contexts" to "strengthening the national economy."

Chapter 3: Liberal Convergence:
The Carter and First Reagan Administrations

1. For an overview of early developments in the industry, see Borrus, Millstein, and Zysman (1983).

2. The founding companies were Intel, Fairchild, Advanced Micro Devices, Motorola, and National Semiconductor. By 1985 the SIA had a membership of forty-eight companies with combined revenues of more than $100 billion, representing nearly 95% of all semiconductors produced annually in the United States.

3. U.S. manufacturing exports as a percentage of the world market had declined from 25% in 1960 to 17% in 1979 (House 1980b, 26).

4. The following discussion is based largely on an interview with a former Carter administration official, Washington, D.C., April 1992. For a discussion of the differing perspectives on the consequences of this development, see Stanfield (1979).

5. The lone representative from the semiconductor industry was Robert Noyce, at the time vice chairman of Intel and a founding director of the SIA. For a full listing of the participants, see Department of Commerce (1979a).

6. In addition, the Commerce Department concurrently had the task of composing the Industry Sector Advisory Committees (ISACs) for the Tokyo

Round negotiations and making certain that these advisory committees functioned smoothly throughout the negotiations. In effect, the department had a parallel system of advisory committees and members already in place.

7. For a delineation of the advisory committee's recommendations, see Department of Commerce (1979a).

8. For allegations that the increased sales of Japanese firms were due to their dumping practices, see the statements by several representatives from the U.S. semiconductor industry to the House Committee on Ways and Means (House 1979).

9. These preferences are articulated in the following sources: statement by Robert Noyce in Senate (1978b); SIA (1978, 60); Can Semiconductors (1979); and SIA (1981, 24–30).

10. See statement by Robert Noyce in House (1980c, 107–8, 124–26).

11. See the statement by Senator Gaylord Nelson (D-WI) to Senate (1979, 6).

12. As one observer notes, DRAMs epitomized the trend that had come to characterize semiconductor devices during the very large scale integration period: "toward the increasing miniaturization of already miniaturized semiconductor devices and towards the increasing integration of highly integrated functions performed by semiconductor devices" (Malerba 1985, 241).

13. See statement by Charles Sporck, president of the National Semiconductor Corporation, quoted in Sanger (1985, sec. 3, p. 8); and a statement by a Mitsubishi executive quoted in *Electronic News* (1986, 1).

14. These preferences are detailed in SIA (1980; 1981; 1983).

15. In 1978 Noyce argued that because the Japanese government supported its industry's investment requirements and these firms operated from an insulated home market, Japanese semiconductor firms had the potential to flood "the American market with underpriced Japanese integrated circuits. American companies, having limited access to the Japanese market and faced with falling prices and bookings in the U.S. market and rising inventories, [will] have no choice but to cut production or go bankrupt" (Moylan 1978, 51).

16. Japan agreed at the Tokyo Round negotiations to harmonize its formal tariffs on semiconductor products to the U.S. level of 4.2% by 1987 and liberalize the procurement practices of the state-owned Nippon Telephone and Telegraph by 1982.

17. A common theme among the government officials interviewed was their belief that Mr. Wolff played the critical role in enabling the SIA to influence U.S. policy.

18. Information regarding the creation of the working group is derived from an interview with a former Reagan administration Commerce Department official, Cambridge, MA, April 1992.

19. These agencies included the USTR, the Council of Economic Advisors, the National Security Council, the Office of Management and Budget, and the Departments of State, Labor, Justice, Treasury, Commerce, and Defense.

20. The 1974 Trade Act institutionalized several of these institutional networks.

Chapter 4: Industrial Policy Without Limits?
Reagan's Second Term

1. The SIA calculated that limited access to the Japanese market had cost American semiconductor firms nearly $600 million in incremental revenues between 1982 and 1984. Many U.S. semiconductor manufacturers believed that the loss of these revenues provided Japanese firms with an enhanced R&D and capital investment capacity, thus, enabling them to preempt the entrance of U.S. firms into the 256K DRAM generation of computer memories (Wolff et al. 1985, vi).

2. The two remaining firms were Texas Instruments and Micron Technology; IBM and AT&T continued to manufacture DRAMs for their internal use. According to Laura Tyson and David Yoffie (1991, 38), "the American merchant firms which exited DRAM production in 1985 did so believing that the Japanese government was committed to maintaining the Japanese industry and that the Japanese companies, with government help and their own deep pockets, would be able to outlast them in a disastrous price war."

3. The following amplifies and modifies Cortell and Davis (1996, 460–63).

4. These findings were due one month after the Section 301 findings. In the end, the June deadline was extended to enable a final agreement, which was reached on July 31.

5. See statements by James Murphy, assistant United States trade representative, and Clyde Prestowitz, counselor to the secretary of commerce for Japan affairs in Senate (1985, 17, 19).

6. Interview, Department of Commerce, Washington, D.C., April 1992.

7. In April 1985 the Economic Policy Committee "effectively absorbed" the Trade Policy Committee (Cohen 1987, 77). The number of departments could have been greater, as the statute provides that the Section 301 committee's members "may be designated by agencies which have an interest in the issues raised by the particular complaint and whose participation is invited by the Chairman of the Committee" (Code of Federal Regulations 1996, 410).

8. Peter Evans (1989, 224) reports that "[t]he administration's failure to initiate Section 301 cases or to retaliate against 'unreasonable' foreign practices when industry-initiated complaints drew attention to them was raised as a primary example of its general lack of aggressiveness in trade policy."

9. At this time, the president also accelerated two cases that were pending against European Community restrictions of canned fruit and Japanese prohibitions on imports of leather and leather footwear.

10. Prestowitz (1988, 160) offers a similar interpretation.

11. Prestowitz (1988, 161) takes credit for bringing the semiconductor industry's concerns to the top of the strike force's agenda: "With the life of the U.S. semiconductor industry ebbing away, the talks under the 301 petition were grinding forward slowly and uncertainly. The relaxed Japanese were handling them with their usual skill and aplomb. With every passing day, the U.S. industry was in worse shape. Some shock treatment was needed in order to get some negotiating leverage. I recommended that the U.S. government do what it had the legal authority to do but never had done before: start its own dumping case on 256K

DRAM chips without waiting for private industry to file a suit, and thus move the government from the position of intermediary to one of advocate."

12. The ITC ruling concerned the individual antidumping petition Micron Technology filed against Japanese semiconductor manufacturers with respect to 64K DRAMs.

13. This suit was filed by Intel, Advanced Micro Devices, and National Semiconductor and alleged that eight Japanese firms dumped EPROMs.

14. The information in this paragraph is drawn from Prestowitz (1988, 161).

15. Interview with a former strike force member, Cambridge, MA, April 1992.

16. On this episode, see Auerbach (1985a; 1985b).

17. For a similar observation on the Japanese reaction, see Cutting Rough (1986, 59).

18. In fact, the president was given discretion as to the type of products, which need not be semiconductors, subject to possible retaliatory sanctions.

19. The action placed $300 million worth of tariffs on only four products: laptop and desktop computers, home power tools, and 18- and 20-inch color televisions. These products were chosen because Japanese-made semiconductors were inputs into them, the products were manufactured by the same companies accused of dumping, and non-Japanese producers supplied the products to the American market. As a result, the U.S. semiconductor and computer industries, and the American consumer would be affected only minimally by the tariffs. Of the total sanctions, $165 million compensated for lack of market access and $135 million for dumping. The latter tariff was suspended in November 1987. Japanese firms avoided the sanctions by relocating their assembly operations.

20. The three largest chipmakers were NEC, Hitachi, and Fujitsu. This calculation excludes IBM and AT&T; no reliable data exist concerning their semiconductor production and revenues, since the two firms manufactured semiconductor devices almost entirely for their own uses. As Tyson (1993, 105, n. 25) writes, "[t]he best estimates suggest that semiconductor production by IBM has been roughly equivalent to that of NEC, Japan's largest producer, and AT&T has roughly a quarter of that volume."

21. This discussion is based on NACS (1989, 11–16).

22. Information concerning this group, its report, and its subsequent implications are drawn from Warshofsky (1988, chaps. 1, 11).

23. At this time, Texas Instruments and Micron Technology were the lone American commercial producers of DRAMs and ostensibly would compete against the proposed consortium. Even so, they planned to participate in the consortium.

24. Among the industry members were several prominent American semiconductor officials including: Larry Sumney, president of the SIA-sponsored Semiconductor Research Corporation (SRC); Jack Kilby, a former Texas Instruments executive and coinventor of the integrated circuit; Erich Bloch, former IBM vice president and then director of the National Science Foundation; and Dr. Robert Burger, then staff vice president of the SRC. Soon after the release of the DSB task force's recommendations, the SIA appointed Sumney executive director of Sematech.

25. According to the chair of the task force, Norman Augustine, these figures were "rough . . . estimates of what we judge would be a reasonable amount of money to undertake what we have proposed. There was no detailed line by line analysis that led to" these numbers (Senate 1987a, 159–60).

26. Much of this dissent reflected the high minimum participation fee of $1 million required of all firms.

27. These firms included: Advanced Micro Devices, AT&T, Digital Equipment Corporation, Harris, Hewlett-Packard, Intel, IBM, LSI Logic, Micron Technology, Motorola, National Semiconductor, NCR, Rockwell International, and Texas Instruments.

28. Members of Semi/Sematech did not have to pay the $1 million entrance fee. Membership in Semi/Sematech ranged from $3,000 to $27,000, depending on a company's annual revenue.

29. This figure represented a fraction of the department's nearly $5.5 billion Science and Technology request.

30. Representatives from the Senate Armed Services Committee also were involved. The information contained in this paragraph is based on an interview with a staff member to that committee, Washington, D.C., April 1992.

31. Although the Department of Defense had played a critical role in developing the American semiconductor and computer industries between 1945 and the late 1960s, this support was primarily in the form of contracts for parts and machines that were to be used in military systems (Flamm 1988).

32. There were at least twelve hearings held on these issues.

33. Interview with Dr. Thomas Dorsey, Office of Management and Budget, Washington, D.C., April 1992.

34. The Sematech initiative was eventually funded in a Department of Defense Appropriations bill that was included in the Omnibus Budget Reconciliation Act of 1987. Funding was frozen until the consortium and the secretary of defense worked out a "memorandum of understanding" governing the use of the funds.

35. Instructive in this regard is the internal memorandum: Freedenberg (1987). This memorandum was received by the author through a Freedom of Information Act request.

36. Interview with Charles Herz, NSF counsel and study group chair, Washington, D.C., April 1992, and National Science Foundation (1987).

Chapter 5: Intervention and Institutional Change: The 1990s

1. For a more detailed treatment of the sources of this institutional change, see Cortell and Peterson (1999, esp. 196–201).

2. Market share data for this period is reported in SIA (2002). Unless otherwise noted, market share data come from this source.

3. U.S. Memories was set up in June 1989 by the American semiconductor firms, Advanced Micro Devices, Hewlett-Packard, Digital Equipment Corporation, Intel, LSI Logic, and National Semiconductor.

4. For discussions of this initiative, see Schoppa (1997) and Mastanduno (1992a).

5. CSPP was established in early 1989 by the CEOs of IBM, Tandem, and Hewlett-Packard to coordinate and represent the interests of computer manufacturers. Nine leading American computer firms comprised the group during this time.

6. See CSPP/SIA Press Release, "Joint Trade Policy Recommendations," October 4, 1990, in SIA (1990, appendix 14).

7. There was a delay in convening the industry members of this committee, given concerns about its duplication with the NACS and the likelihood that there would be overlapping industry memberships on the separate committees. As a consequence, the committee's first report was written in May 1989 based on interviews with industry officials. The under secretary of defense for acquisition issued the first report, which was prepared by the under secretary of commerce for economic affairs (GAO 1989, 19–20).

8. This information was widely reported at the time. See, for example, Pollack (1992).

9. Letter from Senator John Heinz (R-PA) and Representatives Mel Levine (D-CA), Norman Minetta (D-CA), and Majority Leader Richard Gephardt (D-MO) to President George H. W. Bush, November 15, 1989. Letter was received by the author thanks to a Freedom of Information Act request.

10. Majority Leader Richard Gephardt offered a similar sentiment in a nationally broadcast address, June 8, 1990.

11. See the interchange among Representative Joan Kelly Horn (D-MO), T. J. Rodgers, CEO of Cypress Semiconductor, and Dr. William Spencer, president and CEO of Sematech, in House (1991, 112–15).

12. See in particular the testimony of Dr. William Spencer in Senate (1992b, 134–35, 158).

13. These groups included the Campaign for Responsible Technology, a national network of community, environmental, and labor groups, and Silicon Valley Toxics Coalition.

14. LSI Logic and Micron Technology withdrew in January and July 1992. Harris left the consortium in January 1993.

15. Sematech received $90 million for each of the subsequent four years.

16. Among the difficulties in evaluating an industrial policy are the opportunity costs of other policies, interaction effects of other policies, and the criteria used to judge effectiveness. These issues are discussed in chapter 8.

Chapter 6: Emerging Globalization and Intervention: 1970–1980

1. Statement by Sir Arnold Weinstock to the House of Commons Select Committee on Science and Technology in 1971, quoted in Hills (1984, 201).

2. For an illuminating discussion of the powers of the prime minister from an insider's perspective, see Donoughue (1987, chap. 1).

3. For a detailed discussion of the limits to parliamentary influence, see Judge (1990).

4. These mergers involved: first, English Electric with Elliott Automation; second, GEC with Associated Electrical Industries; and third, GEC taking over the English Electric/Elliott Automation combination.

5. The government stipulated that the money go only to wholly British-owned companies (Electronic Components 1973). Perhaps indicative of the weakness of the British firms, it took them six years to use up the funds.

6. According to Grant (1982, 29–30), in making these changes the prime minister "was influenced by the heavy political workload that had been imposed under the Conservatives on the minister in charge of Trade and Industry, and also perhaps by a wish not to give too many important responsibilities to Tony Benn [the leader of the party's socialist left-wing and the government's first industry minister]."

7. For a detailed discussion of this period, see Middlemas (1991, chaps. 1–6).

8. ITT, a U.S. firm, owned 100% of the British telecommunications and electronics company, STC. ITT formed STC in 1883. It began to reduce its stake in STC in the late 1970s, apparently in the hopes of enabling the company to qualify for government support. By the early 1980s, ITT owned only 35% of STC. For details, see ITT May Turn (1977) and Campbell-Kelly (1989, 347–49).

9. The information in this paragraph is drawn from Rodgers (1978), Owen (1978a), and Hills (1984, 204).

10. The MAP provided government assistance for three types of endeavors: worker training courses; a portion of the cost of consultancy work to companies seeking professional advice on how to incorporate microelectronics into their manufacturing processes or end-products; and support for projects involving the use of microelectronics (Government Responds 1978).

11. This context led the Labour government to pursue several other industrial policies that were tailored to the needs of other industries, including the non-ferrous foundries, steel, machine tools, engineering, and clothing industries. For more details on these programs, see Grant (1982, chaps. 3 and 4).

12. Initially, many of Britain's nationalized industries were placed under the NEB's auspices. The NEB's function with regard to these industries was different from the one discussed here. The objectives, priorities, and role of the NEB were the focus of much debate within the Labour Party prior to its assumption of power and continued during its first two years in office. For good discussions of this debate, see Grant (1982, 104–6), Redwood (1984, chap. 5), and Middlemas (1991, 80–84, 131–36).

13. The Labour Party was in power from 1974 to 1979. On Harold Wilson's resignation in 1976, James Callaghan became prime minister. The term Labour governments refers to the governments headed by these two prime ministers.

14. The discussions between the NEB and Plessey were broken off only after the Inmos venture was announced. For information on the discussions between the NEB and Plessey, see Plessey (1978).

15. The remaining shares were given to the firm's three founders and to other selected employees.

16. For details on this period, see McLean and Rowland (1985, chaps. 6 and 7).

17. The information in this paragraph is drawn from Redwood (1984, 78).

Chapter 7: Intervention, Disengagement, and State Transformation: The Conservatives' Turn

1. Jenkin's statement was made in response to the Electronics Economic Development Committee's call for the "government to join with manufacturers and trades unions to chart a selective strategy for the industry's development" (de Jonquieres 1982).

2. This discussion is drawn from Oakley and Owen (1989, 16–33). (Oakley was the civil servant who administered the Alvey Program.) The goal of the Japanese program was to develop the next generation computer, one which was "closer to human beings in their ability to reason and infer from large knowledge databases. . . . Fifth generation computers would not have a single C[entral] P[rocessing] U[nit] slowly grinding its way through data; instead, they would have lots of processors that would be able to solve problems by computing simultaneously" (Callon 1995, 24).

3. In an earlier work (Cortell and Peterson 2001, 786–88), I use some of Thatcher's reforms to illustrate how a reformer can control the consequences of institutional change.

4. Smith (1995) contends that Thatcher's relationship with her supporters enhanced her ability to dominate policymaking.

5. Sharp and Walker (1994) provide a useful overview of Thatcher's strategy.

6. Testimony by A. A. Duguid, assistant secretary, Information Technology Division, Department of Trade and Industry.

7. In 1986–87 alone, £75 million was offered to 111 foreign-owned companies that were expanding existing investments or making new ones (Wren 1996, 189).

8. See testimony of Sir John Clark, Plessey chairman and testimony by Lord Weinstock, managing director of GEC in Lords (1985, 267).

9. Margaret Sharp and William Walker (1994, 428, n. 22) report "that the cost of European programs are borne by their 'sponsor' departments within the overall public expenditure limits set. The result is a total loss of 'additionality' from the EC expenditures which is totally contrary to the spirit of EC initiatives which conceives them as supplementary to existing national expenditures." According to the ECIF, a second problem emerged from the government's unwillingness to provide more than 10 to 15% of project costs (Bullock 1988).

10. The reports' authorship includes any cabinet ministry with jurisdiction over any issue related to industry matters.

11. This document was accessed via the Internet. It has no pagination and, instead, is divided in sections. The two subsequent quotations are from the section entitled "Key Recommendations."

12. The 1997 Treaty of Amsterdam led to a change in the numbers of the articles regulating state aids. Articles 92 and 93 became 87 and 88.

13. For useful overviews of EC policies on state aids, see Lord (1996), Wren (1996, 193–202), and Lavdas and Mendrinou (1999). One indication of the constraints imposed by developments at the EC level is that the DTI has established a State Aid Policy Unit dedicated to providing advice on the EC's state aid regulations. Its website makes clear that "[a]ny Government action which affects the operations of companies will need to involve [all government officials] in understanding and thinking through the effects of Community rules." It provides a detailed overview of current regulations and identifies the Commission's understanding of permissible aid for R&D. See "European Community State Aids," http://www.dti.gov.uk/europe/stateaid/guide.

Chapter 8: Globalization and Domestic Institutions: Conclusions

1. Letter from USTR Clayton Yeutter to Ambassador Nobuo Matsunga, September 2, 1986, contained in SIA (1992).

2. For details, see USTR (1996). The agreement expired on July 31, 1999. At the same time, the Electronic Industries Association of Japan dissolved the Users' Committee of Foreign Semiconductors.

3. Hart and Prakash (2000) provide a useful discussion of this point.

4. Openness to a new strategy in the cases examined here involved a shift away from liberalism and toward intervention. The cases suggest that government officials became more inclined to favor such a strategy when the costs, both political and economic, associated with globalization increased.

5. Smith (1993) provides an insightful discussion on this point.

6. These theories do not provide rigorous measures for relative gains concerns, leading to uncertainty regarding which political or economic dynamics count or how much decline is necessary for such concerns to materialize.

7. For excellent overviews of this aspect of the globalist argument, see Berger (1996), Clark (1999), and Guillén (2001b).

8. This conclusion draws on and extends Cortell and Peterson (2002). For a similar conclusion derived from the experience of the European Union, see Risse, Cowles, and Caporaso (2001).

9. Some (Wilks 1984; Hall 1992, 107) see party competition as creating strong incentives for innovation.

10. For some exceptions, see Moe (1990), Lindsay (1994), Pierson (1996), and Cortell and Peterson (2001).

11. On the importance of viewing one set of institutions in relation to other institutions, see Orren and Skowronek (1994).

12. Manners (1998) provides a useful overview of the remaining British firms.

13. On the significance of investigating a policy's costs in relation to other possible options when attempting to determine its overall efficacy, see Baldwin (1985, 118–31).

14. A similar comment pertains to Alvey: "In some cases, sights were lowered and plans altered during the course of projects, but this should not necessarily detract from the very real accomplishments of the participants. In fast moving technical areas it is important to be able to modify targets as priorities and circumstances shift" (DTI 1991, ii).

15. For an exception, see Davis, Flanders, and Star (1992).

16. IBM also incorporated Inmos's color graphics chip into a line of its personal computers.

17. Simon Lee (1997, 184) explains that "Thorn lacked the industrial and financial resources that rival semiconductor manufacturers had found essential for financing costly innovation and weathering severe and sudden fluctuations in the demand of their products. Thorn-EMI spent several fruitless years and several hundred million pounds in an ultimately fruitless attempt to make Inmos an industrial world-beater."

18. Thomson eventually sold Inmos to QPL, a Hong Kong-based manufacturer.

19. Tyson (1993, 136–43) provides a detailed analysis of some other costs associated with this aspect of the trade agreement. She (Ibid., 132) observes that the agreement "overall was a qualified success with respect to some of its objectives. . . ."

Bibliography

Adams, F. Gerard. 1983. Criteria for U.S. Industrial Policy Strategies. In *Industrial Policies for Growth and Competitiveness*, eds. F. Gerard Adams and Lawrence Klein. Lexington, MA: D. C. Heath and Company.

Allison, Graham. 1971. *Essence of Decision*. Boston: Little, Brown.

Amsden, Alice, and Takashi Hikino. 2000. The Bark is Worse than the Bite: New WTO Law and Late Industrialization. *Annals of the American Academy of Political and Social Science* 570: 105–11.

Art, Robert. 1973. Bureaucratic Politics and American Foreign Policy: A Critique. *Policy Sciences* 4: 467–90.

Atkinson, Michael, and William Coleman. 1989. Strong States and Weak States: Sectoral Policy Networks in Advanced Capitalist Economies. *British Journal of Political Science* 19, no. 1: 47–67.

Auerbach, Stuart. 1985a. White House Backs Off Baldrige Plan. *Washington Post*, 14 December, p. B1 and 2.

———. 1985b. White House in the Chips Again. *Washington Post*, 17 December, p. E3.

Baker, Andrew. 2000. Globalization and the British 'Residual State.' In *Political Economy and the Changing Global Order*, eds. Richard Stubbs and Geoffrey R. D. Underhill. Oxford: Oxford University Press.

Baldwin, David. 1985. *Economic Statecraft*. Princeton, NJ: Princeton University Press.

Bambrick, Richard. 1986. Sematech Gets SIA Go-Ahead; Target Govt, Ind. for Funds. *Electronic News*, 24 November.

Barfield, Claude. 1982. *Science Policy from Ford to Reagan: Change and Continuity*. Washington, D.C.: American Enterprise Institute for Public Policy Research.

Barnes, Fred. 1990. Laying Off. *New Republic,* 21 May.

Barnett, Joel. 1982. *Inside the Treasury*. London: Andre Deutsch.

Barzelay, Michael. 1986. *The Politicized Market Economy: Alcohol in Brazil's Energy Strategy*. Berkeley: University of California Press.

Bello, Judith Hippler, and Alan Holmer. 1990. The Heart of the 1988 Trade Act: A Legislative History of the Amendments to Section 301. In *Aggressive Unilateralism: America's 301 Trade Policy and the World Trading System,* eds. Jagdish Bhagwati and Hugh Patrick. Ann Arbor: University of Michigan Press.

Berger, Suzanne. 1996. Introduction. In *National Diversity and Global Capitalism,* eds. Suzanne Berger and Ronald Dore. Ithaca, NY: Cornell University Press.

Bergsten, C. Fred, and Marcus Noland. 1993. *Reconcilable Differences? United States-Japan Economic Conflict*. Washington, D.C.: Institute for International Economics.

Bird, Jane, and Margaret Park. 1987. Chip Firms Unite to Survive. *Sunday Times* (London), 22 November, p. 85.

Blackstone, Tessa, and William Plowden. 1988. *Inside the Think Tank: Advising the Cabinet, 1971–1983*. London: Mandarin.

Blumenthal, Karen. 1987. Chip Consortium's Organizer Wants U.S. to Provide $125 Million Annually. *Wall Street Journal,* 13 May, p. 12.

Borrus, Michael, James Millstein, and John Zysman. 1983. Trade and Development in the Semiconductor Industry: Japanese Challenge and American Response. In *American Industry in International Competition: Government Policies and Corporate Strategies,* eds. John Zysman and Laura Tyson. Ithaca, NY: Cornell University Press.

Bowen, David. 1994. Case for Helping Your Own. *Independent* (London), 7 August.

Brown, Archie. 2001. From Democratization to 'Guided Democracy.' *Journal of Democracy* 12, no. 4: 35–41.

Brown, Malcolm. 1978. Secrecy of State Electronics Angers NEDO Team. *Times* (London), 2 June, p. 21.

Brown, William. 1993. Waldegrave Rejects the Thatcher Legacy. *New Scientist,* 13 February.

Bullock, R. H. W. 1988. UK Delays Entry into the JESSI Project. *Financial Times,* 28 March, p. 21.

Burch, Martin. 1983. Mrs. Thatcher's Approach to Leadership in Government: 1979–June 1983. *Parliamentary Affairs* 36: 399–416.

Bush, George H. W. 1989a. Statement on the Economic and Domestic Policy Councils. 8 February. http://bushlibrary.tamu.edu/papers/1989/89020802. html (accessed July 9, 2001).

———. 1989b. Statement on United States Action Against Foreign Trade Barriers. 26 May. http://bushlibrary.tamu.edu/papers/1989/89052601.html (accessed July 8, 2001).

———. 1990. Statement on International Trade. 27 April. http://bushlibrary.tamu.edu/papers/1990/90042700.html (accessed July 9, 2001).

Cable, Vincent. 1995. The Diminished Nation-State: A Study in the Loss of Economic Power. *Daedalus* 124, no. 2: 23–53.

Callon, Scott. 1995. *Divided Sun: MITI and the Breakdown of Japanese High-Tech Industrial Policy, 1975–1993.* Stanford, CA: Stanford University Press.

Campbell, John. 2003. States, Politics, and Globalization: Why Institutions Still Matter. In *The Nation-State in Question*, eds. T. V. Paul, G. John Ikenberry, and John A. Hall. Princeton, NJ: Princeton University Press.

Campbell-Kelly, Martin. 1989. *ICL: A Business and Technical History.* Oxford: Clarendon Press.

Can Semiconductors Survive Big Business? 1979. *Business Week*, 3 December, 66–86.

Cane, Alan. 1983. Britain Enters the Great Race. *Financial Times*, 9 May, p. 12.

Cawson, Alan, Peter Holmes, and Anne Stevens. 1987. The Interaction between Firms and the State in France: The Telecommunications and Consumer Electronics Sectors. In *Comparative Government-Industry Relations: Western Europe, the United States and Japan*, eds. Stephen Wilks and Maurice Wright. Oxford: Clarendon Press.

Cawson, Alan, Kevin Morgan, Douglas Webber, Peter Holmes, and Anne Stevens. 1990. *Hostile Brothers: Competition and Closure in the European Electronics Industry.* Oxford: Clarendon Press.

Cerny, Philip G. 1995. Globalization and the Changing Logic of Collective Action. *International Organization* 49, no. 4: 595–625.

———. 1997. Paradoxes of the Competition State: The Dynamics of Political Globalization. *Government and Opposition* 32, no. 2: 251–74.

Chips: The War of Tomorrow's Worlds. 1985. *Economist*, 24 August, 69.

Chira, Susan. 1985. Japanese Chip Dumping Cited. *New York Times*, 5 June, p. D4.

Clark, Ian. 1998. Beyond the Great Divide: Globalization and the Theory of International Relations. *Review of International Studies* 24, no. 4: 479–97.

———. 1999. *Globalization and International Relations Theory.* Oxford: Oxford University Press.

Code of Federal Regulations. 1996. *Commerce and Foreign Trade.* Title 15, sec. 2002.3. Washington, D.C.: Office of the Federal Register.

Cohen, Stephen D. 1987. *The Making of United States International Economic Policy: Principles, Problems and Proposals for Reform.* 3rd ed. New York: Praeger.

———. 1994. *United States International Economic Policy.* 4th ed. New York: Praeger.

Congressional Record. 1985a. 99th Cong., 1st sess. Vol. 131, no. 38, 28 March, S3556.

———. 1985b. 99th Cong., 1st sess. Vol. 131, no. 40, 2 April, H1815.

———. 1988. 100th Cong., 2d sess. Vol. 134, no. 131, 22 September, E3038.

———. 1989a. 101st Cong., 1st sess. Vol. 135, no. 73, 6 June, H2311.

———. 1989b. 101st Cong., 1st sess. Vol. 135, no. 75, 8 June, S6399.

———. 1990. 101st Cong., 2d sess. Vol. 136, no. 33, 26 March, S3206.

———. 1991. 102d Cong., 1st sess. Vol. 137, no. 61, 24 April, H2534.

———. 1992. 102d Cong., 2d sess. Vol. 138, no. 129, 22 September, S14256.

Cookson, Clive. 1992. Love in the Laboratory. *Financial Times,* 27 July, p. 34.

Corina, Maurice. 1976. Planning Sector By Sector for the Industrial Revival. *Times* (London), 10 June, p. 21.

———. 1977. 20m to Make up Lost Ground. *Times* (London), 2 February, p. 25.

Cortell, Andrew P., and James W. Davis, Jr. 1996. How Do International Institutions Matter? The Domestic Impact of International Rules and Norms. *International Studies Quarterly* 40, no. 4: 451–78.

Cortell, Andrew P., and Susan Peterson. 1999. Altered States: Explaining Institutional Change. *British Journal of Political Science* 29, no. 1: 177–203.

———. 2001. Limiting the Unintended Consequences of Institutional Change. *Comparative Political Studies* 34, no. 7: 769–99.

———. 2002. Agents, Structures, and Institutional Change. In *Altered States: International Relations, Domestic Politics, and Institutional Change,* eds. Andrew P. Cortell and Susan Peterson. Lanham, MD: Lexington Books.

Croft, Sally. 1999. UK Formulates Long-Term R&D Vision. *R&D* 41, no. 10.

Cutting Rough with Japan's Chip Makers. 1986. *Economist,* 11 January, 59.

Davis, Evan, Stephanie Flanders, and Jonathan Star. 1992. British Industry in the 1980s. *Business Strategy Review* 3, no. 1: 45–69.

de Jonquieres, Guy. 1982. Jenkin Firm on Private Role in Electronics. *Financial Times,* 6 May, p. 6.

———. 1983. Semiconductor Industry Needs Ministry. *Financial Times,* 18 October, p. 8.

———. 1985a. Electronics Deficit will Deepen. *Financial Times,* 18 February, p. 4.

———. 1985b. The Harsh Imperatives of Survival. *Financial Times,* 24 June, p. 16.

Destler, I. M. 1992. *American Trade Politics.* 2d ed. Washington, D.C.: Institute for International Economics.

Doherty, Michael. 1988. Prime Ministerial Power and Ministerial Responsibility in the Thatcher Era. *Parliamentary Affairs* 41, no. 1: 49–67.

Donoughue, Bernard. 1987. *Prime Minister: The Conduct of Policy under Harold Wilson and James Callaghan*. London: Jonathan Cape.

Doremus, Paul N., William W. Keller, Louis W. Pauly, and Simon Reich. 1998. *The Myth of the Global Corporation*. Princeton, NJ: Princeton University Press.

Dosi, Giovanni. 1983. Semiconductors: Europe's Precarious Survival in High Technology. In *Europe's Industries: Public and Private Strategies for Change*, eds. Geoffrey Shepherd, Francois Duchene, and Christopher Saunders. London: Frances Pinter.

Drezner, Daniel. 2000. Bottom Feeders. *Foreign Policy* 118: 64–70.

———. 2001. Globalization and Policy Convergence. *International Studies Review* 3, no. 1: 53–78.

Dunford, Mick. 1989. Technopoles, Politics and Markets: The Development of Electronics in Grenoble and Silicon Glen. In *Strategies for New Technology: Case Studies from Britain and France*, eds. Margaret Sharp and Peter Holmes. New York: Philip Allan.

Eizenstat, Stuart, Jim McIntyre, and Frank Press. 1979. *Memorandum for the President Concerning the Domestic Policy Review*. Washington, D.C., President's Office, 22 October. Photocopy.

Electronic Components: Mini-support. 1973. *Economist*, 21 April, 90.

Electronic News. 1986. 29 April.

Elliot, John. 1978. Seeking Credibility for the Industrial Strategy. *Financial Times*, 18 January, p. 16.

Elliot, John, and John Lloyd. 1978. The Microelectronics Debate: Scheme to Meet Challenge. *Financial Times*, 7 December, p. 30.

European Community (EC). 1996. Competition Directorate General. *Community Framework for State Aid for Research and Development*. 96/C 45/06, 17 February. http://www.europa.eu.int/comm/competition/state_aid/legislation/96c46_en.html (accessed July 15, 2004).

A European Glut in Semiconductors. 1970. *Business Week*, 22 August, 19.

Eustace, Peter. 1984. Watching the Battle for Europe. *Engineer*, 8 November, 26.

Evangelista, Matthew. 1995. The Paradox of State Strength: Transnational Relations, Domestic Structures, and Security Policy in Russia and the Soviet Union. *International Organization* 49, no. 1: 1–38.

Evans, Peter. 1989. Declining Hegemony and Assertive Industrialization: U.S.-Brazil Conflicts in the Computer Industry. *International Organization* 43, no. 2: 207–38.

———. 1995. *Embedded Autonomy: States and Industrial Transformation.* Princeton, NJ: Princeton University Press.

———. 1997. State Structures, Government-Business Relations, and Economic Transformation. In *Business and the State in Developing Countries*, eds. Sylvia Maxfield and Ben Ross Schneider. Ithaca, NY: Cornell University Press.

Feigenbaum, Harvey. 1985. *The Politics of Public Enterprise: Oil and the French State.* Princeton, NJ: Princeton University Press.

Feigenbaum, Harvey, Richard Samuels, and R. Kent Weaver. 1993. Innovation, Co-ordination and Implementation in Energy Policy. In *Do Institutions Matter? Government Capabilities in the United States and Abroad*, eds. R. Kent Weaver and Bert Rockman. Washington, D.C.: The Brookings Institution.

Fisher, Bart S., and Ralph G. Steinhardt III. 1982. Section 301 of the Trade Act of 1974: Protection for U.S. Exporters of Goods, Services and Capital. *Law and Policy in International Business* 14, no. 3: 569–690.

Flamm, Kenneth. 1985. Internationalization in the Semiconductor Industry. In *Global Factory: Foreign Assembly in International Trade*, eds. Joseph Grunwald and Kenneth Flamm. Washington, D.C.: The Brookings Institution.

———. 1988. *Creating the Computer: Government, Industry and High Technology.* Washington, D.C.: The Brookings Institution.

———. 1996. *Mismanaged Trade? Strategic Policy and the Semiconductor Industry.* Washington, D.C.: The Brookings Institution.

Freedenberg, Paul. 1987. Memorandum for Michael Darby, Assistant Secretary of the Treasury for Economic Policy. Washington, D.C., Office of the Assistant Secretary for Trade Administration, Department of Commerce. 14 July. Photocopy.

Frieden, Jeffry. 1988. Sectoral Conflict and U.S. Foreign Economic Policy, 1914–1940. *International Organization* 42, no. 1: 59–90.

Friedman, Thomas. 1999. *The Lexus and the Olive Tree.* New York: Farrar, Straus and Giroux.

Garrett, Geoffrey. 1998. Global Markets and National Politics: Collision Course or Virtuous Circle? *International Organization* 52, no. 4: 787–824.

Goldstein, Judith. 1988. Ideas, Institutions, and American Trade Policy. *International Organization* 42, no. 1: 179–217.

———. 1993. *Ideas, Interests, and American Trade Policy.* Ithaca, NY: Cornell University Press.

Gourevitch, Peter. 1986. *Politics in Hard Times: Comparative Responses to International Economic Crises.* Ithaca, NY: Cornell University Press.

———. 1996. The Macropolitics of Microinstitutional Differences in the Analysis of Comparative Capitalism. In *National Diversity and Global Capitalism*, eds. Berger and Dore.

Government Responds to the Challenge of Microelectronics. 1978. *Trade and Industry*, 8 December, 492–5.

Graham, Otis. 1992. *Losing Time: The Industrial Policy Debate*. Cambridge: Harvard University Press.

Grant, Wyn. 1982. *The Political Economy of Industrial Policy*. London: Butterworths.

Green, Eric. 1996. *Economic Security and High Technology Competition in an Age of Transition*. Westport, CT: Praeger.

Grindley, Peter, David Mowery, and Brian Silverman. 1994. Sematech and Collaborative Research: Lessons in the Design of High-Technology Consortia. *Journal of Policy Analysis and Management* 13, no. 4: 723–58.

Guillén, Mauro F. 2001a. *The Limits of Convergence: Globalization and Organizational Change in Argentina, South Korea, and Spain*. Princeton, NJ: Princeton University Press.

———. 2001b. Is Globalization Civilizing, Destructive or Feeble? A Critique of Five Key Debates in the Social Science Literature. *Annual Review of Sociology* 27: 235–60.

Haggard, Stephan, Sylvia Maxfield, and Ben Ross Schneider. 1997. Theories of Business and Business-State Relations. In *Business and the State in Developing Countries*, eds. Sylvia Maxfield and Ben Ross Schneider. Ithaca, NY: Cornell University Press.

Hall, Peter. 1986. *Governing the Economy: The Politics of State Intervention in Britain and France*. New York: Oxford University Press.

———. 1989. Conclusion: The Politics of Keynesian Ideas. In *The Political Power of Keynesian Ideas*, ed. Peter Hall. Princeton, NJ: Princeton University Press.

———. 1992. The Movement from Keynesianism to Monetarism: Institutional Analysis and British Economic Policy in the 1970s. In *Structuring Politics*, eds. Sven Steinmo, Kathleen Thelen, and Frank Longstreth. Cambridge: Cambridge University Press.

Hall, Peter, and Rosemary Taylor. 1996. Political Science and the Three New Institutionalisms. *Political Studies* 44, no. 5: 936–57.

Hansen, Patricia. 1987. Defining Unreasonableness in International Trade: Section 301 of the Trade Act of 1974. *Yale Law Journal* 96, no. 5: 1122–46.

Hart, Jeffrey A. 1992. *Rival Capitalists: International Competitiveness in the United States, Japan, and Western Europe*. Ithaca, NY: Cornell University Press.

Hart, Jeffrey A., and Aseem Prakash. 1999. Globalization, Governance, and Strategic Trade and Investment Policies. In *Globalization and Governance*, eds. Aseem Prakash and Jeffrey Hart. London: Routledge.

———. 2000. Coping with Globalization: A Conclusion. In *Coping with Globalization*, eds. Prakash and Hart.

Hay, Colin. 2000. Contemporary Capitalism, Globalization, Regionalization, and the Persistence of National Variation. *Review of International Studies* 26, no. 4: 509–31.

Hayward, Jack. 1983. *Governing France: The One and Indivisible Republic.* 2d ed. New York: W. W. Norton and Company.

Held, David, and Anthony McGrew. 1998. The End of the Old Order? Globalization and the Prospects for World Order. *Review of International Studies* 24, no. 5: 219–43.

———. 2000a. The Great Globalization Debate: An Introduction. In *The Global Transformations Reader*, eds. David Held and Anthony McGrew. Cambridge: Polity Press.

———. 2000b. Part IV, A Globalized Economy? In *The Global Transformations Reader*, eds. Held and McGrew.

Held, David, Anthony McGrew, David Goldblatt, and Jonathan Perraton. 1999. *Global Transformations: Politics, Economics and Culture.* Stanford, CA: Stanford University Press.

Heller, William, Philip Keefer, and Mathew McCubbins. 1998. Political Structure and Economic Liberalization: Conditions and Cases from the Developing World. In *The Origins of Liberty: Political and Economic Liberalization in the Modern World*, eds. Paul Drake and Mathew McCubbins. Princeton, NJ: Princeton University Press.

Heseltine, Michael. 2000. *Life in the Jungle: My Autobiography.* London: Hodder & Stoughton.

Hills, Jill. 1984. *Information Technology and Industrial Policy.* London: Croom Helm.

Hirst, Paul. 1997. The Global Economy: Myths and Realities. *International Affairs* 73, no. 3: 409–25.

Hirst, Paul, and Grahame Thompson. 1996. *Globalization in Question.* Cambridge: Polity Press.

Hobday, Mike. 1989. The European Semiconductor Industry: Resurgence and Rationalization, *Journal of Common Market Studies* 28, no. 2: 155–86.

Holmes, Martin. 1989. *Thatcherism: Scope and Limits, 1983–1987.* New York: St. Martin's Press.

How Inward Investment Affects the UK Economy. 1982. *British Business*, 26 February, 402–4.

How the High Technology Game is Played. 1970. *Economist*, 12 September, 77.

Ikenberry, G. John. 1988. Conclusion: An Institutionalist Approach to American Foreign Economic Policy. In *The State and American Foreign Economic Policy*, eds. G. John Ikenberry, David Lake, and Michael Mastanduno. Ithaca, NY: Cornell University Press.

———. 1994. History's Heavy Hand: Institutions and the Politics of the State. Paper prepared for the conference on The New Institutionalism, 14–15 October, at the University of Maryland.

Ikenberry, G. John, David Lake, and Michael Mastanduno, eds. 1988. *The State and American Foreign Economic Policy.* Ithaca, NY: Cornell University Press.

Immergut, Ellen. 1992. The Rules of the Game: The Logic of Health Policymaking in France, Switzerland, and Sweden. In *Structuring Politics: Historical*

Institutionalism in Comparative Politics, eds. Sven Steinmo, Kathleen Thelen, and Frank Longstreth. New York: Cambridge University Press.

Irwin, Douglas. 1996. Trade Politics and the Semiconductor Industry. In *The Political Economy of American Trade Policy*, ed. Anne Kreuger. Chicago: University of Chicago Press.

The IT 86 Committee. 1986. *Information Technology—A Plan for Concerted Action: The Report of the IT 86 Committee.* London. Photocopy.

ITT May Turn the Knob on the British Electronics Show. 1977. *Economist*, 17 December, 121.

The Japanese Challenge in Semiconductors. 1977. *Business Week*, 11 July, 72–4.

Jenkin, Patrick. 1982. IT in Industry: A Key to Survival. *British Business*, 25 June, 2–3.

———. 1983. Statement to the House of Commons. *Times* (London), 29 April, p. 4.

Jenkins, Peter. 1988. *Mrs. Thatcher's Revolution: The Ending of the Socialist Era.* Cambridge: Harvard University Press.

Johnson, Chalmers. 1982. *MITI and the Japanese Miracle.* Stanford, CA: Stanford University Press.

Johnson, Christopher. 1991. *The Grand Experiment: Mrs. Thatcher's Economy and How it Spread.* Boulder, CO: Westview Press.

Judge, David. 1990. *Parliament and Industry.* Aldershot, UK: Dartmouth.

Katzenstein, Peter. 1978. Conclusion: Domestic Structures and Strategies of Foreign Economic Policies. In *Between Power and Plenty*, ed. Katzenstein.

———. 1985. *Small States in World Markets.* Ithaca, NY: Cornell University Press.

———, ed. 1978. *Between Power and Plenty: Foreign Economic Policies of Advanced Industrial States.* Madison: University of Wisconsin Press.

Kavanagh, Dennis. 1990. *Thatcherism and British Politics: The End of Consensus?* 2d ed. Oxford: Oxford University Press.

Keliher, Leo. 1990. Core Executive Decision Making on High Technology Issues: The Case of the Alvey Report. *Public Administration* 68, no. 2: 61–82.

Kennedy, Paul. 1987. *The Rise and Fall of the Great Powers.* New York: Vintage Press.

Keohane, Robert, and Joseph Nye. 2000. Globalization: What's New? What's Not? (and so What?). *Foreign Policy* 118: 104–19.

King, Gary, Robert Keohane, and Sidney Verba. 1994. *Designing Social Inquiry: Scientific Inference in Qualitative Research.* Princeton, NJ: Princeton University Press.

Kramer, Daniel. 1988. *State Capital and Private Enterprise: The Case of the UK National Enterprise Board.* London: Routledge.

Krasner, Stephen. 1978. United States Commercial and Monetary Policy: Unraveling the Paradox of External Strength and Internal Weakness. In *Between Power and Plenty*, ed. Katzenstein.

Krauss, Ellis. 1993. U.S.-Japan Negotiations on Construction and Semiconductors, 1985–1988. In *Double-Edged Diplomacy: International Bargaining and Domestic Politics*, eds. Peter Evans, Harold Jacobson, and Robert Putnam. Berkeley: University of California Press.

Krauss, Ellis, and Simon Reich. 1992. Ideology, Interests and the American Executive: Toward a Theory of Foreign Competition and Manufacturing Trade Policy. *International Organization* 46, no. 4: 857–97.

Lake, David. 1988. The State and American Trade Strategy in the Pre-Hegemonic Era. In *The State and American Foreign Economic Policy*, eds. Ikenberry, Lake, and Mastanduno.

Lavdas, Kostas A., and Maria M. Mendrinou. 1999. *Politics, Subsidies and Competition: The New Politics of State Intervention in the European Union.* Cheltenham, UK: Edward Elgar.

Lawson, Nigel. 1992. *The View from No. 11: Memoirs of a Tory Radical.* London: Bantam Press.

Lee, Simon. 1996. Manufacturing. In *Industrial Policy in Britain*, ed. David Coates. London: Macmillan Press.

———. 1997. Manufacturing British Decline. In *The Political Economy of Modern Britain*, eds. Andrew Cox, Simon Lee, and Joe Sandersen. Cheltenham, UK: Edward Elgar.

Lehner, Urban. 1982. U.S., Japan Pact Would Bolster Joint Research. *Wall Street Journal*, 11 November, p. 35.

Levine, Richard J. 1979. Business Community Pressing President to Cut Taxes by $20 Billion to $30 Billion. *Wall Street Journal*, 10 December, p. 3.

Lindsay, James. 1994. Congress, Foreign Policy, and the New Institutionalism. *International Studies Quarterly* 32, no. 2: 281–304.

Lord, Christopher. 1996. Industrial Policy and the European Union. In *Industrial Policy in Britain*, ed. David Coates. London: Macmillan Press.

Madison, Christopher. 1982. U.S.-Japan High-Technology Talks Turn on Trade Tactics and Teamwork. *National Journal*, 11 September, 1555–7.

Major, John. 1993. My Ambition: To Help Industry Fight its Battles for Britain. *Daily Telegraph* (London), 12 March, p. 20.

———. 2000. *The Autobiography.* New York: Harper Collins.

Malerba, Franco. 1985. *The Semiconductor Business: The Economics of Rapid Growth and Decline.* London: Frances Pinter.

Manners, David. 1984. It's Chips for Everyone—Except the Europeans. *Times* (London), 10 July, p. 18.

———. 1998. Rest in Peace. *Electronics Weekly*, 25 February.

Mansfield, Edward D., and Marc L. Busch. 1995. The Political Economy of Non-Tariff Barriers: A Cross-National Analysis. *International Organization* 49, no. 4: 723–49.

Marsh, David, and R. A. W. Rhodes, eds. 1992. *Policy Networks in British Government.* Oxford: Oxford University Press.

Mastanduno, Michael. 1991. Do Relative Gains Matter? America's Response to Japanese Industrial Policy. *International Security* 16, no. 1: 73–113.

———. 1992a. Framing the Japan Problem: The Bush Administration and the Structural Impediments Initiative. *International Journal* 47, no. 2: 235–264.

———. 1992b. Setting Market Access Priorities: The Use of Super 301 in U.S. Trade with Japan. *World Economy* 15, no. 6: 729–53.

Mayer, Jeffrey L. 1989. *Sematech: Progress and Prospects*. Report of the Advisory Council on Federal Participation in Sematech. Washington, D.C., Office of Economic Policy, Department of Commerce.

———. 1990. *Sematech 1990: A Report to Congress*. The Advisory Council on Federal Participation in Sematech. Washington, D.C., Office of Policy Analysis, Department of Commerce.

McCalman, James. 1988. *The Electronics Industry in Britain: Coping with Change*. New York: Routledge.

McCarthy, Patrick. 1978a. UK Offers IC Plant Aid. *Electronic News*, 31 July.

———. 1978b. UK Firms Fear Raids to Fill Inmos Talent Needs. *Electronic News*, 21 August.

McCausland, Richard. 1992. Sematech Grapples with Skeptics: Will Offshore R&D Alliances Undercut Competitive Efforts? *Electronic News*, 13 January.

McLean, Mick, and Tom Rowland. 1985. *The Inmos Saga: A Triumph of National Enterprise?* London: Frances Pinter.

Merry, Robert. 1985. Reagan's Aides Split over his Trade Speech and Altered it Sharply. *Wall Street Journal*, 24 September, pp. 1 and 12.

Microcircuits: GEC Bows Out. 1971. *Economist*, 17 July, 72.

Microelectronics Aid. 1977. *Times* (London), 29 December, p. 13.

Microelectronics: American Challenge. 1967. *Economist*, 2 September, 807.

Middlemas, Keith. 1983. *Industry, Unions and Government: Twenty-One Years of the NEDC*. London: Macmillan.

———. 1990. *Threats to the Postwar Settlement*. Vol. 2 of *Power, Competition and the State*. London: Macmillan.

———. 1991. *The End of the Postwar Period, Britain Since 1974*. Vol. 3 of *Power, Competition and the State*. London: Macmillan.

Milner, Helen V. 1988. *Resisting Protectionism: Global Industries and the Politics of International Trade*. Princeton, NJ: Princeton University Press.

Milner, Helen V., and Robert O. Keohane. 1996. Internationalization and Domestic Politics: An Introduction. In *Internationalization and Domestic Politics*, eds. Robert O. Keohane and Helen V. Milner. Cambridge: Cambridge University Press.

Mitchell, Douglas. 1982. Intervention, Control, and Accountability: The National Enterprise Board. *Public Administration Bulletin* 38: 40–65.

Moe, Terry. 1990. The Politics of Structural Choice: Toward a Theory of Public Bureaucracy. In *Organization Theory: From Chester Barnard to the Present and Beyond*, ed. Oliver Williamson. Oxford: Oxford University Press.

Moon, Jeremy. 1995. Innovative Leadership and Policy Change: Lessons From Thatcher. *Governance* 8, no. 1: 1–25.

Morgan, Kevin, and Andrew Sayer. 1988. *Microcircuits of Capital: 'Sunrise' Industry and Uneven Development*. Boulder, CO: Westview Press.

Moylan, Peter. 1978. Noyce Rips Government as Peril to U.S. Semiconductor Industry. *Electronic News*, 9 October.

National Research Council (NRC). 1992. Committee on Japan. *U.S.-Japan Strategic Alliances in the Semiconductor Industry: Technology Transfer, Competition, and Public Policy*. Washington, D.C.: National Academy Press.

Newton, Scott, and Dilwyn Porter. 1988. *Modernization Frustrated: The Politics of Industrial Decline in Britain Since 1900*. London: Unwin Hyman.

Noland, Marcus, and Howard Peck. 2003. *Industrial Policy in an Era of Globalization: Lessons from Asia*. Washington, D.C.: Institute for International Economics.

North, Douglass. 1990. *Institutions, Institutional Change and Economic Performance*. Cambridge: Cambridge University Press.

Oakley, Brian, and Kenneth Owen. 1989. *Alvey: Britain's Strategic Computing Initiative*. Cambridge, MA: The MIT Press.

Odell, John. 1979. The U.S. and the Emergence of Flexible Exchange Rates. *International Organization* 33, no. 1: 57–81.

———. 1990. Understanding International Trade Strategies: An Emerging Synthesis. *World Politics* 43, no. 4: 139–67.

Okimoto, Daniel. 1989. *Between MITI and the Market: Industrial Policy for High Technology*. Stanford, CA: Stanford University Press.

Organisation for Economic Cooperation and Development (OECD). 1992. *Globalisation of Industrial Activities: Four Case Studies: Auto Parts, Chemicals, Construction, and Semiconductors*. Paris: OECD.

Orren, Karen, and Stephen Skowronek. 1994. Beyond the Iconography of Order: Notes for a 'New Institutionalism.' In *The Dynamics of American Politics: Approaches and Interpretations*, eds. Lawrence Dodd and Calvin Jillson. Boulder, CO: Westview Press.

O'Shea, Timothy J. C. 1988. *The U.S.-Japan Semiconductor Problem*. Pew Foundation Cases in International Affairs, no. 139, Graduate School of Public and International Affairs, University of Pittsburgh.

Owen, Kenneth. 1972. Microelectronics: Whitehall Aid Reflects Important Trends. *Times* (London), 29 December, p. 15A.

———. 1974. Ferranti: A 92-Year Tradition of New Ideas In Technology. *Times* (London), 16 September, p. 19.

———. 1978a. Microelectronics: Helping Industry to Meet the Challenge. *Times* (London), 12 May, p. 23.

———. 1978b. NEDO Gives Options on Microcircuit Industry. *Times* (London), 24 June, p. 17.

———. 1978c. DoI Aids Use of Microprocessors. *Times* (London), 5 July, p. 19.

———. 1978d. Microelectronics Support Scheme Worth £70 million over Five Years. *Times* (London), 27 July, p. 17.

Painter, Chris. 1989. Thatcherite Radicalism and Institutional Conservatism. *Parliamentary Affairs* 42, no. 4: 463–84.

Pastor, Robert. 1980. *Congress and the Politics of U.S. Foreign Economic Policy, 1929–1976.* Berkeley: University of California Press.

Perraton, Jonathan, David Goldblatt, David Held, and Anthony McGrew. 2000. Economic Activity in a Globalizing World. In *The Global Transformations Reader*, eds. Held and McGrew.

Peterson, Mark. 1993. Institutional Change and the Health Politics of the 1990s. *American Behavioral Scientist* 36, no. 6: 782–801.

Pierson, Paul. 1996. The Path to European Integration: A Historical Institutionalist Analysis. *Comparative Political Studies* 29, no. 2: 123–63.

Pierson, Paul, and Miriam Smith. 1993. Bourgeois Revolutions? The Policy Consequences of Resurgent Conservatism. *Comparative Political Studies* 25, no. 4: 487–520.

Pine, Art, and Robert Merry. 1985. Reagan Revises America-First Economic Policy As Trade Deficit Forces More Active World Role. *Wall Street Journal*, 29 April, p. 56.

Pine, Art, and David Shribman. 1985. Reagan Attacks Unfair Trade Practices by Foreign Nations with Modest Plan. *Wall Street Journal*, 24 September, p. 12.

Plessey Goes to the NEB. 1978. *Economist*, 8 July, 81.

Plodding into Sunrise. 1985. *Economist*, 23 November, 46 and 47.

Pollack, Andrew. 1991. A Financing Drive Begun by Sematech. *New York Times*, 20 December, p. D1.

———. 1992. U.S. Chip Makers Stem the Tide in Trade Battles with Japan. *New York Times*, 9 April, p. A1.

Poole, James. 1978a. Reversing UK's Microelectronics Programme. *Sunday Times* (London), 25 June, p. 55.

———. 1978b. £15 million Aid to Boost Micro Industry. *Sunday Times* (London), 8 July, p. 55.

Pope, Kyle. 1992. Sematech May Lose Pentagon Funding. *Wall Street Journal*, 17 August, p. B1.

Prakash, Aseem, and Jeffrey A. Hart. 2000a. Coping with Globalization: Introduction. In *Coping with Globalization*, eds. Aseem Prakash and Jeffrey A. Hart. London: Routledge.

———. 2000b. Responding to Globalization: An Introduction. In *Responding to Globalization*, eds. Aseem Prakash and Jeffrey A. Hart. London: Routledge.

Prestowitz, Clyde. 1988. *Trading Places: How We Are Giving Our Future to Japan and How to Reclaim It.* New York: Basic Books.

Pym, Francis. 1984. *Politics of Consent.* London: Hamish Hamilton.

Radcliffe, James. 1991. *The Reorganisation of British Central Government.* Aldershot, UK: Dartmouth.

Rawstorne, Philip. 1980. Government to Give £25 million for Inmos Microchip Plant. *Financial Times*, 30 July, p. 1.

Reagan, Ronald. 1985. United States International Trade: Radio Address to the Nation, September 7, 1985. *Weekly Compilation of Presidential Documents* Vol. 21, no. 37. Washington, D.C.: GPO.

———. 1987. Statement on Tariff Increases on Japanese Semiconductor Products. *Public Papers of the Presidents of the United States: Ronald Reagan, Book I.* Washington, D.C.: GPO.

Redwood, John. 1984. *Going for Broke: Gambling with the Taxpayers' Money.* Oxford: Basil Blackwell.

Rhodes, R. A. W., and David Marsh. 1992. Policy Networks in British Politics: A Critique of Existing Approaches. In *Policy Networks in British Government*, eds. Marsh and Rhodes.

Richards, David, and Martin Smith. 2002. Breaking the Policy Bias: Windows of Opportunity and the Realignment of Structural Constraints in Three Government Departments. In *Altered States*, eds. Cortell and Peterson.

The Rise and Fall of Britain's IC Empire. 1988. *Electronic Business*, 4 April, 40–2.

Risse-Kappen, Thomas. 1991. Public Opinion, Domestic Structure and Foreign Policy in Liberal Democracies. *World Politics* 43, no. 4: 479–512.

———. 1994. Ideas Do Not Float Freely: Transnational Coalitions, Domestic Structures, and the End of the Cold War. *International Organization* 48, no. 2: 185–214.

———, ed. 1995. *Bringing Transnational Relations Back In: Non-State Actors, Domestic Structures, and International Institutions.* Cambridge: Cambridge University Press.

———. 1995a. Bringing Transnational Relations Back In: Introduction. In *Bringing Transnational Relations Back In*, ed. Risse-Kappen.

———. 1995b. Structures of Governance and Transnational Relations: What Have We Learned? In *Bringing Transnational Relations Back In*, ed. Risse-Kappen.

Risse, Thomas, Maria Green Cowles, and James Caporaso. 2001. Europeanization and Domestic Change: Introduction. In *Transforming Europe: Europeanization and Domestic Change*, eds. Maria Green Cowles, James Caporaso, and Thomas Risse. Ithaca, NY: Cornell University Press.

Robertson, Jack. 1982. Galvin: GATT Must Eye Japan Semicon Trade. *Electronic News*, 20 September.

———. 1985. Trade Rep Tells Congress He Ended Efforts to Settle 301. *Electronic News*, 21 October.

———. 1986. Japanese Officials Visit IC Cos. on Dumping. *Electronic News*, 20 January.

———. 1989. Cite Japan on Super 301. *Electronic News*, 29 May.

———. 1990. SIA Fails in Super 301 Attempt. *Electronic News*, 30 April.

Robinson, Brian. 1992a. Sematech Execs Seek Funds to Secure Future. *Electronic Engineering Times*, 16 April.

———. 1992b. Industry Fights Senate R&D Spending Plan. *Electronic Engineering Times*, 28 September.

Rodgers, Peter. 1978. Microcircuit Firms to Get £55 million Aid. *Sunday Times* (London), 5 February, p. 55.

Rodrik, Dani. 1997. Sense and Nonsense in the Globalization Debate. *Foreign Policy* 107: 19–37.

Rose, Richard. 1989. *Politics in England*. 5th ed. Glenview, IL: Scott, Foresman.

Rosenau, James. 2000. Governance in a Globalizing World. In *The Global Transformations Reader*, eds. Held and McGrew.

———. 2003. *Distant Proximities: Dynamics beyond Globalization*. Princeton, NJ: Princeton University Press.

Rosenbaum, Andy. 1989. Semiconductor Makers Bask in the Italian Sun. *Electronic Business*, 6 February.

Rothstein, Bo. 1996. Political Institutions: An Overview. In *New Handbook of Political Science*, eds. Robert Goodin and Hans-Dieter Klingemann. Oxford: Oxford University Press.

Samuel, Gill. 1984. Using a Voice in Whitehall. *British Business*, 21 September.

Samuels, Richard. 1994. *Rich Nation, Strong Army: National Security and the Technological Transformation of Japan*. Ithaca, NY: Cornell University Press.

Sandholtz, Wayne. 1992. *High Tech Europe: The Politics of International Cooperation*. Berkeley: University of California Press.

Sanger, David. 1985. Pushing America Out of Chips. *New York Times*, 16 June, sec. 3, p. 8.

Scholte, Jan Aart. 1997. Global Capitalism and the State. *International Affairs* 73, no. 3: 427–52.

———. 2000. *Globalization: A Critical Introduction*. New York: St. Martin's Press.

Schoppa, Leonard J. 1997. *Bargaining with Japan: What American Pressure Can and Cannot Do*. New York: Columbia University Press.

Sciberras, E. 1980. The UK Semiconductor Industry. In *Technical Innovation and British Economic Performance*, ed. Keith Pavitt. London: Macmillan.

Semiconductor Industry Association (SIA). 1978. Statement of Concern on Matters Relating to International Business and Trade. In U.S. Senate Committee on Commerce, Science and Transportation, *Industrial Technology*, 95th Cong., 2d sess., 30 October, 55–67.

———. 1980. *An American Response to the Foreign Industrial Challenge in High Technology Industries*, Proceedings of an SIA Conference, Monterey, CA.

———. 1981. *The International Microelectronic Challenge: The American Response by the Industry, the Universities, and the Government.* Cupertino, CA: The SIA.

———. 1983. *The Effect of Government Targeting on World Semiconductor Competition: A Case History of Japanese Industrial Strategy and its Costs for America.* Cupertino, CA: The SIA.

———. 1985. *The Impact of Japanese Market Barriers in Microelectronics.* Cupertino, CA: The SIA.

———. 1987. *One Year of Experience under the U.S.-Japan Semiconductor Agreement.* Cupertino, CA: The SIA.

———. 1988. *One and One-half years of Experience under the U.S.-Japan Semiconductor Agreement.* Cupertino, CA: The SIA.

———. 1990. *Four Years of Experience under the U.S.-Japan Semiconductor Agreement: A Deal is a Deal.* San Jose, CA: The SIA.

———. 1992. *The 1991 U.S.-Japan Semiconductor Agreement: Heading towards Crisis.* San Jose, CA: The SIA.

———. 2002. *World Market Shares, 1982–1990.* http://www.sia-online.org/downloads/market_shares_82–90.pdf (accessed July 22, 2004).

Sharp, Margaret, and William Walker. 1991. Thatcherism and Technical Advance: Reform Without Progress? Part II: The Thatcher Legacy. *Political Quarterly* 62, no. 3: 318–37.

———. 1994. Thatcherism and Technical Advance—Reform Without Progress? In *Britain's Economic Performance*, eds. Tony Buxton, Paul Chapman, and Paul Temple. London: Routledge.

Shortcomings of UK Technology Foresight. 1998. *Technology Analysis & Strategic Management* 10, no. 2: 271.

SIA Readies Sematech Business Plan. 1987. *Electronic News*, 4 May.

Silk, Leonard. 1978. Seeking Ways the U.S. Can Spur Research by Industry. *New York Times*, 30 March, p. D5.

Skocpol, Theda. 1985. Bringing the State Back In: Current Research. In *Bringing the State Back In*, eds. Peter Evans, Dietrich Rueschemeyer, and Theda Skocpol. Cambridge: Cambridge University Press.

Skocpol, Theda, and Margaret Weir. 1985. State Structures and the Possibility for Keynesian Responses. In *Bringing the State Back In*, eds. Evans, Rueschemeyer, and Skocpol.

Smith, Martin J. 1993. *Pressure, Power and Policy: State Autonomy and Policy Networks in Britain and the United States*. Pittsburgh, PA: University of Pittsburgh Press.

———. 1995. Interpreting the Rise and Fall of Margaret Thatcher: Power Dependence and the Core Executive. In *Prime Minister, Cabinet and Core Executive*, eds. R. A. W. Rhodes and Patrick Dunleavy. New York: St. Martin's Press.

Solingen, Etel. 1993. Macropolitical Consensus and Lateral Autonomy in Industrial Policy: The Nuclear Sector in Brazil and Argentina. *International Organization* 47, no. 2: 263–98.

Stanfield, Rochelle. 1979. Building a Better Mousetrap—Is Government Getting in the Way? *National Journal*, 1 September, 1436–42.

Stokes, Bruce. 1985. Baldrige Aims for Trade Mark. *National Journal*, 14 December, 2865–6.

Strange, Susan. 1996. *Retreat of the State: The Diffusion of Power in the World Economy*. Cambridge: Cambridge University Press.

Suleiman, Ezra. 1987. *Private Power and Centralization in France*. Princeton, NJ: Princeton University Press.

£10m State Aid for Micro Electronics Industry. 1972. *Times* (London), 22 December, p. 17.

Thain, Colin, and Maurice Wright. 1995. *The Treasury and Whitehall: The Planning and Control of Public Expenditure, 1976–1993*. Oxford: Clarendon Press.

Thatcher, Margaret. 1993. *The Downing Street Years*. New York: Harper Collins.

Thatcher, Mark. 1999. *The Politics of Telecommunications: National Institutions, Convergence, and Change in Britain and France*. Oxford: Oxford University Press.

Theakston, Kevin. 1996. Whitehall, Westminster, and Industrial Policy. In *Industrial Policy in Britain*, ed. David Coates. London: Macmillan.

Thelen, Kathleen, and Sven Steinmo. 1992. Historical Institutionalism in Comparative Politics. In *Structuring Politics*, eds. Sven Steinmo, Kathleen Thelen, and Frank Longstreth. Cambridge: Cambridge University Press.

Thurow, Lester. 1992. *Head to Head: The Coming Economic Battle Among Japan, Europe and America*. New York: Morrow.

Tooze, Roger. 1997. International Political Economy in an Age of Globalization. In *The Globalization of World Politics: An Introduction to World Politics*, eds. John Baylis and Steve Smith. Oxford: Oxford University Press.

Tyson, Laura. 1993. *Who's Bashing Whom? Trade Conflict in High Technology Industries*. Washington, D.C.: Institute for International Economics.

Tyson, Laura, and David Yoffie. 1991. *Semiconductors: From Manipulated to Managed Trade*. Working Paper, Harvard Business School.

Tyson, Laura, and John Zysman. 1983. American Industry in International Competition. In *American Industry in International Competition*, eds. John Zysman and Laura Tyson. Ithaca, NY: Cornell University Press.

U.K. Alvey Committee. 1983. *A Programme for Advanced Information Technology: The Report of the Alvey Committee.* London: HMSO.

U.K. Chancellor of the Exchequer (Chancellor). 1976. Memorandum by the Chancellor of the Exchequer and the Secretary of State for Industry. *Industrial Strategy: The First Stage.* 25 June. Photocopy.

———. 1978. Memorandum by the Chancellor of the Exchequer and the Secretary of State for Industry. *Industrial Strategy.* 25 January. Photocopy.

U.K. Department of Trade and Industry (DTI). 1988. *DTI-The Department of Enterprise.* London: HMSO. Cmnd. 278.

———. 1991. *Evaluation of the Alvey Programme for Advanced Information Technology.* A Report Commissioned by the Department of Trade and Industry and the Science and Engineering Research Council. London: HMSO.

U.K. Electronic Components Sector Working Party (ECSWP). 1979a. *Industrial Strategy: Progress Report 1979.* London: National Economic Development Office.

———. 1979b. *What the Future Holds.* London: National Economic Development Office.

———. 1981. *Progress Report 1981.* London: National Economic Development Office.

U.K. Electronics Economic Development Committee (EEDC). 1983. *Policy for the UK Electronics Industry: Review 1982/1983.* London: National Economic Development Office.

U.K. Foresight Programme. 1995. *Progress Through Partnership: IT & Electronics.* Part 8. http://www.foresight.gov.uk/servelet/DocViewer/docnoredirect=116/ (accessed August 6, 2001).

———. 1996. Information Technology and Electronics Panel. *An Action Plan for the Information Technology, Electronics, and Communications Panel.* http://www.foresight.gov.uk/servelet/DocViewer/docnoredirect=90/ (accessed August 6, 2001).

U.K. House of Commons. 1972. *Research and Development.* Fourth Report of the Select Committee. 1971–1972 Session, Minutes of Evidence.

U.K. House of Lords. 1985. *Overseas Trade.* Report from the House of Lords Select Committee on Overseas Trade. 1984–1985 Session, HL 238-2, Oral Evidence.

———. 1986. *Civil Research and Development.* First Report from the Select Committee on Science and Technology. 1986–1987 Session, HL 20-III, Written Evidence.

———. 1991a. *Innovation in Manufacturing Industry.* Report of the House of Lords Select Committee on Science and Technology. 1990–1991 Session, HL 18-I, Report.

———. 1991b. *Innovation in Manufacturing Industry.* Report of the House of Lords Select Committee on Science and Technology. 1990–1991 Session, HL 18-II, Oral Evidence.

U.K. Information Technology Economic Development Committee (ITEDC). 1984. *Crisis Facing the UK Information Technology.* London: National Economic Development Office.

U.K. National Economic Development Council (NEDC). 1970. *Economic Assessment to 1972: Industrial Report by the Electronics EDC.* London: National Economic Development Office.

U.K. Office of Science and Technology (OST). 1995. *Progress Through Partnership: Report from the Steering Group of the Technology Foresight Programme.* London: HMSO.

U.K. Parliament. 1987. *Civil Research and Development: Government Response to the First Report of the House of Lords Select Committee on Science and Technology.* Cmnd. 185.

———. 1991. *Government Response to the First Report of the House of Lords Select Committee on Science and Technology.* Cm. 1575.

———. 1993. *Realising Our Potential: A Strategy for Science, Engineering and Technology.* Cm. 2250.

———. 1994. *Competitiveness: Helping Business to Win.* Cm. 2563.

———. 1995. *Competitiveness: Forging Ahead.* Cm. 2867.

———. 1998. *Our Competitive Future Building the Knowledge Driven Economy.* Cm. 4176.

U.S. Congressional Budget Office (CBO). 1987. *The Benefits and Risks of Federal Funding for Sematech.* Washington, D.C.: Congress of the United States.

U.S. Defense Science Board Task Force on Semiconductor Dependency (Defense Science Board). 1987. *Report of Defense Science Board Task Force on Defense Semiconductor Dependency.* Washington, D.C.: Office of the Under Secretary of Defense for Acquisition. Microfiche.

U.S. Department of Commerce. 1979a. Bureau of the Census. *U.S. Commodity Exports and Imports as Related to Output 1972 and 1971.* Washington, D.C.: GPO.

———. 1979b. Bureau of the Census. *U.S. Commodity Exports and Imports as Related to Output 1976 and 1975.* Washington, D.C.: GPO.

———. 1979c. *Advisory Committee on Industrial Innovation: Final Report.* Washington, D.C.: GPO.

U.S. Department of State. 1985. *President Reagan: The President's Trade Policy Action Plan.* Washington, D.C.: Bureau of Public Affairs.

U.S. General Accounting Office (GAO). 1989. *Federal Research: The Sematech Consortium's Start-up Activities.* Washington, D.C.: GPO.

———. 1992. *Federal Research: Sematech's Technological Progress and Proposed R&D Program.* Washington, D.C.: GPO.

U.S. House. 1979. Committee on Ways and Means. *Competitive Factors Influencing World Trade in Semiconductors.* 96th Cong., 1st sess. 30 November.

————. 1980a. Committee on Science and Technology. *Technology Trade: Hearing before the Committee on Science and Technology.* 96th Cong., 2d sess. 24 June.

————. 1980b. Committee on Science and Technology, Subcommittee on Science, Research and Technology. *Analyses of President Carter's Initiatives in Industrial Innovation and Economic Revitalization.* 96th Cong., 2d sess. Committee Print.

————. 1980c. Committee on Banking, Housing and Urban Affairs. *Trade and Technology: Part III.* 96th Cong., 2d sess. 15 June.

————. 1982. Committee on Ways and Means. *Trade in Services and Trade in High Technology Products.* 97th Cong., 2d sess. 24 May.

————. 1984. Committee on Foreign Affairs. *United States-Japan Relations.* 98th Cong., 2d sess. 12 June.

————. 1987a. Committee on Energy and Commerce, Subcommittee on Commerce, Consumer Protection, and Competitiveness. *Trade and Competitiveness (Part 2).* 100th Cong., 1st sess. 10 March.

————. 1987b. Committee on Energy and Commerce, Subcommittee on Commerce, Consumer Protection, and Competitiveness. *Competitiveness of the U.S. Semiconductor Industry.* 100th Cong., 1st sess. 9 June.

————. 1987c. Technology Policy Task Force of the Committee on Science, Space, and Technology. *Communications and Computers in the 21st Century.* 100th Cong., 1st sess. 25 June.

————. 1990. Committee on Energy and Commerce, Subcommittee on Commerce. *U.S.-Japan Trade Issues.* 101st Cong., 2d sess. 10 May.

————. 1991. Committee on Science, Space, and Technology, Subcommittee on Technology and Competitiveness. *Semiconductors: The Role of Consortia.* 102d Cong., 1st sess. 23 July.

————. 1992. Committee on Armed Services. *National Defense Authorization Act for Fiscal Year 1993.* H. Rept. 102–527.

U.S. International Trade Administration. 1983. *High Technology Industries: Profiles and Outlooks: The Semiconductor Industry.* Washington, D.C.: GPO.

U.S. National Advisory Committee on Semiconductors (NACS). 1989. *Strategic Industry at Risk: A Report to the President and the Congress from the National Advisory Committee on Semiconductors.* Washington, D.C.: GPO.

————. 1992. *Attaining Preeminence in Semiconductors: Third Annual Report to the President and the Congress.* Washington, D.C.: GPO.

U.S. National Science Foundation (NSF). 1987. *The Semiconductor Industry: A Report of a Federal Interagency Staff Working Group.* Washington, D.C.: National Science Foundation.

U.S. Office of Technology Assessment (OTA). 1991. *Competing Economies: America, Europe and the Pacific Rim.* Washington, D.C.: GPO.

———. 1993. *Multinationals and the National Interest: Playing by Different Rules*. Washington, D.C.: GPO.

U.S. Office of the U.S. Trade Representative (USTR). 1991. *Arrangement Between the Government of Japan and the Government of the United States of America Concerning Trade in Semiconductors*. 11 June. Photocopy.

———. 1996. Joint Statement by the Government of the United States and the Government of Japan Concerning Semiconductors. 2 August. http://www.mac.doc.gov/japan/source/menu/semiconductors/semis.html (accessed July 25, 2001).

———. 1997. *Foreign Share of the Japanese Semiconductor Market Reaches 35.8% in Second Quarter*. Press Release, 10 December.

U.S. Office of the White House Press Secretary (Press Secretary). 1979. *Fact Sheet: The President's Industrial Innovation Initiatives*. Mimeograph.

U.S. Senate. 1978a. Committee on Commerce, Science and Transportation. *Oversight of Science and Technology Policy: Parts 1 and 2*. 95th Cong., 1st sess. 14 February.

———. 1978b. Select Committee on Small Business. *Capital Formation: Part 1*. 95th Cong., 2d sess. 8 February.

———. 1979. Committee on Commerce, Science and Transportation. *Industrial Innovation*, 96th Cong., 1st sess. 31 October.

———. 1984. Committee on Foreign Relations. *United States-Japan Trade: The $30 Billion Gap*. 98th Cong., 2d sess. 3 October.

———. 1985. Committee on Banking, Housing and Urban Affairs. *Semiconductor Trade and Japanese Targeting*. 99th Cong., 1st sess. 30 July.

———. 1987a. Committee on the Judiciary, Subcommittee on Technology and the Law. *Issues Confronting the Semiconductor Industry*. 100th Cong., 1st sess. 3 March.

———. 1987b. Committee on Armed Services, Subcommittee on Defense Industry and Technology. *Department of Defense Authorization for Appropriations for Fiscal Years 1988 and 1989*. 100th Cong., 1st sess. 9 March.

———. 1987c. Committee on the Judiciary. *Competitiveness and Antitrust*. 100th Cong., 1st sess. 7 May.

———. 1987d. Committee on Armed Services. *National Defense Authorization Act for Fiscal Years 1988 and 1989*. 100th Cong., 1st sess. Rept. 100-57.

———. 1989. Committee on Finance. *Confirmation of U.S. Trade Representative*. 101st Cong., 1st sess. 27 January.

———. 1990. Committee on Commerce, Science, and Transportation, Subcommittee on Science, Technology, and Space. *Semiconductors and the Electronics Industry*. 101st Cong., 2d sess. 17 May.

———. 1991a. Committee on Foreign Affairs, Subcommittee on International Economic Policy. *Prospects for a New United States-Japan Semiconductor Agreement.* 101st Cong., 2d sess. 20 March.

———. 1991b. Committee on Finance, Subcommittee on International Trade. *Renewal of the United States-Japan Semiconductor Agreement.* 102d Cong., 1st sess. 22 March.

———. 1992a. Committee on Governmental Affairs, Subcommittee on Government Information and Regulation. *Technology Policy and Competitiveness: The Federal Government's Role.* 102d Cong., 2d sess. 12 March.

———. 1992b. Committee on Armed Services. *Department of Defense Authorization for Appropriations for Fiscal Year 1993 and the Future Years Defense Program.* 102d Cong., 2d sess. 18 March.

———. 1992c. Committee on Armed Services. *National Defense Authorization Act for Fiscal Year 1993.* S. Rept. 102–352.

Vestal, James. 1993. *Planning for Change: Industrial Policy and Japanese Economic Development, 1945–1990.* Cambridge: Cambridge University Press.

Wade, Robert. 1990. *Governing the Market.* Princeton, NJ: Princeton University Press.

———. 1996. Globalization and its Limits: The Reports of the Death of the National Economy Are Greatly Exaggerated. In *National Diversity and Global Capitalism,* eds. Berger and Dore.

Wall Street Journal. 1977. 9 November, p. 26.

Waltz, Kenneth. 1979. *Theory of International Politics.* Reading, MA: Addison-Wesley.

Warshofsky, Fred. 1988. *The Chip War.* New York: Charles Scribner's Sons.

Weaver, R. Kent, and Bert Rockman, eds. 1993a. *Do Institutions Matter? Government Capabilities in the United States and Abroad.* Washington, D.C.: The Brookings Institution.

———. 1993b. Assessing the Effects of Institutions. In *Do Institutions Matter?* eds. Weaver and Rockman.

———. 1993c. When and How do Institutions Matter? In *Do Institutions Matter?* eds. Weaver and Rockman.

Weinraub, Bernard. 1985. Reagan Proposes Export Subsidies to Gain Markets. *New York Times,* 24 September, p. A1.

Weiss, Linda. 1998. *The Myth of the Powerless State.* Ithaca, NY: Cornell University Press.

———. 1999. Globalization and National Governance: Antimony or Interdependence? *Review of International Studies* 25, no. 5: 59–88.

———. 2003a. Introduction: Bringing Domestic Institutions Back In. In *States in the Global Economy,* ed. Weiss.

———. 2003b. Is the State Being 'Transformed' by Globalization? In *States in the Global Economy,* ed. Weiss.

———, ed. 2003. *States in the Global Economy: Bringing Domestic Institutions Back In.* Cambridge: Cambridge University Press.

Wilkinson, Mary. 1988. State Cash Helps British Electronics R&D Catch Up. *Electronic Business*, 1 April.

Wilkinson, Max. 1978. A Giantkiller v. the U.S. and Japan. *Financial Times*, 19 September, p. 31.

———. 1979a. Working Party Rebukes NEB. *Financial Times*, 2 February, p. 40.

———. 1979b. Microelectronics Will Employ at Least Another 15,000. *Financial Times*, 1 February, p. 8.

Wilks, Stephen. 1983. Liberal State and Party Competition: Britain. In *Industrial Crisis*, eds. Kenneth Dyson and Stephen Wilks. New York: St. Martin's Press.

———. 1984. *Industrial Policy and the Motor Industry*. Manchester, UK: Manchester University Press.

———. 1985. Conservative Industrial Policy 1979–83. In *Implementing Government Policy Initiatives: The Thatcher Administration, 1979–83*, ed. Peter Jackson. London: Royal Institute of Public Administration.

Willetts, David. 1987. The Role of the Prime Minister's Policy Unit. *Public Administration* 65, no. 4: 443–54.

Williams, Nigel. 1995. U.K. Tries to Set Priorities with the Benefit of Foresight. *Science*, 12 May.

Wolff, Alan R., Michael Gadbaw, Thomas Howell, and Timothy Richards. 1985. *Japanese Market Barriers in Microelectronics: Memorandum in Support of a Petition Pursuant to Section 301 of the Trade Act of 1974, as Amended*. Washington, D.C.: Dewey, Ballantine, Bushby, Palmer, and Wood, 14 June.

World Trade Organization (WTO). 1994. *Agreement on Subsidies and Countervailing Duties*. Uruguay Round Agreements. http://www.wto.org.

Wren, Colin. 1996. *Industrial Subsidies: The UK Experience*. New York: St. Martin's Press.

Yoffie, David, and John Coleman. 1991. The Semiconductor Industry Association and the Trade Dispute with Japan (A). Rev. ed. Harvard Business School Case No. 9-387-205. Boston: Harvard Business School Press.

Young, Hugo. 1989a. *The Iron Lady: A Biography of Margaret Thatcher*. New York: Farrar, Straus, Giroux.

———. 1989b. *One of Us: A Biography of Margaret Thatcher*. London: Macmillan.

Young, Stephen. 1974. *Intervention in the Mixed Economy*. With A. V. Lowe. London: Croom Helm.

Zhu, Tianbiao. 2003. Building Institutional Capacity for China's New Economic Opening. In *States in the Global Economy*, ed. Weiss.

Zürn, Michael. 2002. From Interdependence to Globalization. In *Handbook of International Relations*, eds. Walter Carlsnaes, Thomas Risse, and Beth A. Simmons. London: Sage Publications.

Zysman, John. 1983. *Governments, Markets, and Growth: Financial Systems and the Politics of Industrial Change*. Ithaca, NY: Cornell University Press.

Index

American Patriotism in a Global Society—Betty Jean Craige

The Political Discourse of Anarchy: A Disciplinary History of International Relations—Brian C. Schmidt

From Pirates to Drug Lords: The Post–Cold War Caribbean Security Environment—Michael C. Desch, Jorge I. Dominguez and Andres Serbin (eds.)

Collective Conflict Management and Changing World Politics—Joseph Lepgold and Thomas G. Weiss (eds.)

Zones of Peace in the Third World: South America and West Africa in Comparative Perspective—Arie M. Kacowicz

Private Authority and International Affairs—A. Claire Cutler, Virginia Haufler, and Tony Porter (eds.)

Harmonizing Europe: Nation-States within the Common Market—Francesco G. Duina

Economic Interdependence in Ukrainian-Russian Relations—Paul J. D'Anieri

Leapfrogging Development? The Political Economy of Telecommunications Restructuring—J. P. Singh

States, Firms, and Power: Successful Sanctions in United States Foreign Policy—George E. Shambaugh

Approaches to Global Governance Theory—Martin Hewson and Timothy J. Sinclair (eds.)

After Authority: War, Peace, and Global Politics in the Twenty-First Century—Ronnie D. Lipschutz

Pondering Postinternationalism: A Paradigm for the Twenty-First Century?—Heidi H. Hobbs (ed.)

Beyond Boundaries? Disciplines, Paradigms, and Theoretical Integration in International Studies—Rudra Sil and Eileen M. Doherty (eds.)

Why Movements Matter: The West German Peace Movement and U.S. Arms Control Policy—Steve Breyman

International Relations—Still an American Social Science? Toward Diversity in International Thought—Robert M. A. Crawford and Darryl S. L. Jarvis (eds.)

Which Lessons Matter? American Foreign Policy Decision Making in the Middle East, 1979–1987—Christopher Hemmer (ed.)

Hierarchy Amidst Anarchy: Transaction Costs and Institutional Choice—Katja Weber.

International Relations Under Risk: Framing State Choice—Jeffrey D. Berejikian

Globalization and the Environment: Greening Global Political Economy—Gabriela Kütting

Sovereignty, Democracy, and Global Civil Society—Elizabeth Jay Friedman, Kathryn Hochstetler, and Ann Marie Clark

Imperialism and Nationalism in the Discipline of International Relations—David Long and Brian C. Schmidt (eds.)

United We Stand? Divide and Conquer Politics and the Logic of International Hostility—Aaron Belkin

Globalization, Security, and the Nation State: Paradigms in Transition—Ersel Aydinli and James N. Rosenau (eds.)